Words in Search of Victims

Words in Search of Victims

The Achievement of Jerzy Kosinski

Paul R. Lilly, Jr.

THE KENT STATE UNIVERSITY PRESS
Kent, Ohio, and London, England

Library of Congress Cataloging-in-Publication Data

Lilly, Paul R.
    Words in search of victims.

    Bibliography: p.
    Includes index.
    1. Kosinski, Jerzy N., 1933-   —Criticism and interpretation.
I. Title.
PS3561.08Z77   1988   813'.54   88-3021
ISBN 0-87338-366-4 (alk. paper) ∞

British Library Cataloging-in-Publication data are available.

The following publishers have generously given permission to use quotations from copyrighted works by Jerzy Kosinski: From *The Art of the Self: Essays a Propos Steps*, © 1968 by Jerzy Kosinski, reprinted by permission of Scientia-Factum and Jerzy Kosinski. From *Being There*, © 1970 by Jerzy Kosinski, reprinted by permission of Harcourt Brace Jovanovich, Inc. From *Blind Date*, © 1977 by Jerzy Kosinski, reprinted by permission of Houghton Mifflin Company, Bantam Books (paper edition, 1978), and Jerzy Kosinski. From *Cockpit*, © 1975 by Jerzy Kosinski, reprinted by permission of Houghton Mifflin Co. and Jerzy Kosinski. From *The Devil Tree*, © 1973 by Jerzy Kosinski, reprinted by permission of Harcourt Brace Jovanovich, Inc. From *The Future is Ours, Comrade* (Joseph Novak, pseud.), © 1960, reprinted by permission of Doubleday and Company. From *Notes of the Author on The Painted Bird*, © 1965, 1966, 1967 by Jerzy Kosinski, reprinted by permission of Scientia-Factum and Jerzy Kosinski. From *No Third Path* (Joseph Novak, pseud.), © 1962, reprinted by permission of Doubleday and Company. From *The Painted Bird*, 2d ed., © 1976 by Jerzy Kosinski, reprinted by permission of Houghton Mifflin Co. and Jerzy Kosinski. From *Passion Play*, © 1979 by Jerzy Kosinski, reprinted by permission of St. Martin's Press and Jerzy Kosinski. From *Pinball*, © 1982 by Jerzy Kosinski, reprinted by permission of Bantam Books. From *Steps*, © 1968 by Jerzy Kosinski, reprinted by permission of Random House, Inc.

For my wife, Barbara

Contents

Preface

I first read a Jerzy Kosinski novel during a year-long NEH seminar in American humor held at the University of New Mexico and directed by Professor Hamlin Hill. *The Painted Bird* came up in a discussion about the relationship between humor and pain, and although I subsequently completed an essay on Kosinski's use of the picaresque in his novels through *Cockpit* my interest in his fiction soon expanded beyond humor. At the conclusion of the seminar in May 1979 Kosinski's reputation as a writer was growing; he had just published *Blind Date* and was regaling viewers of the "Dick Cavett Show" with anecdotes of his life as a writer in America. As he continued to publish novels I examined the issues in his writing that emerged for me—his use of violence, the nature of his moral code, the writer as victimizer, and the reader as victim. These studies led me to explore a new and, for me, intriguing development in his fiction: the notion that writers' words can be turned against them, that book writing is double-edged, that the printed word can sometimes compose a cage for the writer. By the time I saw I needed a book-length study, the amount of criticism on Kosinski had grown considerably. My own insights have been sharpened by the presence of these and other writers on Kosinski: Paul Bruss, Andrew Gordon, Jack Hicks, Frederick J. Karl, Jerome Klinkowitz, Norman Lavers, Ivan Sanders, and Barbara Jane Tepa.

My book's title claims that Kosinski's words seek victims, and if seeking those words have made me a victim, I am a willing one. In doing so, however, I have concentrated on the words which define him as a novelist, preferring to look at the numerous interviews of Kosinski over the years as well as his own comments on his texts only when these illuminate my perceptions of the novels themselves. "Trust in the worth of a word," Kosinski wrote recently. This book attempts to assess the worth of his eight novels.

I am deeply grateful to several individuals for their assistance during various stages of the work. Professor Richard Giannone has been generous with his responses to my earlier writings on Kosinski. Professors Jerome Klinkowitz and Morton P. Levitt have offered thoughtful suggestions for improving the manuscript. My editor at Kent State University Press, Jeanne West, is a model of patience and skill. Most of all I am indebted to my wife, Barbara, for her loving encouragement throughout the writing of the book.

Introduction
Writing as an Exit

Kafka's thirteenth aphorism in "Reflection on Sin, Fame, Hope, and the True Way" is also his shortest: "A cage went in search of a bird." By means of the unexpected transference of vitality and flight from the bird to the inanimate cage, Kafka forces us to see the cage as having needs, seeking out its counterpart in order to define itself. Kafka's tantalizing symbiosis of cage and bird is an apt metaphor as well for Jerzy Kosinski's novels, each of which individually delineates the relationship between freedom and repression, victim and oppressor, writer and reader, bird and cage. On more than one occasion Kosinski has borrowed a metaphor from his most famous novel, *The Painted Bird* (1965), to refer to his own life.[1] He sees himself as a painted bird still—that is, as vulnerable, often ostracized, surrounded by those who represent emotional, economic, and political conformity. Several of his fictional protagonists also perceive themselves in terms of birds. Aside from the Boy in *The Painted Bird*, Tarden in *Cockpit* (1975) is both "a bony old bird" and a "hummingbird," a writer in *The Devil Tree* (1973) is "an angry hawk," and Levanter in *Blind Date* (1977) is compared with a "bird of prey."[2] Each of these protagonists, moreover, sees himself surrounded by some kind of cage. For Novak in Kosinski's first two books, both non-fiction, the cage is the Soviet Union in particular and communism in general. For the narrators of his first two novels, *The Painted Bird* and *Steps* (1968), the cage is not so specific: the bars surrounding these speakers undergo continual transformations, from Nazi occupation, to brutalized peasant life, to the repressive institutions of socialism. For Tarden and Levanter, protagonists of *Cockpit* and *Blind Date*, the cage takes on the trappings of mass consumption, television-induced conformity, and a willing surrender of personal freedom to the corporate life. In all of these avatars of bird and cage, the bird succeeds in exiting from the cage.

So it has been, in a sense, with Kosinski's own life, especially his flight from Communist Poland in 1957. "The creative man in a police state," Kosinski said in 1972, "has always been trapped in a cage where he can fly as long as he does not touch the wires. The predicament is: how to spread your wings in the cage."[3] For those who need more room to fly—including all artists—there is only one hope: escape. Kosinski, reflecting again on his former life in Poland, saw his escape from that cage in terms of an act of language. "To exit is a very important verb. When I reached the United States, I said to myself that since photography, unfortunately, requires such expensive equipment, my exit would have to be language itself, writing prose."[4] The writer's written words ensure him the exit he needs to spread his wings, unafraid of touching the wires. Kosinski once described Poland as a cage of words placed around him by the most powerful writer of his time. "I saw myself imprisoned in a large 'house of political fiction,' persecuted by a mad best-selling novelist, Stalin, and a band of his vicious editors from the Kremlin, and quite logically I saw myself as a protagonist of his fiction."[5] Writing prose eventually provided Kosinski with an exit, but he reminds us that the cage he fled from was a book in which he was character rather than author, victim rather than oppressor. Writing can free; writing can also imprison.

Kosinski's reference in 1972 to the bird and the cage only partly resembles Kafka's aphorism. Spoken at a time when his own career as a novelist was unfolding in surprising and successful ways, his departure from Poland nearly fifteen years in the past, Kosinski's statement did not hint at the possibility of his exit leading to still another cage, as if the cage itself were in pursuit of the bird. But by

1975, with the publication of *Cockpit*, Kosinski's concept of the bird and the cage began to take on a new complexity: the act of language that once brought the writer freedom might actually assist the cage in catching up to the bird. *Cockpit*, and *Blind Date* after it, show us that the bird is never fully free. The exit that writing once granted becomes for Kosinski—and for his many writer-protagonists—the testing of new space for the inevitable rush of wings against the wires of still another cage.

Kosinski's fiction, I am proposing, is about the art of writing fiction—but I qualify this statement in two ways. First of all, Kosinski has not been attracted to the self-conscious fiction we encounter in the likes of Donald Barthelme's "The Balloon" or John Barth's "Lost in the Funhouse." Although at one point *Steps* was discussed in the context of writers like these,[6] Kosinski does not invent new ways to underscore our awareness that a fiction is only a pattern of words after all. Rather, his power as a writer derives from the narrow rhetorical stance he chooses to impose on his material. He creates a voice limited by what it sees, a kind of eyeball, although certainly not a transparent one. Kosinski's fictive eyeball looks through a keyhole, as it were, seeing but not being seen. Thus Tarden of *Cockpit* describes how he once was forced to dress and undress himself repeatedly while, unknown to him at the time, he was being watched. His telling of the scene years later allows him to watch himself being watched—and the reader in turn watches that, completing this circle of a narration that comments on some of the ironies of narration while it continues to narrate.

My second qualification: Kosinski's novels confront the art of writing fiction from a unique and personal viewpoint. He is a writer whose past includes a rejection of his mother tongue in order to seize on an alien one. Although he has by now been a writer in English longer than he lived in Poland, the nature of his relationship to his "stepmother tongue" remains for him a persistent point of reference in a novel as recent as *Pinball* (1982). For all its practical wisdom in terms of survival (he had to learn English in 1957 simply to live), his determination to write in an alien tongue entailed a willed vulnerability, a conscious choice to exchange mastery of his native language for apprenticeship to an adopted one. His comment in 1971 that "no prison is as impregnable as language" can be taken two ways: it is difficult to break out of the prison of one's native speech, but it is also difficult for a foreigner to break into that prison from the outside. Freedom, imprisonment: his remarks during the early 1970s about using English for his art touch on not only the predictable difficulties of writing in another language (he claims his methods of composition once included dialing telephone operators to confirm the sense of his sentences)[7] but the elation he felt at freeing himself from anxieties associated with his mother tongue. The writer in an alien language, he said on one occasion, is free from the trauma of childhood links with particular words. "One is traumatized by the language when one is growing up. In our society the adults use the language as a reprimanding device. A child often cannot help feeling that certain words hurt just as much as certain gestures do. A native, because of this, is at the same time more idiosyncratic to certain aspects of his language, of his self, than a foreign-born writer who adopted a new language long after his formative years."[8] In a 1977 interview Kosinski expanded the implications of writing in a new language. "By the time I was 25, in America, my infancy in English had ended and I discovered that English, my stepmother tongue, offered me a sense of revelation, of fulfillment, of abandonment—everything contrary to the anxiety my mother tongue evoked."[9] For each of these images of release, of "revelation," Kosinski often provides a counterimage, one that suggests confinement, a cage as necessary to his art as is the accompanying sense of "abandonment." "A writer who writes in an accepted language which he has learned as an adult," he once wrote, "has in that language *one more curtain* that separates him from spontaneous expression [italics Kosinski's]."[10] Such a writer, restrained from the risk of verbal excess by his outsider's knowledge of the language, gains, he feels, a built-in editing process: "I think that a foreign-born writer who manipulates the adopted language (as opposed to the native who is more manipulated by the language) more consciously selects from the 'verbal environment' its pivotal aspects."[11] Kosinski's version of himself as a beginning writer in America makes a virtue out of the necessity imposed upon him as an alien. But it also suggests that the process of sorting out the problems of writing in an adopted language—with its attendant images of children, pain, reprimands, tongues, curtains, mothers—might occasionally be a subject compelling enough for fiction itself.

I want to pursue briefly Kosinski's account of how he turned a handicap into a style because it tells us something of the aggressive nature of his fiction. Writing in a new language forced him, he said, to pare down words to the bare minimum needed to instill a particular response in the reader. "For me to evoke more means to describe as little as possible. . . . I tend to believe that 'the more' of the language, the less evocative its power." The fewer the words, the sharper the impact. On the surface, all this is conventional enough, but Kosinski's accompanying analogies often picture for us a concept of words as weapons, as if the aim were not clarity but intimidation. "If you pierce someone with a small needle," Kosinski conjectures, "the response might be greater than, let's say, twenty-five moderate blows."[12] The alien writer's engagement with his new language—an act which ordinarily would disclose his unfamiliarity and thus his vulnerability—provides him instead with unexpected strength, allowing him to victimize the native reader. At least for this alien writer, penning words in his adopted tongue provided him with an alternative kind of power than that wielded by the novelist Stalin over his millions of characters, one of whom was Kosinski. Writing is not only an exit, it can imprison someone else. Or, to imprison a reader is a way of escaping one's own prison.

Kosinski's books—whatever else they accomplish—inevitably involve protagonists who see themselves moving along an imaginary language scale that ranges from powerlessness to mastery, from mute victimization to words arranged to transform readers into victims. Language is never a given, a mere means of expression, but a continual battle. His fiction dramatizes protagonists who not only wage war with words but do so as writers, whether they are what I term "protowriters," such as the narrators of *The Painted Bird* and *Steps*, or actual writers, such as those in *Passion Play* (1979) and *Pinball*. His consistent concern in all of these novels has been to describe a writer who first seizes power by mastering a language and then exits from the cage by means of the flight of words. In Kosinski's first novel, *The Painted Bird*, the Boy dreams of becoming a writer like the "great man" that Gorky once was; in a later novel, *Pinball*, Domostoy aspires to write music that would captivate an audience while revealing nothing of the composer. Domostoy wants to speak, as he says, a "language without an accent." Each of Kosinski's books tests anew the premise that the writer's words can gain for him the power to flee from the cage of his own life by dominating the reader. For Kosinski, the meaning of the writer's power—and his vulnerability—has undergone several transformations over the years. As he confronts the task of writing each new book, he is a different writer. He cannot write except from within the context of his previous achievement as a writer, and this context he transforms in novels like *Passion Play* and *Pinball* into imaginary cages. Kosinski said in 1980 that "Like Fabian [the protagonist of *Passion Play*], I think that I have a sense of destiny now which I didn't have before. Because I have written the books that I have written—they form my destiny as it has been lived until now. There is a pattern."[13] This pattern of what he has written and published—and, to a lesser extent, how his work has been received—shapes his next writer-protagonist. Since every pattern is also a confinement, the novels thus confront not only the paradox of the nature of writing but also the paradox of his career as a novelist whose words have both released him from cages and imprisoned him in new ones. Few writers have been so radically transformed by the publication of a book, and it is perhaps understandable why Kosinski is drawn to the notion of writing as an exit: his first book, *The Future Is Ours, Comrade* (1960),[14] transformed him from a Polish refugee—drifting between jobs at Kinney parking lots, scraping rust from tramp steamers, or driving truck-loads of hats throughout the Southwest—to a successful writer, serialized in *Reader's Digest*.[15] Before the publication of his second book, *No Third Path* (1962), one of his many readers married him. And his writing not only won him a wife, that woman, Mary Hayward Weir, was one of the wealthiest persons in the United States.

The Novak Books

Kosinski's two books on the sociology of the individual in the Soviet Union tell us much of the novelist he would soon become. For *The Future Is Ours, Comrade* he created a fictional narrator, "Joseph Novak,"[16] who arranges his Russian experience into chapters that bring the reader within earshot of representative Russians who talk to Novak about everything—housing, monuments, street life, police on horseback, vodka, nudity, labor unions, the Party. Novak himself is reticent about his own identity. We learn little of his personal past, his family, his national origin, how he managed to become a "minor bureaucrat from one of the satellite countries," (15) or how he succeeded in escaping to the West to write the book. What is clear is that Novak's words examine a cage he has left behind. The enigmatic narrator is a device that allows Kosinski to place the reader in the scenes as a secret listener, overhearing the conversations of Russians who are unaware their words are being preserved. Deception is the order of the day. Just as the American reader of *The Future Is Ours, Comrade* in 1960 was unaware that Novak was a mask for Jerzy Kosinski, so too the many Russians in the book were unaware that the "minor bureaucrat" was not only an inveterate note taker, but a writer learning his art.

Kosinski's prose is suggestive rather than explanatory or tendentious. In his foreword, Novak recalls a train ride to Moscow with a party official, who boasts of the diversity of Russia while he carefully peels the "golden skin of a banana" (12). Wearing a heavy gold watch, the official is obviously a privileged member of the Soviet state. As the train stops for a time in a remote country station, a small boy stares greedily through the window at the official's plate of fruit.

"His keen eyes discovered the oranges and bananas on the table in front of us" (12). The scene prepares us to trust the narrator's ability to stage a scene without an explicit evaluation. Here, the prideful words of the bureaucrat contrast with the silent stare of the hungry boy.

The exchange between Novak and the official is a model as well for Kosinski's attitude toward language in *The Future Is Ours, Comrade*. The spoken words of Party officials, soldiers, and workers clash against the grim reality of experience, often revealed by the hopeless, silent gesture—such as the hungry boy's stare—rather than by words. The words that are spoken frequently hide fear, and so language itself becomes a mask. Survival depends on adjusting the mask successfully, of saying the right thing. Novak, moving from cramped apartment to crowded street to small village, begins to see that every individual is a potential snare. One citizen confides to Novak, "A friend is a dangerous thing. He knows everything about you. A friend is a luxury that I, personally, can't afford. I'd rather buy a radio" (88).

For Novak, the entire experience in Russia begins to resemble a deadly game between victim and oppressor. Obligatory group meetings that demand self-criticism from each member force even dedicated party functionaries into deception, and each deception makes that member vulnerable to eventual exposure. One successful party official, and a friend from the past, Dymitrij, reveals to Novak how he has worked his way to an important party position:

> The organization of our daily life forces us into these activities. All the parts of our life are closely tied to them. If a man wants to live—and what man doesn't—he must change as his surroundings change. Each of us is a small wheel in a large machine, and there is no way out of it. You can change places with another wheel, but you can't change the machine itself. And you can't live outside the *organized group*. (213)

Thus even the Dymitrijs of the Soviet world must confront daily the "hazards of satisfying ambition, fighting competitors, struggling to hold their own position, or trying to capture a position occupied by

someone else" (213). At any moment the oppressor might make a
mistake and become victim again. To survive, continues Dymitrij,
the individual must acquire continual vigilance so that victimization
can be conferred on others, rather than on oneself. Dymitrij then
confides to Novak how he has risen through the ranks by winning
the game of survival, namely, by transforming individuals into
victims. "To be always attacking others, to bring to life the Party
line, and at the same time not to come into conflict with that line is
the most difficult game" (212). The game's risky nature parallels the
role of the writer. Without knowing it, Dymitrij is an artist: he
transforms people into characters confined within an invented plot,
the Party line. His "stories" give him power as they create victims.
But these same stories can be used against him.

In a country full of victims, learning the game of survival is
imperative. Novak now focuses on still another survivor, a former
high functionary in a labor union who was arrested in 1936,
tortured, and sentenced to life at hard labor in a quarry. After
eighteen years he is released. Novak interviews him in a Leningrad
restaurant. The man's hands, broken and twisted by years of torture,
lie on the white tablecloth in front of Novak.[17] "The joints were
swollen and jutted out and to the sides. On some fingers the nails
were ingrown. They stretched out and their layers formed shapeless
lumps. The flesh was blue and brown. . . . It was difficult for me to
realize that these were the hands of a living man, hands that had been
so terribly violated by other human beings" (140). The man with the
broken hands seems to Novak, who is becoming a writer, an example
of the power of the state to crush writing itself.

Revenge, power, escape. The words begin to reverberate through
the final chapters of The Future Is Ours, Comrade. Every victim he
meets becomes for Novak a living testament to the need to obtain
power. Earlier in his Russian experience Novak felt he was in a cage
with no exit; now he realizes there is an exit: deception, principally
through the mask of language. Dymitrij had confided to him, "A
man is only what others think he is, nothing more" (220). The right
mask must be worn. The right language must be mastered.

The book ends with Novak's plane flight from Russia, the exit from at least one cage. But the narrator is silent about the exit from the nameless "East European" country of which he was once a minor bureaucrat. Novak's plane rises above the Russian countryside, heading west but not, for the time being, to the West. "The plane climbed higher. The steamy, curling clouds which hugged it tightly fell away. The sky contrasted sharply with the earth below, on which darkness had already fallen" (286).

Kosinski's assertions about the influence of the Soviet military on political life, his analysis of the hold of the Party on the common citizens, psychiatric confinement of dissidents, widespread bribery, and Soviet anti-Semitism are surprisingly relevant today.[18] The book was well received;[19] more importantly, *The Future Is Ours, Comrade* is a book in which the author comes to terms with his own material—the transmutation of his past experience in Russia into compelling narrative. The most memorable scenes of the book are not so much his insights into Soviet political institutions as the many vignettes which reveal glimpses of people struggling at the game of victim and oppressor: the crushed and broken hands folded on a white table-cloth, a girl waving a silent good-bye from a receding train station, a boy staring through glass at forbidden fruit. In these scenes the writer is both observer and participant, publicly open but privately deceptive, alone behind his mask of conformity, dreaming of power while looking for an exit from the cage.

Kosinski's success with his first book determined the scope and method of his second, *No Third Path* (1962).[20] Kosinski's persona, Novak, had become an author whose book, *The Future Is Ours, Comrade*, brought him recognition in the West while permanently barring him from returning to the world he wrote about, the subject of his research. In his foreword, Kosinski reveals a few more details about the background of Novak, but continues to be reticent about Novak's national origin or age. Only once in the book do we see Novak's personality analyzed by another Russian. The situation concerns Zina, a girl Novak knew in Sevastapol, who is a dedicated Communist, and of whom Novak had asked a sexual encounter to prove the sincerity of their relationship. Zina's attack on Novak gives us the first extended—if hostile—analysis of the young Novak's state of mind:

> And yet you are a little egoist, wrapped up in yourself! Your own nose, which you consider too long, your naturalistic remembrances of childhood and the war, your hatred of village life and primitive conditions, your 'exercise of intimacy'—all this causes the world of today to reach you in a *distorted image.* You refract it, as it were, in a prism. . . . Where will your 'philosophy of the distorted image' lead you in the long run? . . . In the name of what humanism are you fighting against the Soviet humanism, you, *the man on the fence,* the worst phenomenon of the coexistence of two social systems? (58–59)

After this outburst Novak breaks with Zina; but her tirade further delineates our own image of Novak in Russia—a loner, driven by painful childhood memories, increasingly suspicious of socialism, willing to use sexual intimacy as a means of enhancing an emotional life that can be hidden from the prying eyes of the state, but above all—a writer willing to put himself at risk.

As in *The Future Is Ours, Comrade,* Novak finds himself surrounded by people caught in the relentless bond that ties victim and oppressor, hunter and hunted. One Muscovite, K., works as a bookkeeper. He confides to Novak that he "feels as free as a bird" because he has carefully kept out of sight, out of politics, and is not even a Party member. "All philosophy," K. says, consists in knowing "not to distinguish oneself" (53). For K., the great good place in Moscow—and the safest—is a public toilet. "You enter, the entire room is so clean that it glitters, you lock the door behind you, and you are *alone.* . . . *No one* has the right to disturb you. . . . You sit—like a Greek god!" (54). The scene in which K., alone in the toilet, enjoys temporary freedom from surveillance, anticipates a character in Kosinski's novel, *Steps*—"The Philosopher," a student who hides in the public toilets to escape similar oppression. K., having revealed his own philosophy to the younger Novak, asks Novak for his. Novak's answer represents the first revelation of his true feelings to another person: "I—I would like to depend on nobody. You know, to tailor my life to my own yardstick, and not to rifle around in ready-made-clothes stores. . ." (53). K. is an antiwriter; he sits in safety producing only his own waste. Novak needs the freedom to "tailor" his experience, which means composing the words that threaten his exposure.

Novak continues his search for patterns of escape, for people who have succeeded in one way or another in achieving some form of freedom. The few he finds are secret artists, who, like himself, disguise their personal vision behind a mask of conformity. One is a pianist and a member of the Moscow Conservatory. Peter G. composes music for his audience "in accordance," he tells Novak, "with the principles of the socialist music which I accept as historically correct and in step with the progress of art" (84). But underneath the pile of officially sanctioned compositions in his apartment, Novak comes across one labeled "Experimental." Novak urges Peter to play it for him, which he agrees to do after first securing a promise from Novak not to tell anyone that he indulges in "such wild musical fancies between serious *work*" (83). Novak hears what he considers a brilliant composition. Peter then admits that his piece can never be played in public because it is "a classic example of the modernism and formalism which our music rejects as completely alien" (84). This artist writes his compositions to no one but himself. The pianist's secret compositions are paradigms of Novak's own writing, which he can show to no one. Novak's words expose the victim-oppressor bond of Soviet society, and that bond, he sees, is largely maintained by language. Both he and Peter G. are in a cage of words.

In a chapter called "The Price of Being Different," Novak meets a Russian girl by the name of Varvara, who describes her own alienation from the Soviet system. She first sensed the plight of the nonconformist as a young girl.

I remember how once a group of us kids caught a sparrow in a trap. . . . We then painted him purple and I must admit he actually looked much better—more proud and unusual. After the paint had dried we let him go to rejoin his flock. We thought he would be admired for his beautiful and unusual coloring, become a model to all the gray sparrows in the vicinity, and they would make him their king. He rose high and was quickly surrounded by his companions. For a few minutes their chirping grew much louder and then—a small object began plummeting earthward. . . . In a mud puddle lay our purple sparrow—dead. . . . He had been killed by the other sparrows, by their hate for color and their instinct of belonging to a gray flock. Then, for the first time, *I understood.* (107)

The episode of the painted sparrow epitomizes not only Varvara's life as an outcast, but that of anyone who would defy conformity in Russia. As an image, it is also the most striking link between Kosinski's brief career as a writer of social science and his present one as a novelist.

In the epilogue of *No Third Path*, Novak offers a terse summary of the genesis of the book and his vision of a more creative and colorful life than that which awaited him under a socialist system. "The descriptions contained in this book do not propose moral codes and involve no judgments: they are sketches" (21). But these sketches *do* propose moral judgments. They do so not by direct statement but by implication. Varvara's plight as a symbolic painted bird (as well as the crippled hands on the white tablecloth in the first Novak book) indict a whole political system as morally bankrupt. This indictment is no less strong for being our own inference from the text of such sketches. Kosinski's denial of the presence of moral codes is a half-truth; and that is to the good of his art as a writer. But even at this early point in his career, we cannot accept his pronouncements about his writing at face value.

With the publication of his second book, Kosinski must have felt that the material of his own past, even as far back as his own childhood (those "naturalistic remembrances" that Zina spoke scornfully about) would yield new material for his growing mastery of the art of his tale-telling. The tales in this next book would concern another figure like himself, nameless, one who went through discoveries of pain somewhat the way Varvara did when she painted a gray sparrow purple.

Kosinski's first two books on Soviet life reveal a gradual shift from a study of institutions to a dramatization of psychological states of mind—especially fear and its relation to the imagination. The books also reflect Kosinski's interest in the effect of the collective on the individual psyche, how it forces the psyche either to submit and become victim or to respond in imaginative, often deceptive ways, of which the most deceptive is simply to write about it. The strongest scenes focus on the role playing that the collective forces on the individual—bureaucratic games of confrontation and intimidation, masks, paranoia. Different versions of such scenes later turn up in a number of his novels: George Levanter's friend, Romarkin, challenging a professor in a hushed lecture hall (*Blind Date*), sexual experimentation to test a willingness to explore the underside of society (*Cockpit* and *Passion Play*), a pianist's experimental work and his role as outcast (*Pinball*).

By the time of the last reviews of his second book in 1962, Kosinski had created a public image of himself as a writer that, for complex reasons, shortly became one he wished to escape. He had transformed himself from an unknown immigrant into a successful writer; both his books had been serialized in *Reader's Digest* and ultimately earned for him, one critic claims, $150,000.[21] But this public perception of himself as a writer on the Soviet system could not be sustained through still another book.[22]

For the first time—but not for the last—Kosinski's own writings seemed to have placed him inside a cage. His new American audience perceived him as Novak, the journalist and social scientist positioned on the inside track to understanding the Soviet Union. But he could never return to replenish the collection of interviews that helped create his image. The life he was now living with Mary Haywood Weir, replete with elegant hotels and private jets—could only have emphasized the contrast between Kosinski's image of himself in 1957, alone in New York clutching laboriously recorded notes written in Polish, and the image of himself five years later, the acknowledged author of the "Novak" books. If he felt in a cage, only a new kind of writing would release him. After all, the real interest in his first two books—the behavior of the self under pressure from

five-novel cycle

society, the intimate relationship between victim and oppressor, and the exhilarating if risky power of the writer's deception—was by no means confined to his travels in the Soviet Union.

The Constant in Kosinski's Evolving Aesthetic

Because of the open-ended nature of Kosinski's continual probing of what it means to be a writer, and the unique and often bizarre range of personal experience he can bring to bear on that probing (as of June 1982 he is free to add what it is like to be a writer accused of not writing his own books, an issue which I address in the appendix), Kosinski's work needs a reassessment. It is not enough to rely on his often scintillating remarks on the nature of fiction he once made in his essay, *Notes of the Author on The Painted Bird* (1967), because a number of these comments, such as those on Jung and the unconscious, do not illuminate his later work. His disdain for the use of plot, first advanced in *The Art of the Self: Essays a Propos Steps* (1968) does not survive the composition of *Passion Play* and *Pinball*, both of which depend on conventional understandings of the function of plot. Kosinski has spoken of the "constant pruning"[23] he forces on his sentences as he composes, but the sparse, unadorned style we associate with *Steps* and perhaps *Being There* (1971) does not always characterize the pages of either *The Painted Bird*, written earlier, or *Passion Play* and *Pinball*, written more than a decade after *The Painted Bird*. Kosinski's own appraisals of his work, moreover, need to be looked at in the light of both his more recent comments and the direction of his fiction since *Blind Date*. When, for instance, he said in 1976 that he wrote *The Painted Bird* as the first of a five-novel cycle, he was looking back from a specific moment in his career, one which of course included the publication of five novels. He saw his work then as methodically advancing a specific thesis: "As the story began to evolve, I realized that I wanted to extend certain themes, modulating them through a series of five novels. This five-book cycle would present archetypal aspects of the individual's relationship to society.''[24] But the subsequent novels, *Blind Date* through *Pinball*, reveal a more exacting and personal relationship than that between the individual and society. Kosinski's recent fiction—and in fact all of his novels, including his first two books on the social system of the Soviet Union—tests the dynamic and often antagonistic relationship between the artist and his audience, the writer and his reader. Here is one of several remarks Kosinski made on the duplicitous, manipulative energy of the writer's words as they provoke, victimize, and ultimately transform the reader: "By engaging my reader, on one hand, in the concrete, visible acts of cunning, violence—assault, and disguise—(as opposed to its diluted, camouflaged violence of our total environment) my fiction is, on the other, purging his emotions, enraging him, polarizing his anger, his moral climate, turning him *against* such acts (and against the author as well).''[25] Still, it is not clear just why the reader should turn against acts of "cunning" and "violence" described in a fiction *and* against the author as well. We certainly do not turn against Dostoyevski (to choose a writer Kosinski himself quotes) for narrating Raskolnokov's axing of an old woman. But if Kosinski is perhaps self-serving here (he is attacked only because his art is powerful), he is nevertheless correct to emphasize that the relationship between his fictive narrator and the reader in *The Painted Bird* and *Cockpit* is one of provocation, deception, and victimization.

Kosinski's abundant references to other writers in both his fiction and essays consistently underscore the paradoxical combination of power and vulnerability that constitutes the act of writing. His quotations from Melville, Proust, Dostoyevski, de Sade, Camus, Saint-Exupéry, and John Milton collectively point to the subversive, double life of the writer, who is simultaneously deceiver and truth teller, manipulator and victim. "O what a mask was there, what a disguise!," prefaces Kosinski's *The Art of the Self*. This line from Milton's "The Passion" sums up the moment when Christ, the "sov'ran Priest," enters the "Poor fleshly Tabernacle" of the human form at Bethlehem. Milton's version of the disguised and masked Christ is one of Kosinski's many evocations of the writer engaged in his art—simultaneously deceiving the reader while releasing an unpredictable energy. A selection from Proust that prefaces *The Devil Tree* is another variation of the image of the writer as deceiver. "Sometimes the future dwells in us without our knowing it and when we think we are lying our words foretell an imminent reality." The artist's success depends on the strength of his deception, but the audience's response to his disguise is volatile, unpredictable; the artist's lies may turn into truth.

Or, they may turn the writer back into a victim, as if the cage were to catch up to the bird. In one episode of *Cockpit*, the protagonist-narrator assumes for a time the role of the reader as avenger. Tarden reads through the work of a successfully published writer and discovers his powers as a reader can unmask this writer. "As I read, I dictated brief bursts of thoughts into a tape recorder. Only when I finished scanning everything the writer had produced, did I become aware how flat and unchallenging the topography of his work was" (92). Here, the writer's words (which once marked his exit from obscurity to fame) have become the bars of still another cage, unwittingly providing the "map" that exposes the writer's work as "flat and unchallenging." The passage expresses Kosinski's first hint that a writer's words may not grant him an unqualified exit—but that the cage left behind might well have, as in Kafka's aphorism, unexpected powers of pursuit. *Cockpit* suggests that the writer's power over his reader is subject to sudden shifts, that the predator-prey relationship Kosinski once described as "the struggle between the book (the predator) and the reader (the victim)" might on occasion reverse itself.[26] These unpredictable reversals of the flow of power—first analyzed by Novak in *The Future Is Ours, Comrade* in terms of abrupt transformations of Party members from oppressors into victims—remain an important aspect of Kosinski's attitude toward the act of writing. Just as the victim-narrator in the Novak books, as well as those in *The Painted Bird* and *Steps*, might seize briefly the oppressor's role, usually by means of a specific act of language, so too the oppressor is continually subject to unwelcome transformations back into victim. Such pairings of dialectical forces—victim and oppressor, writer and reader, bird and cage—suggest the dynamic nature of Kosinski's fiction.[27] The vision that animates the novels relies on continual testings, tentative articulations about the writer's self that inevitably emerge from clashes between opposite psychic and linguistic forces. Modes of language are pitted against one another. The Boy in *The Painted Bird* embraces the Russian language, refusing to speak his mother tongue, because he senses that the power he needs to redeem himself from victimization lies hidden within the speech of the Soviet soldiers who have befriended him. If speech can make one a victim, the Boy reasons, speech—the right kind—can also make one an oppressor. In a similar way, the writer's words seek to make victims of his readers in order to ensure escape from his own sense of powerlessness. But these same words may, as Tarden discovered, provide maps that the reader can use to expose the identity of the writer, returning him to victimization, such as when Tarden's employer, the director of a spy agency of the United States, agrees to blackmail the writer whose map Tarden has successfully read. Similar scenes from *Cockpit* through *Pinball* test new and often painful insights about the writer's power and vulnerability, about writing as escape and writing as entrapment.

I have arranged Kosinski's eight novels into four pairings, discussing each pairing in a chapter. The four chapters on the novels explore his unique probings into the art of writing. When on occasion I turn to the relationship between Kosinski's life and his fiction, a relationship about which Kosinski has often invited speculation, I follow this assumption: his personal experiences are not factors in assessing the quality of either individual novels or his work as a whole. Whatever really happened to Kosinski as a boy in Poland during World War II or as an adult riding in a taxi in Los Angeles,[28] these experiences were not composed of printed words arranged for specific artistic effects. What counts obviously is the art of each novel. Here, too, I would admit the need for caution about seeing his work in terms of a cycle or overall pattern for which each novel is more or less an equal contribution. Concepts like "cycle" and "development" are apt to mislead in Kosinski's case because they imply uniform movement or progress. But if the novels display thematic connections—and I am claiming that all reveal the writer as both caged and released by language—they are uneven in quality. *The Painted Bird* is not only his first but undeniably his best; I would rank *Cockpit* next, ahead of the prize-winning *Steps*. In short, rather than focusing too much on how the novels aim at a larger design, we should regard each as an individual discovery, a renewed look at still more dimensions of the paradox of the writer. Some of these discoveries, like those in *Cockpit* and *Steps*, generate their own energy independently from prior Kosinski novels. Other passages seem forced and contrived, such as certain scenes from *Passion Play, The Devil Tree*, and *Pinball*. The notion of a cycle, moreover, suggests the image of a writer looking ahead to a gradually unfolding concept which guides the book he is writing. Since *Blind Date*, the novels look as much to their predecessors for confirmation and clarification of design.

one
Meat in Cans
The Painted Bird and *Steps*

The Painted Bird[1] is primarily a book about language testing. Its main character, the unnamed Boy, is also the narrator grown old, an adult who has mastered the right language and who can look back at his childhood, at his desperate unlearning of a speech that brought him only the status of victim. Between that point of desperation—perhaps symbolized by the muteness the narrator experienced, his tongue, as he says, flapping "helplessly in my mouth"—and the point that we, his readers, first listen to his language, lies a great abyss. The actual telling of the story gives us only a partial glimpse into the abyss. The story ends as the speaker reaches adolescence, and we never learn who the speaker has become as an adult or what motivated him to confine his viewpoint to the child he no longer is as he writes. But the telling does reveal to us how the narrator, whose "voice was too weak to rise above the earth" (25), discovered the speech that redeemed him from victimization.

Like all novels, *The Painted Bird* tells a tale, but this telling also involves the conscious discarding of tales, the necessary learning of new tales, and the disquieting relationship between the teller and his listener, the victim. The Boy's story, first of all, is a painful giving up of stories. His actual voice—as opposed to the brief paragraphs in the third person which provide a historical preface for the narration—begins to speak after the worst of a child's deprivations, the loss of parents, has already taken place. "I lived in Marta's hut," the

Boy begins, "expecting my parents to come for me any day, any hour" (3). The Boy invents compensations, tests them as anodynes, discards them as useless. "Crying did not help," he says. He looks to Marta, a crone who lives apart from the village where her services as a healer are valued. Marta mutters to herself, says the Boy, "in a language I could not quite understand," but he knows he must learn it to survive, and to learn it means to repress his mother tongue. Inside Marta's hut he can still hear his mother's voice. "I could see my mother sitting at the piano. I heard the words of her songs" (8). But the words of her songs cannot erase the present. Like his own tears, they do not help. He thinks of his past as a false language, "an illusion like one of my old nanny's incredible fables" (8). He is ready to learn from Marta, and begins by listening carefully to the language of animals. "She encouraged me to play in the yard and make friends with the household animals. . . . These animals had their own life, their loves and disagreements, and they held discussions in a language of their own" (4). With barely a first lesson mastered, the Boy loses his teacher, Marta, who goes up in smoke. As he watches Marta's hut burn and senses that he is once more abandoned—nanny, nurse, and mother before Marta—he is left to face a savage world with little more than a "story my mother told me" about a witch. He must abandon not only his mother's story but her way of telling, with its rhetorical assumption of a loving speaker and a dependent, nurtured hearer. The Boy's survival depends on his ability to master new and cruel stories more appropriate for his new environment, such as the tale he tells to a murderous carpenter of war booty hidden in an abandoned pillbox. This tale, a painful weaning from his mother's mode of telling, is based on a rhetoric of hate: the teller turns out to be a deceiver, the hearer the victim. Thus the tale not only saves the Boy's life but it destroys his listener, the carpenter, literally cutting the cord that binds together torturer and victim. Further on in this painful learning of a language, Garbos, a sadistic peasant, orders the Boy to tell him Gypsy stories, but all he can do is recite "poems he heard before the war," poems in his mother tongue. The poems bring about only an increase in Garbos's abuse.

But the story Garbos himself tells the Boy reveals to him something about the kind of tale needed to survive: Garbos tells the Boy about a man who is impaled on a stake sharpened like "a gigantic pencil," an image which suggests the writer's power, the tale-teller's hold over his victim. Garbos's story suggests the nature of the tale the Boy has not yet learned to tell, but it is the Boy transformed into the adult narrator—speaking from the other side of the abyss—who tells it so well: "Now hanging under the ceiling I could almost see the man and hear him howling in the night, trying to raise to the indifferent sky his arms which hung by the bloated trunk of his body. He must have looked like a bird knocked out of a tree by a slingshot and fallen flabbily onto a dried-out, pointed stalk" (138). In the imagination of the suffering Boy, man-victim becomes bird-victim, the sharpened pencil one of nature's lethal stabbings.

Rainbow the tale-teller is another of these narrators who are victimizers. "In the evenings when he entertained his neighbors he could talk for hours about rainbows. Listening to him from a dark corner, I learned that a rainbow is a long arched stalk, hollow as a straw" (106). Rainbow's story of fish swimming through rainbows from pond to pond cannot be separated from his rape of a Jewish girl; his power over the girl is analogous to the now grown narrator's power over his readers, us. Thus does the Boy learn the unspeakable connection between tale-telling and torture, words and victims. His slow learning, his testing of modes of telling in his search for the right language, is also the story of the transformation of the Boy into an aspiring writer, the same writer who finds, eventually, the right language to tell his story.

For much of this story the Boy's quest is for a particular language, for whatever speech is necessary to avoid victimization. When he is tormented by peasants after Marta's death, he finds that because he cannot speak their language he is treated the way some boys once tortured his pet squirrel. "I hopped around like a squirrel while he continued whipping me" (16). The Boy tries to speak this new peasant dialect, knowing that his ignorance of it marks him as an outsider and natural victim. "I tried to tell them something, but my

language and the manner in which I spoke it only made them giggle"
(17). The only words he knows with which to protest, to implore,
brand him as victim and provoke further the cruelties of the
peasants.

In one of the book's first scenes, the Boy, who is temporarily living
with Olga the Wise One, catches a fever. To cure him, Olga digs a
hole and buries him up to his neck. "I lost all awareness. Like an
abandoned head of cabbage, I became part of the great field" (23).
Early the next morning a flock of ravens begins to attack him. Here
too, his cries and shouts only provoke the birds. He hears the flock's
raven speech, "the language of their own," but he cannot speak it.
Crazed by their beaks, the Boy sinks into unconsciousness. "I was
myself now a bird. I was trying to free my chilled wings from the
earth. Stretching my limbs, I joined the flock of ravens. . . . I
soared straight into a ray of sunshine. . . . and my joyous cawing
was mimicked by my winged companions" (25). Only in his imagination does he pass over into the world of this new language of
joyous cawing, in which now the ravens must practice his sounds.
His old language is buried in the fields below him. After this first
imprisonment in the earth, the Boy endures one form of persecution
after another. He is whipped, pushed below the ice of a frozen pond,
left to drown in a river, tossed into a cesspool, and suspended from
hooks over a bloodthirsty dog. In each case, the Boy learns that
survival depends on observing the behavior of the oppressor,
decoding the oppressor's language, and eventually learning to speak
that language. When he hears from Olga the Wise One that he
possesses an "evil spirit," he stares at the eyes of some of his peasant
tormentors forcing them to look away. Attacked by dogs, he instinc-
tively counterattacks, taking on for the moment the behavior and
voice of a wild animal. "I crouched before the fence, waving my
hands vigorously, hopping like a frog, howling, and throwing stones.
The dogs halted astonished, uncertain of who I was and how to act. A
human being had suddenly acquired dimensions unknown to them"
(61). The Boy's spontaneous mimicking of dog speech, his "howling," resembles an earlier ruse in which he "hissed like a snake"

(32), confusing a dog long enough to snatch from its owner a flaming "comet."

The Boy's whirling comet, much like the gigantic pencil, suggests the power of the writer's art, and, like Prometheus's own, the fire smoldering in the tin can is stolen. The comet's glowing arc signals the presence of a demonic energy, a defiant inspiration; it forms a circle of defense, a "fortress," an "indispensable protection against dogs and people" (29). Inside this circle of flame carved out of the darkness the Boy earns temporary refuge but also a separateness as bleak as that of any of Melville's "isolatoes." Once the Boy even ties himself to his comet, wrapping "some of the wire attached to the handle around my wrist" (30); the gesture suggests a self-manacling, a willing surrender of freedom of movement in exchange for the restraining discipline of the comet's fire, and as such represents the opposite of that other wrist tying, the cord that once bound the Boy to his tormentor, the carpenter. Here, wrist and comet bring to mind not only the writer's inspiration but the mundane, pen-in-hand travail of his craft.

not so—the comet is a weapon & source of security

The Boy's first mentor of this speech of animals is one who speaks it himself, Lekh the bird trapper. The birds Lekh encloses in his cages of woven twigs are his prisoners and his listeners. Lekh could "imitate the carefree call of the cuckoo, the screech of the magpie, the hooting of the owl" (42). He speaks to birds as much as he does to the Boy, whose tiny cagelike bed is itself enclosed by bird cages. "At the very bottom of one of these cages a narrow space was found for me" (43). Lekh's tales about birds define the terms of the Boy's own entrapment as well as the temporary exhilaration of release. Cuckoos are "noblemen" imprisoned inside bird bodies, "begging God in vain to turn them back into humans" (45). Swallows, Lekh says, spend the winter in ponds sealed by ice. The Boy can make no distinction between Lekh's tales and his actions: both are texts to be read; both provide a place for him in the plot. Two stork parents argue over the presence of a gosling in the nest (placed there by Lekh); the father stork, aided by other storks, pecks to death his seemingly unfaithful wife, while the abandoned gosling, "shedding bitter tears,'' watches helplessly, duplicating the Boy's own grief at the loss of his parents. When Lekh releases his frustrations on the hapless birds by painting them gaudy colors, the Boy reads Lekh's silent acts as exempla, unspoken testimonies of his status, but also timely warnings to escape the plot Lekh has designed for his birds. The Boy watches as a released bird, unaware of its damning marks, is singled out for death by its own flock. "We saw soon afterwards how one bird after another would peel off in a fierce attack. . . . When we finally found the painted bird it was usually dead" (51). The pile of thrashing painted birds signals to the Boy the need to invent alternate tales, to break out of the plot that seems to constrict his life. All around him hostile tellers invent tales in which he is the central character, and always his role is victim. He hears that his stare causes sickness, that his hair extracts lightning from the sky. To survive, he must tell new tales of himself, and, above all, abandon the mode of telling of his "mother and my nurses," those stories of the nurturing female. The time calls for stories invented by the killer male, tales of men impaled on pointed poles as sharp as the pencils needed to write them.

Freed of Lekh, the Boy tells a story to an injured horse. It is a story with a happy ending. "I spoke to him about the warm stable, the smell of hay, and I assured him that a man could set his bone and seal it with herbs. I told him about the lush meadows still under snow, only awaiting spring" (80). The Boy is sincere and wishes the horse well. But his tale is deceptive: its purpose is to enhance the status of the teller, to ingratiate himself with the horse's owner. Ultimately, the Boy's tale leads the horse to a brutal death. When the farmer examines the Boy somewhat the way the Boy first sized up the horse, the Boy senses he is in danger of appropriating the role he had earlier assigned to the horse—victim. Instead, carefully censoring "any stories which might arouse his suspicions" (81), the Boy invents a new tale about himself. "I swore on everything and everybody I could think of that I was a good Christian and an obedient worker" (81). The farmer accepts this story and orders him to tell more. In time he becomes an exotic pet, a captive storyteller, forced to perform at parties, weddings. He is Scheherazade, spinning stories on cue that manage to defer the fate allotted to him by his listeners, who, when he is silent, become again his tormentors. Listening to him, they lose some of their power over him. His words are so captivating that the peasants cannot swallow their dinner. "They were entirely convulsed by the fables and rhymed stories about animals. Listening to stories about a goat traveling across the world in search of the capital of goatland, about a cat in seven-league boots, the bull Ferdinand, Snow White and the Seven Dwarfs, Mickey Mouse, and Pinocchio, the guests laughed, choking on their food and sputtering vodka" (83). Here, tale-telling temporarily saves him. But his speech, which he defines as "urban" (83), is at odds with the language of his tormentors, peasants of "slow, deliberate speech" who measure their words carefully. Their custom, the Boy says, requires them "to spare words as one spares salt" (82). Unwillingly, the Boy finds himself on a battlefield in which modes of speech are at war, and he must choose between the taciturn or loquacious. The Boy is forced by the peasants to recite still more fables and rhymed stories about animals in front of an audience which is hostile to eloquence. He senses that his brand of speech forces him again to play victim: "whenever I recited poetry at great speed, the peasants opened their eyes wide in amazement, thinking that I was out of my mind and that my fast speech was some sort of infirmity" (83). In the minds of the Boy's oppressors, verbal agility is a weakness, even dangerous. Although his voice suggests a certain power—he says his "city talk" was "full of hard consonants" and "rattled like machine-gun fire"—his speech lacks the power to oppress. The peasants choose a stronger power that they sense lies in silent action. At a wedding in which the Boy is again forced to display his fast speech and vulnerability, he becomes the lone witness to a murder: a peasant wordlessly stabs another peasant. The Boy, watching the death agony of the stabbed man, recognizes not only a fellow victim but the vulnerability of mere human speech in the face of silent, brutal power. "The stabbed man tried to rise. He looked around with glassy eyes; when he saw me he tried to say something, but all

that came out of his mouth was a half-chewed piece of cabbage"
(85). Again, silent brutality defines the victim, reduces his words to
bits of spit-out cabbage, recalling the image of the Boy's head as a
cabbage, immobile and speechless in the face of his tormentors.

The Boy's wedding tales cannot postpone for long the telling by
others of tales which claim for him a role in them. He thinks of the
power of the Germans to invent—clever bomb fuses, first of all, but
also verbal inventions on a grand scale. The German claim of racial
superiority the Boy sees as a story powerful enough to draw him into
its plot. "If it was true that the Germans were capable of such
inventions, and also that they were determined to clear the world of
all swarthy, dark-eyed long-nosed, black-haired people, then my
chances of survival were obviously poor" (91). Soon, he sees this
German-invented story claim its victims. "Then a new kind of train
appeared on the line. Living people were jammed in locked cattle
cars" (96). Rumors of the burning of Jews and Gypsies reach the
village. The peasants accept these new "stories," interpreting them,
reducing them to elements of a much longer story with an older plot.
"The peasants listened to these stories thoughtfully. They said the
Lord's punishment had finally reached the Jews. They had deserved
it long ago, ever since they crucified Christ. God never forgot. If He
had overlooked the sins of the Jews so far, He had not forgiven them.
Now the Lord was using the Germans as His instrument of justice"
(96). The Jews themselves, rolling to their deaths in cattle cars,
undergo a parallel deprivation of language. As they are caught up in
the plot of the German story, they are robbed of words, their written
messages go astray. A few manage to toss from the trains scraps of
paper with words "scribbled in handwriting obviously shaken by
fear or the motion of a train. The words were often washed off by the
morning dew or bleached out by the sun" (102). The Boy recognizes
that these erased words constitute the language of the victim, his
speech, the one he is trying to unlear. His personal discarding of
those texts and modes of telling structure the rest of the book.

The Boy wanders to a church and hears the "different language" of
a priest saying Mass. Clearly, he senses, this language of Christian

prayer is superior to Olga's remembered "magic incantation." Olga
was an outsider; the priest, surrounded by peasant believers, wields a
power greater than Olga's. His voice seems to the Boy even to "but-
tress the dome of the Church" (121). The priest eventually teaches
the Boy certain prayers by rote (the Boy cannot yet read), and this
new language promises the Boy a way of inventing still another story
of himself. His desperate prayers broker specific doses of heavenly
power, which he hopes will offset the power of his latest torturer,
Garbos, who has already invented for him a plot in which he hangs
from hooks over a dog named Judas. "I visualized my name being
mentioned at the councils of angels, then at those of some minor
saints, later at those of major saints, and so closer and closer to the
heavenly throne" (127). But the Boy cannot master this language of
Christian prayer. Its written text, the "Holy Book filled with sacred
prayers collected for the greater glory of God by the saints and
learned men throughout the centuries" (137), literally rises against
him as he attempts to lift it during a High Mass. The book tips him
backward, crushes him to the altar floor, turns him into the sacri-
ficial victim of the ceremony. The weight of the book expels from
him "an involuntary shout" which becomes the last sound to pass
his lips for years. The peasants, enraged by the Boy's disruption of
the Mass, carry him to a nearby open cesspool. "When I realized
what was going to happen to me, I again tried to shout. But no voice
came from me" (139). The pit into which he is tossed is a "maw,"
but his own mouth is silent, confirming the Boy's enforced silence.
"I tried to cry out, but my tongue flapped helplessly in my open
mouth" (140). Wordless, his mouth can release only vomit; the lips
that once uttered tales of Puss and Boots revert to mere aperture, one
end of the food tube.

   The entire scene in which the cesspool's maw devours the Boy represents a turning point in both the Boy's life and the structure of *The
Painted Bird*. Up to this scene the narration is episodic: the Boy's
voice describes discrete tales consisting of untitled, numbered units
which we can refer to as the Boy and Marta, the Boy and Olga, the
Boy and Miller the Jealous, and so on. These units are linked to-

gether by the Boy's random wandering or outright flight from one to the next. Each is a claustrophobic cell in which a "strange dialect," as the Boy calls Olga's speech, must be learned in order to escape. The reader moves through these tight, circular units somewhat the way the Boy himself floats away from Olga's village on an inflated fish bladder. "Round and round the bladder swirled, pulling away from and returning to the same spot" (25). With each new unit we feel, as perhaps the Boy does, that we have been here before. But when the Boy climbs out of the cesspool unaided, voiceless, he exhibits a new energy, linear rather than circular in its direction. "The time of passivity was over," he says (160). He has moved beyond the role he described in the episode of Miller the Jealous in which he vowed to "remember everything I saw" (40). Now he is determined to find a way of expressing all he saw. The remainder of the novel constitutes the steps he takes toward becoming a writer, the only one who has the power to open and close the doors to the kinds of cages he has so far passed through. The book's final scene shows him manipulating his newly returned voice, preventing it from escaping "through the door that opened onto the balcony" (251). *The Painted Bird* thus ends with the Boy as stern gatekeeper of this final cage, which is both a hospital room (he is recovering from a skiing accident) and a metaphor of the writer in control of his own voice.

With this overall view of the novel in mind I want to return to the moment in which the Boy emerges from the cesspool and flees into the forest, where his rough cleansing of his skin with pieces of tree bark suggests the even harsher interior scrubbing away of his hopes for heavenly assistance. Transformed into a mute, the Boy wanders through the dark countryside, thinking that the power he needs—if it does not reside in God—must belong to the Devil. "God had no reason to inflict such terrible punishment on me. I had probably incurred the wrath of some other forces" (141). Soon he meets Ewka, a girl a few years older than he, and has his first sexual experience. Their moment of silent caress takes place in a wheat field, a brief return to the maternal nest which is surrounded by protective circles. "I scanned this golden river of wheat, noticing the bluebottles timidly hovering in the sun's rays. Higher up the swallows promised good weather with their intricate gyrations" (152). But their refuge in the wheat field, like Lekh's stork nest, is really a trap. Ewka is corrupt; within a few weeks the Boy witnesses Ewka coupling with a goat under the encouragement of her own father. The Boy is crushed, but believes he has discovered the hidden source of power he has been seeking all along. "I tried to visualize the manner in which the evil spirits operated. The minds and souls of people were as open to these forces as a plowed field, and it was on this field that the Evil Ones incessantly scattered their malignant seed" (152).

The dark insight he learns from observing Ewka's willing liaison with the Evil Ones suggests to him that he might obtain a similar power from the same source. "Only those with a sufficiently powerful passion for hatred, greed, revenge, or torture to obtain some objective seemed to make a good bargain with the powers of Evil" (152). The more cruelty one inflicts, he concludes, the more power is available. And the Germans, because of the scale of their cruelty, are the most powerful. "Success was a vicious circle: the more harm they inflicted, the more secret powers they secured for evil" (153). All this probing of the relationship between evil and power bring about still another transformation in the Boy. He changes from passive victim to active inflicter of pain. "I felt stronger and more confident. . . . Now I would join those who were helped by the Evil Ones" (154). Skimming over an ice pond on a pair of crude skates, he thinks he hears in the wind satanic voices. "The Evil Ones were interested in me at last. To train me in hatred they had first separated me from my parents, then taken away Marta and Olga, delivered me into the hands of the carpenter, robbed me of my speech, then given Ewka to the he-goat. . . . I was in their power, alone on a glassy sheet of ice which the Evil Ones themselves had spread between remote villages" (158). The Boy's ecstatic flight over the ice, aided by "the frenzied power of the wind," is a Dionysian dance, a surrender of the self to the unpredictable energy of inspiration, which the Boy sees as satanic in origin: "Flying along that endless white plain I felt free and alone like a starling soaring in the air, tossed by every flurry, following a stream, unconscious of its speed, drawn into an abandoned dance" (157). The makeshift skates inscribe markings on the ice which record his passing as they propel his escape, suggesting once more the analogous power of the writer, whose markings on white sheets both reveal his identity as they promote his imaginative flight.

As the war comes to an end, and with it the Nazi occupation, the Boy makes friends with some Soviet soldiers, including Gavrila, who teaches him to read and write. The Boy relishes this new design of printed words. Their order contrasts sharply with the disorder of his life. "I also liked poetry. It was written in a form resembling prayers, but was more beautiful and more intelligible. . . . The smooth, polished words meshed with each other like oiled millstones ground to a fine fit" (187). Gavrila presides over the Boy's divestiture of entrapping stories about prayer, God, religion. "They were all tales," Gavrila teaches him, "for ignorant people who did not understand the natural order of the world, did not believe in their own power, and therefore had to take refuge in their belief in some God" (187). Gavrila then tells the Boy a new tale meant to supplant the Boy's previous stories of God and prayer. The sacredness of this new story is confirmed by the devotion of the Soviet soldiers who have saved him. It is the story of Stalin. "The soldiers said that the windows of Stalin's study in the Kremlin were lit late into the night and that the people of Moscow, along with all the working masses of the world, looked toward those windows and found new inspiration and hope for the future. There the great Stalin watched over them, worked for them all, devised the best ways of winning the war and destroying the enemies of the working masses" (189). But this tale too, told so relentlessly, does not survive the Boy's growing talent for measuring stories for their capacity to provide him with power. Variations of the Stalin story seem to him more enclosures, cages even stronger than the one he is in. The vagaries of Party discipline are as unpredictable as his previous life wandering from one village to the next. It is not until Mikta takes him on a sniping attack that the

Boy quietly rejects even this last of the sacred texts, the story of
Stalin and the masses. Mikta's telling shots from the seclusion of a
tree suggest to the Boy that there are "many paths and many ascents
leading to the summit" (206). New tales need to be learned.

Gavrila's gift to the Boy is reading. But the discovery of the power
of words arranged in patterns, its promise of escape from the harsh-
ness of life by means of an imaginative one, and its glimpse into the
hidden life of others all encourage him to think that he himself might
become a writer, might change the plot of his life. The printed word
becomes for the Boy the latest in a series of discoveries about power
and remains the only one to survive the test of his own experience.
All other sources of power—prayers, God, Satan, witchcraft, even
communism—turn out in the course of the book to be empty promises. Here is the Boy analyzing his first contact with printed words:

> Books impressed me tremendously. From their simple printed pages
> one could conjure up a world as real as that grasped by the senses.
> Furthermore, the world of books, like meat in cans, was somehow richer
> and more flavorful than the everyday variety. In ordinary life, for
> example, one saw many people without really knowing them, while in
> books one even knew what people were thinking and planning. (186)

The Boy recognizes that literature not only intensifies life but reveals
some of its mysteries, especially the seemingly inexplicable behavior
of his adult oppressors. Perhaps, he thinks, literature might permit
the reader to anticipate the pitfalls of life and thus to become
stronger. Knowing what people are thinking and planning is a form
of vicarious unmasking, a penetrating device that anticipates trouble
by exposing its motivation. If books could certify vicarious strength
to the reader, how much more power might accrue to the writer of
books?

Sometimes, the Boy continues, a certain book seems to describe
the pattern of one's life, offering a glimpse of a more hopeful future.
When he reads his first book, *Childhood*, by Maxim Gorky, he is
struck by the way the plot urges him to think of his own life in terms
of similar patterns: "I read my first book with Gavrila's assistance. It

was called *Childhood* and its hero, a small boy like myself, lost his father on the first page. I read this book several times and it filled me with hope. Its hero did not have an easy life either. After his mother's death he was left quite alone, and yet despite many difficulties he grew up to be, as Gavrila said, a great man" (186). The Boy is as fascinated by the status of the writer—in this case, Gorky—as he is by Gorky's story of his childhood. The Boy is a reader, but also an embryonic writer waiting for his birth into printed language. If he could learn to control words himself, he might someday gain the status of "the great man," transforming himself from silence and weakness to eloquence and power. Meanwhile, the Boy draws strength from his daily reading of *Pravda*'s account of the impending Soviet defeat of the Nazis. He also becomes a student of Gavrila's teaching about the "collective," in an effort to learn not only Russian but whatever power it is that causes Gavrila's spoken words to animate the Soviet soldiers. That power is, Gavrila says, "the Party," the ultimate reader capable of perceiving in the text of reality not "meaningless jumbles" of human activity but "a definite pattern." "The Party could see farther than the best sniper" (191). The Boy is attracted to this source of power, and his written messages to Gavrila (his only way of using words since becoming mute) constitute his first effort as a writer. "I absorbed Gavrila's every word, writing questions which I wanted answered on the slate he had given me" (195). The Boy's intensity marks the degree to which he has come to rely on words to discover his identity and destiny. "I tried to memorize Gavrila's teaching," he says, "not to lose a single word" (195). But the words he hears about the Party—he even eavesdrops on Party meetings held in an army tent—gradually convince him that the Party's "many eyes" may well misread him, simply because he himself has not fully discovered who he is: "What was my deepest core: a healthy core like that of a fresh apple, or a rotten one like the maggoty stone of a withered plum?" (194). After he leaves the care of Gavrila and Mitka, clutching their final gifts—books with "inscriptions"—the Boy surreptitiously reads *Pravda*, which he sees is the only proven source of strength in his new environment, an orphanage. When the authorities threaten to remove his Soviet uniform, and with it his recently acquired identity as a student of Gavrila's, he turns to written words to exact vengeance. It is his first piece of fiction:

> I broke from the clumsy women and ran out into the street. There I accosted four quietly strolling Soviet soldiers. I signaled with my hands that I was a mute. They gave me a piece of paper on which I wrote that I was the son of a Soviet officer who was at the front and that I was waiting for my father at the orphanage. Then I wrote in careful language that the principal was the daughter of a landlord, that she hated the Red Army, and that she, together with the nurses exploited by her, beat me daily because of my uniform. (211)

The success of the Boy's first story surprises even him: while Gorky lost his father "on the first page" of *Childhood*, the Boy gains a father in his first paragraph. His new father outranks the four soldiers; his enemy, the principal, now has been transformed into an enemy of the Party. All this he accomplishes simply by "careful language." When he returns to the orphanage, he writes on the blackboard his defiant claim that his identity will be defined only in terms of his newly acquired language, Russian. "Even the teachers ignored my refusal to learn reading and writing in my mother-tongue. I wrote in chalk on the blackboard that my language was Russian" (211). He uses written words to reverse the flow of power. Now he is the teacher, the teachers are his students. He writes, they read, victims of his careful language.

As the war ends and the Boy is claimed by his parents, he seems fully aware that the power aligned with the writing of books is an uncompromising, even dangerous one to live with. When his father takes him from the orphanage, he helps him, as the Boy says, to "carry my books," thus sharing the responsibility for the Boy's aspiration to be a writer. Later, a four-year-old child his parents have adopted interrupts the Boy's reading and knocks over his books. The child's crime is to break the Boy's power of concentration, and so he breaks the child's arm. The Boy's vengeance implies that reading and writing (he is barely a writer) are powers nurtured by hatred itself. Breaking a child's arm may be a hateful act, but hatred is the source of the survivor's strength.[2] The power to avenge is the heritage of the survivor, especially the writer-survivor who can then carry out justice as he sees it. Survival and vengeance become twin hallmarks of the writer's power. He must hate in order to see, avenge in order to survive.

If Gavrila's gift to the Boy is reading and writing, Mitka the Cuckoo, the Soviet sniper, provides a consistent vision for the Boy's future writing. Mitka's single-minded revenge for the killing of some of his friends reinforces the Boy's growing belief that each man "lives mainly with himself," but that he can achieve a sense of power on his own. Mitka's polished rifle, with its delicate scope that can transform a victim from a blurred mass to an individual human face, resembles the writer's own source of power: the pen as weapon, the character as victim. Mitka is a surrogate voice for the mute Boy, speaking a different kind of bird speech than that of Lekh. Like his namesake the cuckoo, Mitka sounds his call again and again with deadly monotony. Mitka's call on one level is merely gunfire; the Boy interprets its deeper meaning this way: "Man carries in himself his own private war, which he has to wage, win or lose, himself—his own justice, which is his alone to administer" (206). The Boy comes to savor the power of wordless action epitomized by Mitka. After he is placed in the orphanage, he allies himself with another wordless avenger, the Silent One. They discover a railroad switch that would allow them to shunt a crowded passenger train into a river. The power the two boys feel, the Boy realizes, is the same as "the men who had ordered and organized" the "gas chambers and crematories" (220); he has turned the German story of racial superiority against itself, escaping that plot by, in effect, writing a new one in which his peasant persecutors ride the train to their deaths instead of himself.

At the end of the novel when the Boy regains his speech, he revels in the power of his newly returned voice: "I spoke loudly and incessantly like the peasants and then like the city folk, as fast as I could, enraptured by the sounds that were heavy with meaning, as wet snow is heavy with water, convincing myself again and again and again that speech was now mine and that it did not intend to escape through the door which opened onto the balcony" (234). Although he now has the capacity to speak—and to speak country or city speech at will—he also knows no one else knows of his transformation from mute to speaker. He can continue to play mute, or he can speak city or peasant speech. Either way, the words he uses will function to claim not hearers but victims.

The Painted Bird, then, is a book that charts a character's transformation from helplessness to lonely power, from injury to retribution, from silent impotence to writer of the words that testify to his survival. The Boy, in his early teens at the end of the narration, confides that he has learned what he considers the final truth. He is beyond illusion. "Every one of us stood alone, and the sooner a man realized that all Gavrilas, Mitkas, and Silent Ones were expendable, the better for him" (233). He even learns to turn his weakness into a strength: because he is mute, he can be trusted with delivery of contraband to underworld characters, who regard his muteness as "an asset which ensured my discretion when I carried out my missions" (232). For each situation he has trained himself to read the plot quickly, so that a new one of his own invention might be substituted.

Kosinski's first novel dramatizes language's multiple roles: how the speech of victims is shaped by the commands of the oppressor, how words can confer either weakness or power, confinement or freedom. Sometimes human speech seems inferior to silent action; certain gestures, such as the Silent One's refusal to use speech, or Mitka the Cuckoo quietly lining up victims between the cross hairs of his rifle, or the Boy himself, mute, dropping bricks into the dark on unseen enemies, seem refutations of the power of speech, or suggest that power increases as words diminish. Other times, spoken words have the power to transform reality, such as when Lekh's description of Stupid Ludmila changes her into a "strange-colored bird flying to faraway worlds, free and quick, brighter and more beautiful than other creatures" (49). But it is only when words are written—such as Gorky's tales or Stalin's splendid press runs—does the Boy see that language can be more powerful than action, capable, as the Boy says, of conjuring up alternative words as real as the one "grasped by the senses."

Between these two extremes of silence and writing lies another area of experience for the Boy—the world of sounds. For much of *The Painted Bird* the Boy finds himself at the center of a whirligig of sounds: howling dogs, buzzing bluebottle flies, the screams of victims of partisans, the "strange humming sound of the human throng" of Jews packed into railroad cars, and whose sound is "neither groan, cry, nor song" (101). Any one of these sounds may emerge into a code, a message, and so he is all ears, an absorber of sounds that by chance may signify a language he needs to know. Some people exist for the Boy almost exclusively in terms of sound —or its absence. The Nazi SS officer, for example, seems to overpower the Boy by the mere "granite sound of his language" (119), while a helpless mute whom the Boy remembers once seeing possesses "words" but they are "unforthcoming" (147). Stalin, who soundlessly weaves the "colored threads" of his narrative design of Soviet society, is an omnipotent author, his power measured by the lavish texts he creates. The Red Army's library, Gavrila proudly claims to the Boy, "owed all its beautifully printed and bound books to him" (188). Even inanimate objects take on a life of language for this intense listener of sounds. Alone in the forest the Boy hears "the confession of the mosses" (60), and later recalls the "shrill cries" (75) of chandeliers as they tumbled to the street from a bombed apartment house. The very trees of the forests he wanders in contain voices of ghouls "trying to bore their way out from inside their trunks" (32).

The Boy's movement away from silent victimization toward the power of eloquence, which is the structure of his narration, is also a tale of a writer's slow progress from silence to spoken to written words. *The Painted Bird* is thus filled with images of writing, and, like Kafka's fable of the printing press as an instrument of torture in "In the Penal Colony," Kosinski's images of writing devices have a deadly side: the comet's fire of inspiration can scorch those approaching the circular limit of its centrifugal force, the gigantic pencil is posed to impale, the Boy's skate blade can stab out eyes as well as cut designs like pens on a white surface, and axe cuts in the bark of living trees are inscribed messages of vengeance. The train tracks, which crisscross the narrative of *The Painted Bird*, resemble the narrative lines of life stories or death stories, depending on authorial whim. "They had the power to decide whether the points of thousands of railroad spurs would be switched to tracks leading to life or to death" (220). Here the Boy is referring to the Nazi's power to bring their elaborately constructed story of the Jews to its logical conclusion. As victim, the Boy is attracted to this power, which resembles the power of the writer over his characters. "To be capable," he says, "of deciding the fate of many whom one did not even know was a magnificent sensation" (220).

Kosinski's interest in the behavior of language in *The Painted Bird* has still another dimension—his determination as a writer to find a unique language for his fiction, more suggestive than the detached and laconic style of his first two books. *The Painted Bird* is not only a character's quest for a new language that would confer on him power but a first novelist's quest for a style that would grant him an immediate and lasting hearing. To effect such a language, Kosinski's narrator combines the vocabulary of an adult with the limited comprehension of a child.[3] Each moment of the narration is gauged by the reader in terms of the difference between what the child-speaker describes and what the reader infers is happening. When the Boy sees Marta engulfed by flames, for example, the reader knows she has been dead for a day, but the Boy can grasp neither the reality of death nor the danger of fire; he remains fascinated by the way the flames seem to touch her "tenderly," licking her hands "as might an affectionate dog" (12). The Boy watches Marta burn and wonders why she—like a snake he had observed—does not "discard her skin like the snake and start life all over again" (8). Later, when he witnesses an angry peasant scoop out both eyes of a youth who is attracted to the peasant's wife, the Boy is struck more by the marvel of two eyes rolling on the floor than by the suffering of the blinded youth. When the Boy reflects that he would like to keep the eyes in his pocket, "taking them out when needed" in order to place them over his own "to see twice as much," the reader must balance conflicting emotional responses—caused, in this case, by the spectacle of the blinded youth and the earnest literalism of the Boy.

This disturbing tension between the imagery of the Boy's descriptions and his limited comprehension of its full meaning is repeated on a smaller scale in the Boy's vocabulary, which moves back and forth between the polar images of confinement and flight, between the world of vegetables, which is the sign of his powerlessness, and the world of birds, which suggests freedom. He is simultaneously imprisoned by society because of his "swarthy" physical features and freed from his tormentors by willed flights of imagination. He is an "abandoned head of cabbage" imprisoned in the earth as well as a raven soaring "straight into a ray of sunshine" (25). The Boy's descriptions are filled with words that suggest the tactile physicality of his peasant tormentors: potatoes, cabbages, rats, manure, lice. He watches boxcars of captive Jews roll by and thinks of their confinement in terms of "cornstalks." When he loses speech, he pictures his former voice as a bird, escaped from his body to wander like "a solitary duck straying over a huge pond" (140). Told of the power of prayer, he thinks of God admiring all the Boy's prayers "lying in huge heaps like potatoes piled high at harvest time" (136). But when he later loses faith in prayer, he wonders where all his prayers have flown: "Were they perhaps circling in the empty heaven like a flock of birds whose nests had been destroyed by boys?" (190).

Kosinski's achievement as a stylist in *The Painted Bird* demonstrates a dramatic break from the world of Novak in *The Future Is Ours, Comrade* and *No Third Path*. The point of view of the Boy provides the reader with a complex disharmony between the words of the narrator and the narrator's comprehension of the experience he is describing, often creating for the reader a rich range of emotional response, from disgust to grim amusement. The language of the Boy's narration, oscillating between vegetable and bird life, confinement and flight, offers a verbal pattern that contrasts markedly with Kosinski's previous work, and indeed with his next novel as well. The Boy at the end of the novel is nearly an adult. He savors his newly restored speech as a prized captive, testing his voice over and over to make sure "it did not intend to escape" (234). The Boy has become keeper of his own language, literally his own master. He is not far from the mentality of the adult narrator who, years later, writes his story. The first sentence of this story, "I lived in Marta's hut, expecting my parents to come for me any day, any hour," brings us to the edge of the abyss he has passed over.

Steps Out of the Cage

The critical success of *The Painted Bird* prepared the way for an interested and ultimately favorable reception of Kosinski's second work of fiction, *Steps*.[4] Much shorter than *The Painted Bird*, *Steps* represents a break in form from his first novel as well. The unnamed Boy in *The Painted Bird* arranges his narration in a chronological sequence, starting from his childhood and ending with his early teenage years; this movement is paralleled by the historical sequence of events in Eastern Europe, from Nazi to Soviet occupation. *Steps* consists of forty-eight scenes or vignettes, mostly narrated by a nameless young man.[5] Some are only a few sentences long, and all echo back and forth between different times and places, none of which is specifically named. One sequence, consisting of twelve italicized dialogues between the narrator and an unnamed woman, functions as a dramatic counterpoint to the detached, cool voice of the narrator. At first glance the vignettes seem to fit no particular pattern, but the reader gradually becomes aware that each falls into one of two distinct stages in the narrator's growth from abject victim to his status as credit card wielding master of an alien language. Although at one point this narrator denies to a priest that he intends to write an article about a caged woman, there is no doubt that his narrative charts the steps necessary to write the narrative we read as *Steps*.

The vignettes cross back and forth as well as between two separate worlds of the narrator, each of which is described in an abstract, "non-figurative" language so as to avoid specific identification.[6] The country of his birth, which can be identified only as one with a "Party" ruling it—even the phrase "East Europe" of *The Painted Bird* is avoided—is the place where twenty two vignettes occur. The second world, "the West," which includes an unnamed city resembling New York and a few foreign countries, one of which has a "palm-fringed" capital, consists of twenty-six vignettes. The first world, the East, is a claustrophobic environment of peasant villages, compulsory military service, political intrigue at a university, and the endless criticism and surveillance of Party organizations such as the kind described by Novak in *The Future Is Ours, Comrade*. In the East, victims abound, and the narrator is often one of them. Here a student called "The Philosopher" wanders from one public toilet to another in a futile effort to escape the daily monitoring by student and Party organizations, a deranged woman is kept in a cage, and the narrator himself, surrounded by victims, learns to fight off victimization either with physical violence (he drops beer bottles on an old man) or with duplicity (he mimics the voice of a military officer and thus destroys a student officer who offends him). Throughout this time, the narrator learns that sexual experiments, besides offering relief from convention and tedium, have a subversive political dimension as well.

The second world, the West, is an equally treacherous environment, where the narrator begins as a victim because he can hardly speak the language. Eventually, as in the previous world of the East, he transforms himself from a victim forced to steal food to survive to a manipulator of instruments of power. He drives fast cars, learns how to use complex electronic eavesdropping devices, and flashes a wallet full of credit cards. The narrator's journey from victim to oppressor in the West is brief and passes through a series of underworld contacts. Our last glimpse of the narrator finds him moving in the more respectable world of apartment houses, bank and law firm contacts, and impulsive plane flights to foreign countries. Power in the West means money, which confers on its owner the special freedom that the narrator at first yearns for and then, as he says, "requires"—freedom to thrust himself into a variety of human encounters, many of them sexual, freedom to seek out victims, freedom to speak the language of the oppressor. Thus the narrator's experience in the West can be divided into two kinds: those in which the narrator does not have money (nine vignettes) and those in which he does (five). If we include the twelve printed in italics (the dialogues between the narrator and the woman) in this second period of the West, then the number of scenes which deal with the narrator's power in the West become seventeen, or about a quarter of the book's pages.[7]

Steps, then, is the narrator's account of two related transformations of himself from the status of a character plotted against to that of a writer who does the plotting. One transformation takes place in a Communist country, one in the West. In both places, the narrator begins as an outsider, speaking the language of victimization. In both, he masters the language of his oppressor and then proceeds to work his will on his enemies, first by escaping from the East, second by acquiring the possessions needed in the West to remain independent —income, credit, mobility. The transitional point in the novel is the plane's flight from East to West, which, in the mind of the narrator, seems to be fixed outside of the flow of time. Could he have done so, he says, "I would have remained there, timeless, unmeasured, un-judged, bothering no one, suspended forever between my past and my future" (107). Only on that flight does he experience a respite from the necessary and endless task of fending off victimization. When he lands, he enters a specific time, culture, and social system, and so he is victim all over again. At the conclusion of the book, the narration changes to third person: the narrator is gone, "departed," says the porter to a woman who is looking for him. "He said he wasn't coming back" (147).

two related transformations [handwritten marginal note]

Another way of looking at the structure of *Steps* is to see the novel framed by two vignettes, the first and the last, each of which demonstrates the level of power that the narrator has achieved in the West. In both he is visiting a foreign country with a woman, and he retains the financial and psychological power to continue or terminate the liaison. The choice is his alone; the partner has no say. In the opening scene, the narrator is "traveling farther south" by car in a vaguely Mediterranean country characterized by "white-washed" villages. He lures a simple peasant girl to a nearby city with the promise of freedom and riches possible by means of his credit cards, which she has never seen before. "I promised her that the two of us would travel to different cities and even countries," says the narrator (5). She agrees, and the vignette closes with the narrator alone with the girl in a hotel room, surveying the fruits of his freedom—a relationship in which he is the controller, she the willing captive. The book's final scene is a mirror image of the first. Another woman, grown dependent on the narrator, finds that he has departed from a seaside resort hotel, leaving her behind. He has controlled the relationship by ending it. Between these two scenes, the book presents dozens more which demonstrate the narrator's sequence of moments (perhaps these are the "steps" of the title) that chart his transformation from "everybody's victim" to a man capable of imposing his will, his identity, on any given situation, which is the prerogative of the writer as well.

The narrator is attracted to three sources of power that will grant him the particular freedom he desires—money, sex, and language. It is this last aspect—language—that makes *Steps* Kosinski's most original experiment with style. Somewhat like the Boy in *The Painted Bird*, the narrator of *Steps* tells his story by utilizing a special language, one that would bring him release from victimization. If the Boy showed mastery of the language of oppression only at the end of his narration, the narrator of *Steps* speaks it from the opening sentence: "I was traveling farther south. The villages were small and poor; each time I stopped in one, a crowd gathered around my car and the children followed my every move" (3). The narrator is the center of attention, and he is alone. He is no longer one of the children envying adult power, as he was in the peasant village of his own childhood. The children surrounding the car represent what he once was. The narrator's voice, with its sparse and laconic vocabulary, its reticence about personal details or even names of actual places, and its detached tone is a voice in the act of inventing a style. The often bizarre anecdotes that compose the narrator's tale become parables of language's powers and pitfalls.

As in *The Painted Bird*, Kosinski dramatizes in *Steps* the psychological state of victimization in terms of language, and so certain scenes in *Steps* that take place in the East inevitably remind us of the world of *The Painted Bird*, with the earlier narrator's sense of helplessness, his affinity for the animal world, and his compulsion for retribution. The narrator of *Steps* recalls his childhood as a "vagrant" in a peasant village: "To amuse himself the farmer with whom I was finally boarded would take hold of me by my collar, drag me up close and then strike me" (35). As a boy he was "everybody's victim," and when he comes to realize that only his own efforts will affect a change in his status, he takes the initiative: observing the agony of a sheep that had swallowed shards of glass, he decides to feed the daughter of the abusive farmer balls of bread filled with fish hooks. "For each lash I received my tormentors were condemned to pain a hundred times greater than mine. Now I was no longer their victim; I had become their judge and executioner" (37). But this vignette, with its reference to "the camps where the furnaces smoked day and night" is the only one in *Steps* that takes place during World War II, the time during which most of *The Painted Bird* is set. The rest of *Steps*'s vignettes about the East function as a sequel to the Boy's experiences in *The Painted Bird*.[8] The narrator of *Steps* is older, a reluctant and potentially subversive participant in the university, military, and political life of a Communist country. This narrator sees early that the social system will claim him as a victim unless he acts against that claim. At the University he finds he has a fellow student who is his enemy. Both are members of the "para-military student defense corps," and when his antagonist is appointed guard commander for a weekend, the narrator, having practiced a "brusque military voice," orders him by phone to lead the university unit in an attack on the city arsenal. The ruse works, and the narrator's victim is destroyed without knowing the identity of his oppressor. The narrator's ability to teach himself the language of power—in this case epitomized by the brusque military voice—permits him to eliminate at least one of his tormentors. But in the world of the East—as Novak had found out—the state victimizes the citizen, and any triumphs by its victims are few and transitory. Nevertheless, the narrator, like Novak, is sympathetic to the plight of victims around him, whose efforts to avoid being victimized by the state reflect his own. One of the narrator's friends, nicknamed "The Philosopher," resembles the bookkeeper K. in *No Third Path*. He seeks refuge from the surveillance of the state in public lavatories, which he calls "Temples." "Here your privacy is absolute: you can contemplate and enjoy your own world" (68). But the Philosopher is eventually driven to commit suicide, which he accomplishes, appropriately enough, in one of his "temples." Another victim of the state, a scientist whose entire family "had been exterminated during the purges" takes his revenge by pinning "foil-wrapped contraceptives" on the lapels of unsuspecting Party members gathered at a crowded reception. As restless with his status of victim as both "The Philosopher" and the scientist, the narrator chooses another way to enact revenge—through exotic sexual liaisons, each of which says something about the subversive nature of writing.

In *The Future Is Ours, Comrade,* Novak discovered that the official public language of the state had no word for certain sexual acts, and so sexual life was a potentially subversive activity. In *Steps* the narrator seeks escape from the role of victim assigned to him by means of calculated and often bizarre sexual encounters. When his student union, dissatisfied by his "lack of involvement," banishes the narrator to four months in an obscure agricultural settlement, he is attracted to a visiting circus acrobat. He sees in this woman's body an assertion of silent physicality that is an antidote to the months of political lectures and meetings he has been enduring. The grace the acrobat displays with her body represents for the narrator the control he would like to have over his own experience. "It seemed as though her whole body were molded from a single flexible fiber, so fluid were the complex positions into which she bent herself" (73). The narrator meets her alone in the woods for a private performance. Naked, and without speaking, she coils herself from a handstand into a circle. "With her face framed between her thighs, and her knees bending, she brushed against my face her mouth and womb" (77). Her coiled body becomes a silent statement that pushes past the limits of human conventions. The performance is also a political act, one in which the narrator and the girl withdraw from the shared values of the collective. Finally, the image of the girl, circular like the Boy's comet, is an image for this narrator of a possible style—a fluid fiber of words as stripped of adornment as the girl's skin.

During his time in the East, the narrator turns to a variety of sexual encounters that cordon off a separate world from the collective. Employed as a ski instructor near a tuberculosis sanatorium, he seeks an affair with a female patient. They become intimate, but their encounters take place not in her sick bed but in their imaginations: "We would make love again: she standing as before in front of the mirror, and I, a pace away, my sight riveted upon her" (17). He photographs her in front of the mirror, and as she becomes sicker, he is left alone, possessing her in his imagination. "I looked at these pictures as if they were mirrors in which I could see at any moment my own face floating ghost-like on her flesh" (18). The photographs and mirrors are ways the narrator extracts from the relationship those qualities that intensify his own awareness of himself. His imaginative encounters with the dying woman explore the limits of sexual union while they intensify the narrator's sense of creating a version of himself he had not known before. These continual meetings in the privacy of her hospital room—because of their obvious unconventionality—bring disapproval from the authorities. One of the nuns who staff the hospital accuses him of being a "hyena." "Men of my kind, she said, lurked around bodies that were dying; each time I fed upon the woman, I hastened her death" (17). The charge is only partially true; he *is* a feeder on the emotional life of the woman. But she feeds on his own healthy life as well and creates an alternate world of sensuality from the world of sickness in which she is condemned to live. Both of the narrator's affairs, then, are related: the circus girl's healthy body is forced beyond normal physical limits to create a sexual encounter that defies conformity and strengthens each self's awareness of its uniqueness; the dying woman's body is forced beyond the conventional expectations of deterioration and decline to live briefly as an object of desire rather than of pity or repugnance. Both represent a mode of escape for the narrator as well as an opportunity to increase the boundaries of his will, his control. Although these relationships contain an element of exploitation on the part of the narrator, each of his sexual partners is a willing participant in the plot he has devised for them, and each is delivered for a brief time from the circumstances of her own life.

Other sexual encounters of the narrator seem more deliberately exploitative, one-sided affairs, in which the narrator dominates the female, or sees her as an object to be controlled, a field on which his fantasies may romp without restraint. One vignette begins as the narrator is walking with a girlfriend through a park at night. A group of men subdue him and rape her. But after witnessing the rape, the narrator feels she is "polluted." "I couldn't think of her except as a body to make love to" (56). He abuses her, testing the extent to which she will permit him to victimize her. "My curiosity about her body intensified. Abruptly and forcefully I subjected her to various experiments, stimulating her responses, exploring and violating her in spite of her pleas and protests" (57). He encourages her decline into sexual promiscuity and ends the relationship by attending a boisterous party with her and then offering her as "my gift to the host and his guests; if they would devise the situation, each could have his pleasure" (59). The scene at the party closes with a replication of the original rape, but the narrator is neither a participant nor a witness. He elects to leave, and so his voice becomes silent. He turns the act of imagination over to the reader, who must "devise" the situation of the girl's fate unaided.

In a similar sexual encounter, the narrator engages in a complicated stratagem to become the lover of a woman without her knowledge. With the aid of a friend who has made the woman his mistress, he plots the fulfillment of his desire. "She had become his instrument, and if I was ready to possess her, he could arrange it" (98). The girl agrees to submit herself, blindfolded, to a stranger. As the narrator then watches the woman lying on a bedroom floor, he is exhilarated by the sudden sense of power over her. "I was aware that to her I was no more than a whim of the man she loved, a mere extension of his body, his touch, his love, his contempt" (99). Although he has succeeded in establishing a master-slave relationship, his realization that he has only possessed her physically, that she is unaware of him as a person, leaves him frustrated, his mind divided between his perception of her as a woman working in his office and his knowledge of her nakedness. His attempt to win for himself complete freedom with her results in his own imprisonment. She is the first in a series of characters who slip out of the role designed for her by the narrator.

master-slave relationship thwarted

(link to woman in cage) →55

The conflict between role playing and physical need, between will and desire, intrigues the narrator, and prompts him to make discoveries about his personality, which he sees is also in conflict with itself. One side of him is calculating, will-oriented, and rational, while the other is spontaneous and emotional. He wants to engage in acts of sexual abandon while simultaneously observing—almost as a scientist—his own and his partner's behavior. He recalls, for example, an affair with a girl when he was in high school. While making love to her in his parents' house, he heard the telephone ring. The narrator answered the phone, talking for a while with a friend; then he attempted to resume love making. But the girl was offended by the power of his concentration, the detachment of his self-control. "It upset her, she said, that I could have an erection purely through an act of will—as though I had only to stretch my leg or bend a finger. She stressed the idea of spontaneity" (26). But spontaneity for this narrator threatens his sense of control. Increasingly, he can only sustain one kind of sexual relationship—his partner must be a victim, and he, the oppressor. The highest level of human intimacy

Spontaneity

becomes for the narrator also a moment when two human bodies form the most bizarre contortions. It is a time when human defenses are dropped, physical and psychological. If nakedness is one aspect of intimacy, then vulnerability is another, and the narrator is convinced that the only way to defer vulnerability is to reduce his partner to the status of victim.[9]

The narrator's concept of his sexual partners as inevitable victims links his two worlds, East and West. Perhaps his most extensive analysis of this concept appears in the twelve italicized vignettes. All are in present tense and seem to emerge from the period in the narrator's life in which he has managed to transform himself into a man of power and mobility, a solitary master of Western technology and pleasure. All twelve are fragments from an ongoing relationship between the narrator and a woman on whom he imposes a variety of controls. When he returns to the city after a trip, for instance, he interrogates her about her activities, probing for inconsistencies in her answers. While away he had ordered for her the services of a skilled masseur at a private club. Now he questions her as to how she felt under the probing hands of the man. "I wanted to know what you would do: how you would behave in that sort of situation" (43), as if she were a character in a fiction he was writing, and he, the author, were determined to circumscribe her life, literally writing a circle around her, a prison of words. His obsession with controlling her behavior is authorial; his frustration results from her refusal to remain within the confines of his plot. When he confronts her with the fact that she had an affair with another man while he was absent, her retort reveals just how far outside the role he has designed for her she is willing to venture. "I felt I had an obligation to know myself better—apart from the self you have brought me to know" (44). For each, then, the relationship consists of mutual testing, judgment, and analysis that expands their perceptions of themselves and of their attitudes toward each other. Questioned by her about his use of prostitutes, he replies, "Money extends my potency; without it I couldn't be what I am. I wouldn't be able to meet you where I do and in the fashion I do. I wouldn't be living the way I do, nor could I afford the experience I require" (61). Money provides for the narrator freedom first to escape victimization and then to select his experience, to probe and extend the outer edges of himself, to extricate himself from the trap of predictability. His relationship with the women he sees in terms of a mirror; just as he had made love to the dying woman in the East, now, equipped with mobility and the appropriate technology, he can sustain a relationship that mirrors his identity:

> I want you, you alone. But beyond you and me together, I see myself in our love-making. It is this vision of myself as your lover I wish to retain and make more real.
>
> But you do want me for what I am, apart from you, don't you?
>
> I don't know you apart from myself. When I am alone, when you are not here, you are no longer real: then, it's only imagining again.
>
> Then, all you need me for is to provide a stage on which you can project and view yourself, and see how your discarded experiences become alive again when they affect me. Am I right? (131)

Not only is she right but her words illuminate for us the dynamics of writer, character, and reader that are at work in *Steps*. The woman senses the extent to which she has been made over into a character by her male lover. He, whom we know as the narrator, uses their relationship as a "stage" on which to project versions of himself. (They are "discarded" because they are now part of the narrator's past.) These versions, like Kosinski's words that make up the scene, "become alive again" when they affect the reader.

The woman's objection is neither denied nor further analyzed by the narrator. This exchange—like the other eleven—is a self-contained, discrete moment in a larger but necessarily inferred dialectic between the two voices, narrator and lover, manipulator and victim, writer and character.

The narrator's control over his partner, his reduction of her to a stage on which to act out his fantasies of escape from political, economic, and psychological systems, represents the high point in his long quest for power that originated with his wanderings through peasant villages in the East. But if the narrator needs money to extend his potency, the steps he takes to acquire it represent most of the vignettes that occur in the West (excluding the twelve italicized ones). These vignettes, nine of them, are some of the most memorably rendered in *Steps*. All are characterized by a sense of powerlessness. Speaking the language of victim at first, the narrator gropes toward mastery of the speech of power. At the end of his long flight to the West, the airplane's door opens to yet another cage, this one composed of words he does not know. His suitcase, "loaded with dictionaries," bursts apart "like a giant clamshell," provoking ridicule and marking him as an outsider. Wandering through grocery stores in order to steal food, he finds himself watched by "panoramic mirrors" in which "I saw myself grotesquely enlarged or flattened like a griddle against a background of exotic fruits" (110). The image recalls the opening of *The Future Is Ours, Comrade*, in which the small boy stares through the glass window at fruit equally inaccessible; here the narrator sees his own words as useless baggage, and silently determines to acquire the language of power. He soon becomes involved in underworld activities—a protection racket, chauffeuring for a black gambler, drugs. As he becomes a more skillful driver, he is invited to participate in betting contests called "book-knock-off," in which he speeds past parked cars, each of which has a book taped to its door. "I could not see the books from behind the steering wheel, but I knew they were there, waiting motionless to be prized off like limpets, their crumpled pages bound tightly between the stiff leather of the gilt bindings" (125). The narrator's steps toward this language of power are marked with fragments of the printed word—dictionaries on airport floors, expensively bound books on the streets of a city. Since his speech marks him as a foreigner ("I hardly spoke the language"), he chooses to discard speech altogether, relying on the kind of silent action favored by the peasants of his youth in the East.[10] In a moment of despair, he wishes he could divest himself of his identifying speech and looks with envy at the seemingly uncomplicated lives of slum-dwelling blacks in the city. They are at least free of possessions and "the symbols of ownership—credentials, diplomas, deeds" (133). He says, "I envied those who lived here and seemed so free, having nothing to regret and nothing to look forward to" (133). Like the Boy in *The Painted Bird*, imagining an escape from his identity through a miraculous change of his features, the narrator of *Steps* imagines himself absorbed into the life of the blacks. "If I could magically speak their language and change the shade of my skin, the shape of my skull, the texture of my hair, I would transform myself into one of them" (133). But while he dreams of speaking the language of power, he takes action to neutralize the impact of his foreign speech by performing a "deaf-mute charade." Now, with his potential oppressors convinced of his permanent victimization, the narrator is free to exploit each situation. In one, a woman who holds parties for figures of "the underworld" takes him as her lover, thinking he is incapable of revealing their affair. As the narrator makes love to her, his feigned muteness releases in her a secret language. "Swaying like a clump of weed in the sea, she quivered, a rushing stream of words broke over her lips like foam. It was as if I were the master of all this fluid passion, and her tumbling words its final wave" (142). The narrator has become the master of still another language—the pent-up eloquence of the woman, who feels free to speak only because she believes her words cannot be heard: "In her last outpouring she broke into a language I could understand, and spoke of herself as a zealot entering a church built long ago from the ruins of pagan temples . . . she cried out again and again, as though trying to detach into speech what had been fused with her flesh" (142). The woman's passionate flow of words constitutes the self she has kept hidden until this moment, but she does what the narrator avoids—she exposes her identity by her language and becomes, unknowingly, a victim of this master of her words.

Language and sex in *Steps* can be either a source of power or a sign of weakness, depending on how the relationship between the two principals, that is, between speaker and hearer or between sexual partners, establishes itself. The narrator sees both language and sex in terms of the interaction of will. Each activity involves role playing, and the only roles available are victim and oppressor. The narrator manipulates the words of the woman who thinks he is a deaf mute; the operators of the concentration camps control the language of their victims and thus capture and destroy their identity. In a dialogue between the narrator and his lover the narrator describes how his friend—a former citizen of a foreign country—designed concentration camps just before World War II. The narrator explains his friend's attitude toward his work as an architect of the camps. Rats are not "murdered," he says, "we get rid of them; or, to use a better word, they are eliminated; this act of elimination is empty of all meaning. There's no ritual in it, no symbolism; the right of the executioner is never questioned. That's why in the concentration camps my friend designed, the victims never remained individuals; they became as identical as rats" (64).[11] The executioners rule over the words as well as the lives of their prisoners. By using "better" words, they manage to remove the opprobrium attached to "murder"; thus the prisoners, bereft of words and identity, are reduced to a problem of "hygiene."The elimination of the symbolic impact of certain words, in short, precedes the elimination of those victims who would utter them.

Kosinski's probing of the darker side of the functions of both speech and sex often result in a grotesque combination of the two, a kind of blending of the separate roles of each in startling ways. Just as words can be eliminated by oppressors to prevent their normal impact ("murder" expunged in favor of "elimination" or "hygiene") so too human sexuality can be severed from its conventional role of reproduction. No womb in *Steps*, for example, produces offspring; instead, the womb—like that of the acrobat—is turned by the narrator's words so far from its natural function that it forms an image of consumption rather than production. The womb becomes a mouth, brushing not just against the face of the narrator but against his imagination. In one scene, for example, the narrator watches a woman visiting a city aquarium. She is gazing at an octopus that is slowing eating its own tentacles. "Each time the octopus bit into itself, some of the spectators shuddered as if they felt it eating their own flesh" (22). The woman's unexpected fascination with the octopus arouses the narrator, who confides to her that he "couldn't free [himself] from the images she excited" in him (23). Instead of shuddering at the octopus consuming itself, "there was a serenity about her that went beyond unconcern" (22). This serenity—inspired by the mouth of the octopus turned against its own body—draws the narrator into a brief affair with her; he is "captivated" by images of distortion inspired by the woman. The grace of the acrobat, the serenity of the woman in the aquarium, and the sexual vitality of the tubercular woman—all these encounters are the narrator's attempts to free himself from the confinement of the expected, the predictable. In another of the twelve dialogues with his lover, the narrator urges intercourse while she is menstruating, an act that asserts a discontinuity between coitus and conception. She resists, pointing out the disquieting—for her, at least—blend of womb and mouth: "I feel the blood staining our bodies as if your hardness made me bleed, as if you had flayed my skin, and had eaten me, and I was drained" (54). Some of the sex-as-food images seem conscious acts of defiance by the narrator against conventional behavior, especially against those sanctioned by Judeo-Christian tradition. In the tuberculosis hospital, for instance, a nun, "whispering some secret language" into the ears of the dying woman, later accuses the narrator of feeding on her patient's flesh. In still another of the dialogues, the narrator listens while his lover describes to him the sensation of fellatio with him. She once went to confession and "received absolution from the priest" for merely thinking of it; now she exults in the act itself, which, she knows, severs her from her religion as well as her former friends who had warned her that "it was degrading, almost like eating living flesh" (82). She says to him, "It could choke me—or I might bite it off. And as it grows, it is I who give it life; my breathing sustains it, and it uncoils like an enormous tongue" (83). Her description conflates the images of mating and eating, sperm and food.

Sexual encounters like these, in which the narrator deliberately seeks out unpredictable and unconventional sexual ties in order to stimulate a sense of freedom from religious, political, or cultural restraint, often end up as sheer exploitation, even sadism. As readers, we wonder what restraints, if any, the narrator of *Steps* feels obligated to impose on himself in a given encounter. One scene, in which the narrator discovers a woman in a cage, does reveal the narrator's attitude toward his own impulse to exploit a human relationship. Wandering alone by car through an unfamiliar countryside, the narrator discovers a deranged woman kept in a cage inside a barn. Marks on her naked body suggest that she has been sexually abused by the owner of the barn. For a moment the narrator senses that no one but the woman knows he is present. "It occurred to me that we were alone in the barn and that she was totally defenseless" (86). The situation is "tempting"; complete dominance over the woman is possible, which he sees as an encounter in which "one could become completely oneself with another human being" (86). What holds him back, he soon realizes, is that the woman, the potential victim, cannot recognize how he is using her. "What I required, however, was the other's recognition of this: the woman in the cage could not acknowledge me" (86). He turns away and reports the incident to the police, who promptly release the woman and arrest the owner of the barn. But the narrator's motive is not compassion; he sees only that she is useless to provide for him new discoveries of himself.

The scene of the woman in the cage—certainly one of the most strikingly told units of *Steps*—reveals even more to us about the narrator's notion of himself, and perhaps Kosinski's attitude toward his narrator. Some time after the trial in which the farmer who had kept the woman in the cage was convicted, the narrator returns to the village to confront the priest, whom he accuses of knowing all the while what was in the barn. The priest, enraged, denies the accusation, but the narrator's description of the priest's rectory suggests the priest is implicated in the same male dominance of the female as are the peasant farmers whom he passionately defends. The priest sits beneath an "enormous painting of a female saint" who holds a pair of shears. "In front of her, on a platter, lay her breasts" (93). The icons of the painting, breasts and shears, tell us the woman is Saint Agatha, a third-century martyr whose refusal to submit to a Roman official evokes an image of willing sacrifice that contrasts with the sordid abuse of the caged woman. In a sense, the priest lives in his own cage, a prisoner of the attitudes of his culture. Just before the narrator leaves the village, he visits the local church, watching the old women line up before the confessional. After the last woman confesses into the "wooden grill," the "bony hand" of the priest inside "thrust out of the darkness of the confessional. The woman leaned over and kissed it; the hand crossed the dank air and withdrew" (93). The image of the hand pulling itself back into the box repeats the narrator's first glimpse of the woman in the cage. "A white hand stretched toward me through the bars" (85). Disembodied hands, severed breasts—the images suggest a division of the self into fragments. The woman, the priest, even the narrator live inside cages; only the narrator is willing to risk breaking free from culturally sanctioned attitudes to test the openness of experience.[12]

But even the narrator carries his cage with him. He has determined in advance that despite the diversity of human relationships, only two are ultimately genuine: the role of victim and that of oppressor. The episode that appears immediately after the scene with the caged woman is one in which the narrator speaks of a murder trial he participated in as a juror. He is impressed by the dispassionate, detached manner in which the defendant explains his action. "He never admitted or even seemed to realize that what he had done was a brutal crime; he never argued that he had lost control or had not known what he was doing or that he would never do anything like it again. He just described his encounter with the victim without exaggeration, and in the most ordinary terms" (93). The murderer's account of how he created a victim is impressive to the narrator in the way that the narrator's account of his own experience in *Steps* is impressive. We, like the narrator listening to the testimony of the defendant, expect conventional responses: remorse, regret, promises to reform, denial—any emotion that would succeed in keeping the event, the murder, within the boundaries of the extraordinary, the exceptional. We want to distance ourselves from the act, surround it with the lurid details that would prevent its acceptance as routine. But the defendant does not cooperate; nor does Kosinski in the writing of *Steps*. The book places us in the world of victim and oppressor without providing for us the conventional moral framework with which to judge the experience. We look in vain for signals that would support our natural inclination to believe that what we see is remote from us, that we remain safe, unimplicated. Kosinski's descriptions of the narrator's encounters with victims are told "in the most ordinary terms," and it is this very ordinariness that seems most upsetting.[13]

In his defendant-jury scene, then, Kosinski dramatizes his theory of reader contribution. The jury acts as his readers. They listen to the dispassionate account by the defendant, who, like the voice of the narrator in *Steps*, provides them with no easy way to disclaim their own identification with him. "Many of us," says the narrator of his fellow jurors and listeners to the tales of the defendant, "could easily visualize ourselves in the act of killing, but few of us could project ourselves into the act of being killed in any manner. We did our best to understand the murder: the murderer was a part of our lives; not so the victim" (94).

This brief vignette perhaps sums up Kosinski's attitude toward his creation, the narrator, who becomes "a part of our lives" in a way that none of his victims do. The emotional force of *Steps* and *The Painted Bird*, and the later *Cockpit*, derives from Kosinski's conviction that, like it or not, our imagination gravitates toward the pole of the oppressor's voice. The vitality of the oppressor's language— however much we as readers are offended by the acts of the oppressor—takes precedence over the silent suffering of his victims. We simply cannot project ourselves into being victims.

Within the year of its publication Kosinski was awarded the National Book Award for *Steps*. Less than ten years after entering the country speaking little English, he had published four books in that language. He had also reworked a great deal of personal anecdote and memories from his pre-American life. He now faced some important choices. Should his next novel rely so heavily on memories of his life first in Poland and then in New York? The voice in *Steps* is that of a mature young man. Should he continue with a "sequel" or strike out in a new direction?

two

Blank Pages
Being There and
The Devil Tree

In one of the last scenes in *Being There*, Skrapinov, Soviet ambassador to the United Nations, presents as a gift to Chance, the novel's protagonist, a rare copy of the fables of Ivan Krylov (1768–1844). Skrapinov inscribes on the frontispiece this quotation from Krylov: "One could make this fable clearer still: but let us not provoke the geese." Skrapinov's choice of Krylov's words hints that he and Chance share a personal secret—not only that Chance is fluent in Russian but that the two understand one another politically. To reveal this secret, Skrapinov implies, would be to provoke unnecessarily the geese, the Beautiful People surrounding them both who are not privy to their secret. In this way Skrapinov uses Krylov's cautionary words to his nineteenth-century readers in order to highlight Skrapinov's assumed relationship with Chance, whom he sees as a fellow reader of Krylov. Because Chance knows nothing of Skrapinov's meaning, and is not only ignorant of Russian but illiterate in English, Skrapinov's communication about hidden meanings is understood only by himself, whose delusion renders him a kind of prisoner, the walls of his cell, so to speak, becoming the words of Krylov. The quotation from Krylov also suggests the fabulous nature of *Being There*, which, like Kosinski's first two novels, dramatizes the way language can establish a duplicitous relationship between speaker and hearer, writer and reader. Skrapinov assumes that Chance wields a mysterious power and that Chance's language must be its outward sign. Like so many who listen to Chance speak, Skrapinov is eager to assert the presence of an original style.

Being There, then, is a fable about a perfect language, one that captivates the listener while revealing nothing of the identity of the speaker. Kosinski's third novel continues his analysis of the embryonic writer testing one new language after another until this writer-survivor discovers the one that both ends his victimization and confers power. Being There's main difference from The Painted Bird and Steps is that the protagonist Chance has no will power, no desire to create a language. The narration is not his, as it was the Boy's, and so the fable about the nature of writing we must infer ourselves. Chance can represent a style of pure persuasion, but he cannot articulate it. He is an embryo of potential speech, suspended, as if before birth, in the vegetable world of his garden. The green hose he pulls from bush to bush tethers him to this garden and acts like an umbilical cord. The Boy in The Painted Bird knew that his vegetable world was a prison and so attempted to flee it, to transform himself from an immobile head of cabbage into a flying raven. Chance is unaware that his garden is a prison; knowing no other place since his birth, the garden is to him a refuge: "It was safe and secure in the garden, which was separated from the street by a high, red brick wall" (4). His movements through the garden's narrow paths can be sustained without conscious choice, a kind of perpetual motion without awareness of origin or ending: "Chance could start to wander, never knowing whether he was going forward or backward, unsure whether he was ahead of or behind his previous steps" (4). In one sense, Chance walking in his garden reminds us of Adam in the garden of Eden. But Chance's steps through the garden also resemble our perception of the narrative structure of Kosinski's previous novel, Steps, in which individual episodes were arranged so that the reader also wandered, unsure of the chronological relationship between them. Moreover, fragments of sentences from Steps reverberate in Being There, underscoring Kosinski's penchant for inserting in a novel certain echoes of an earlier one. When EE tells Chance of his sexual power over her, for instance, her words bring to mind those of the narrator's lover in *Steps*: "You uncoil my wants," says EE, "desire flows within me, and when you watch me my passion dissolves it. You make me free. I reveal myself to myself and I am drenched and purged" (116). In *Steps*, the lover says "it uncoils like an enormous tongue. . . . I felt as though I were being christened: it was so white and pure" (83). The contrast between the two male listeners of these words is ironic: the narrator of *Steps* brings about the submission of his lover by enhancing her sense of herself; Chance, of course, wills no such power over EE, but receives it unasked, "uncoiling" her passion without ever realizing it.

Being There functions within a context of other books—Krylov's fables, the book of Genesis, and the previous novels of Kosinski, in which protowriters sought to captivate their listeners the way Chance manages to captivate his without even trying. Still another book, *The Career of Nikodem Dyzma*, reverberates in the background of *Being There*. Written by Tadeusz Dolega-Mostowicz and published in Poland in 1932, the year before Kosinski's birth, this book was enormously popular in its own time, flourishing during Poland's final period of cultural freedom. By coincidence, the German invasion of Poland in 1939 ended not only that culture but the family life of Kosinski's childhood. Years later, living in another culture, Kosinski must have felt personal affinities for Dolega-Mostowicz, whose novel once captured a reading public while it satirized a government. Parallels between the two books are limited but intriguing. Nikodem Dyzma, an impoverished postal clerk, comes to Warsaw to seek his fortune. By accident he secures an invitation to a dinner at the prime minister's palace, and he shortly fools all the aristocrats attending into believing that he is someone of importance. An old but powerful man befriends him, invites him to his home (where Dyzma later is seduced by the young wife of his host) and provides Dyzma with enough fragments of inside political knowledge that Dyzma succeeds—in spite of his crudity and limited intelligence—in rising to a position of power. The following scene from a fashionable salon shows how Dyzma's literal-mindedness inadvertently bestows on him the reputation of a wit:

They talked about Mrs. Przelecka. The baroness was sure Mrs. Przelecka was absolutely over fifty; the Count asserted that she hadn't even
hit forty-five yet. Nikodem considered it only fair to straighten out this
matter. "Mrs. Przelecka is only thirty-two." Everyone looked at him with
astonishment. The bald count asked him "How do you know that, Mr.
Chairman? Isn't that estimate rather low?" "By no means," answered
Dyzma angrily. "It is a very accurate one. She told me that herself." He
said it in all honesty, and was surprised that the entire room again
exploded with laughter.[1]

Dyzma, although uneducated and crude, is cunning and knows
what he wants. Chance is without will power, ambition, or even
consciousness. Only in plot do the two works invite comparison: in
both, a man without a past, unaware of his limitations, falls by
chance into situations that unintentionally increase his power over
others, and both books conclude with the protagonists about to win
political office—in one case the president of the Republic, and in the
other, vice president of the United States. Kosinski's use of parallels
between Dyzma and Chance suggests his willingness to dramatize the
nature of literary inspiration within his own fiction. Like Dolega-
Mostowicz, Kosinski (at the time of composing *Being There*) had also
written a successful novel which described the plight of a victim
searching for a language that would ensure power.

Being There turns some of the themes of Kosinski's first two novels
inside out. Chance discovers that the only language he knows—the
vocabulary of the garden and the stereotyped gestures of television
performers—works very nicely to secure a power vaster than that
dreamed by either the Boy or the narrator of *Steps*. Unlike the Boy,
Chance never learns to read or write; his admission that he is
ignorant of these skills is taken by his listeners as a sign of
independence and freethinking. And yet, for all Kosinski's ironic
comparisons between the mindless Chance and the protowriters of
The Painted Bird and *Steps*, Chance is intimately involved in the
world of words. In two crucial scenes he is surrounded by written
texts. The dying Old Man's bedroom is "lined with built-in shelves,
filled with books" (9), and Chance is confronted by the lawyer in a

"narrow, dim book-lined room" (15) where Chance learns that his identity has not been recorded by words. "Chance was surprised that in so many papers spread on the desk his name was nowhere mentioned" (15). Because no words have defined him, there is no "trace" of him. He is free of the prison of words but ignorant of the meaning of his extraordinary freedom from everyone else's perception of him. Chance is a tabula rasa, a blank page waiting for others to inscribe words on him.[2] In another sense, Chance is not an embryonic writer seizing the right language; he *is* that language to all those who hear him. Each of his listeners attributes to him an original style that penetrates reality as no other speaker. Tom Courtney of the *New York Times* listens to Chance's voice and claims he is "very laconic and matter-of-fact" (59). Benjamin Rand, EE's husband, claims Chance has a "gift" of being "natural," speaking "directly to the point" (72). A woman praises Chance for having an "uncanny ability of reducing complex matters to the simplest of human terms" (106), and a German diplomat admires Chance's "naturalistic approach." All of these terms are variations of a single illusion of a language that captures listeners without rendering the speaker vulnerable. Chance, moreover, is offered all the rewards of a successful writer ("a six-figure advance" plus royalties)—without suffering a bit of the writer's angst: others will write his words for him, the editor Stiegler assures him. "We can provide you with our best editors and research assistants" (104). The Boy in *The Painted Bird* dreams of becoming a writer; Chance—in the mind of Stiegler—already is one.

While all he meets convince themselves that Chance possesses a unique and powerful language, Chance is by no means unwilling to assume the style they think is his. Invited to appear on television, Chance not only readily agrees, he takes the first step that would demonstrate to millions of viewers that he *is* a style. "He wanted to see himself reduced to the size of the screen; he wanted to become an image, to dwell inside the set" (61). When he was earlier expelled from the garden to wander the streets of the city, Chance could rely only on metaphors about the garden and his belief in television plots.

Even his own television set seemed to promise him the power to create, to become an image. "He sank into the screen. Like sunlight and fresh air and mild rain, the world from outside the garden entered Chance, and Chance, like a TV image, floated into the world, buoyed up by a force he did not see and could not name" (6).

Thus does Chance go forth from the garden, uttering fables of plant life and expecting people to behave the way they do on television. A more unpromising hero could hardly be imagined, yet Chance masters the hostile environment of the streets, mimics the trappings of wealth, seizes the tools of power (electronic media), and ultimately wins both fame and lady—all without knowing it.

We first see Chance deprived of both the presence and love of parents. The narrator paraphrases the words of the Old Man, Chance's protector and jailer, admonishing the young Chance. "His name was Chance because he had been born by chance. He had no family. Although his mother had been very pretty, her mind had been as damaged as his: the soft soil of his brain, the ground from which all his thoughts shot up, had been ruined forever" (8). The Old Man refuses to tell Chance "who his father was" (although we sense the Old Man himself might be the father) and orders Chance to "limit his life . . . to the garden" (8), warning him that otherwise "he would be sent to a special home for the insane where, the Old Man said, he would be locked in a cell and forgotten. Chance did what he was told" (8).

The Old Man's threat of enclosing the boy Chance in a cell is effective; Chance docilely stays within his garden cage in a way that reminds us of the once-wild rabbit of *The Painted Bird*. But when he is confronted by the lawyer of the Old Man's estate and asked to sign a document that would waive any claim, Chance recoils from this first act of writing. "Chance knew that he should not reveal that he could not read or write. On TV programs people who did not know how to read or write were often mocked or ridiculed" (23). Like the Boy, Chance knows he needs a new language. His television watching has taught him that when "one was addressed and viewed by others, one was safe. Whatever one did would then be interpreted by the others in the same way that one interpreted what they did. They would never know more about one than one knew about them" (34). Armed with such naive defenses—we think of the Boy who believed that by staring at the teeth of his oppressors he could ward off their power—Chance ventures out of the garden to test them. The comedy of the Boy's belief in the power of his stare is that we discount the Boy's hope in advance because we know it will fail; the comedy that Chance provokes is that his defense actually works—far better than he ever realizes. The moment he exits from the Old Man's house, he becomes the victim of a car accident. The limousine carrying Benjamin Rand's wife, EE, backs into Chance's leg and slightly injures him. EE mishears Chance's utterance of his name—Chance the Gardener—and she unwittingly renames him Chauncey Gardiner. He realizes her mistake, but he "assumed that, as on TV, he must use his new name from now on" (31). Although unconscious of the process, Chance is already transforming himself from victim to victimizer. After Benjamin Rand's doctor examines Chance in Rand's mansion, he tells EE that "your victim is very handsome" (33); at this point Chance has won EE's fascination. When he models his response to her on a remembered scene from television he wins her affection and eventual passion. "Thinking that he ought to show a keen interest in what EE was saying, Chance resorted to repeating to her parts of her own sentences, a practice he had observed on TV. . . . Her words seemed to float inside his head; he observed her as if she were on television" (37).

The combination of his simple images from the garden and his soft-spoken mannerisms that he mimics from television makes a profound impression on not only EE but Rand himself. They both believe Chance's words—and his mind—are original. Chance's speech about the literal garden in which he once worked moves Rand to exclaim, "Yes, Chauncey, what an excellent metaphor! A productive businessman is indeed a laborer in his own vineyard!" (40). The dinner scene in Rand's mansion shows us Chance's listeners stumbling over themselves in the rush to proclaim the power of his speech. Rand even attempts to speak this extraordinary language. Musing on his impending death, Rand tells EE and Chance, "I feel like a tree whose roots have come to the surface" (42). As Chance is introduced to more and more powerful people, each tries to imitate Chance's language. The president of the United States, after hearing a sample ("There are spring and summer, but there are also fall and winter") quickly adopts it as his own. When the news breaks that the president has been impressed by Benjamin Rand's friend, the media people cannot project this new speaker into the homes of the entire country soon enough. As Chance faces the cameras, he sees them not as a threat but as a source of safety—the audience can only know him as an image. "They would never know how real he was, since his thinking could not be televised" (65). Confident that his language cannot expose his identity, Chance repeats his speech about the garden, and more listeners are taken in. "Chance's last words were partly lost in the excited murmuring of the audience. Behind him, members of the band tapped their instruments; a few cried out loud bravos . . . the applause mounted to an uproar" (67). The scene displays Kosinski's concern about the collective power of television to create dependency in millions of viewers.[3] But the main point is that Chance's language manipulates his audience more completely than any writer, even Stalin, ever could.

By the end of Kosinski's tale Soviet computers have "analyzed Gardiner's vocabulary, syntax, accents" and find that it is impossible to detect Chance's ethnic background or origins in any American community. Chance, reports the Soviet agent, is a "blank page," and this phrase becomes Chance's code name. Independently, the FBI comes up with the same conclusion. Thus, for Kosinski, Chance achieves the status that no other of his protagonists reaches—his language is not a mark of identity, vulnerability, or victimization. Language as pure power, divested of its inherent signals of personal origin, past, and community, is the language that the despairing narrators of The Painted Bird and Steps often imagine speaking. Chance manages to do it just by opening his mouth, and the book ends before anyone is the wiser. "Bewildered" by all the attention he is receiving, Chance breaks away from still another VIP reception to gaze at a small garden. "Not a thought lifted itself from Chance's brain. Peace filled his chest" (140).

In *The Painted Bird* a boy struck dumb learns to write his way to power. We deduce the kind of power he has won from the artistry of the narration he composes years later. The leap from this speechless boy alone in a forest to Chance in double-breasted suit basking in the lights of a television studio may expand the fictional setting for Kosinski's studies of writing and power, but it does so at a price. The novella-length *Being There* lacks not only the unpredictability of *The Painted Bird* or of *Steps* but also the sentence-by-sentence richness of those books. To cite an example, a character confides to an uncomprehending Chance that "when we dream of reality, television wakes us" (107). The phrase asks us to reflect on another text, this one the Prufrockian utterance about lingering "till human voices wake us, and we drown." Kosinski's text in *Being There* defers textual complexity in favor of extratextual echoes.

Whalen as a Writer

Kosinski's fourth novel, *The Devil Tree*, avoids the comic exaggeration of *Being There*, attempting instead to assemble a mosaic of brief, realistic scenes of American life, all centering on the main character, Jonathan James Whalen, who is both a twenty-one-year-old heir to a steel fortune and a writer manqué. If *The Devil Tree* trots out familiar Kosinski themes—the freedom of initiative that wealth affords, the child as victim looking for a language that would open his cage—it also looks more closely than his previous novels at the complex and risk-laden relationship between writer and reader. The book's epigraph is from Proust: "Sometimes the future dwells in us without our knowing it and when we think we are lying our words foretell an imminent reality." Proust's words prepare us for the treatment of a particular concern—the duplicitous nature of writing, especially the gap between the intention of the writer and the public perception of his achievement. Whalen is even more of a protowriter than the Boy or the narrator of *Steps*. He uses written words not only to discover the meaning of his pampered and unhappy childhood but to structure for himself an entirely new identity. Whalen narrates about half of the 136 brief vignettes that make up *The Devil Tree*. His comments in both tone and format resemble diary jottings, notes, observations of his own behavior and consciousness—a notebook of the writer as neophyte. A number of Whalen's comments probe the nature of writing from different perspectives—as therapy, disguise, or discovery. Whalen's initial determination to assume the role of cool-headed observer of his own life reminds us of Kosinski's own description of the writer looking at himself in a mirror. Writing gives Whalen the objectivity he needs to analyze his life, which he sees in a state of flux. "Now I explore my memories," he says, "trying to discover the substructure hidden beneath my past actions, searching for the link to connect them all" (25). Whalen's efforts at writing about himself in order to create himself prove to be too great a strain. It is as if he were a novelist inventing a character on whom he must then model his own life.

In one of Whalen's early written analyses of himself, he feels that his first need is for a sympathetic audience, a reader who could understand him. His girlfriend Karen becomes, for a while, the reader on whom he must depend. He turns over to her all his notes on his past life as a pill-popping drifter through Burma, India, and Africa. "I gave them to her because I wanted to show her something tangible from my past to make her understand it. At the same time I wonder what this new knowledge about me will mean to her. I am always afraid that some incident from my past will destroy other people's affection for me. . . . But with Karen I'm not so frightened. With her there is no need to hide those things in me that seem bizarre or ugly" (31). Although Whalen's efforts as a writer are tentative and brief, this passage shows Whalen's paradoxical sense of writing: it is both a form of self-discovery and a source of exposure. Whalen is also self-conscious about his motivation for writing all these notes. He recalls that he knew while he wrote that he was designing his sentences not for himself alone but for another reader. The fact that this awareness shaped his words seems to him a betrayal of his reliance on writing to discover himself. Whalen's image of the writer is schizoid; he must be honest to discover himself but deceptive to lure another reader. Knowing the reader is looking over his shoulder, so to speak, Whalen wonders if what he wrote could ever be free of this awareness. If not, then the writing becomes, as Proust said, "lying." Here is Whalen's pondering the point. "When I gave Karen the notes, I told her I had written them for myself. Perhaps I even believed it. No doubt it made me uneasy to think I had not written those words purely for my own gratification. Yet I must have known that Karen would read them. I must have known that someday they would belong to her" (32). Karen turns out to be less than the sympathetic reader needed by this vulnerable writer. She is, in fact, a rival writer. Whalen has read her poems and seen that she too is reluctant to become vulnerable through her writing. "She agreed, but said she was afraid of exposing her real self. I suggested that she write in the third person and project her own sensibility onto her protagonists" (83). Her personal life, especially her need for promiscuous relationships, makes Karen a reader who is untrustworthy. When Whalen says "she vacillates between seeing herself as the predator and as the prey," he describes how the writer-reader relationship he desired has turned against him. Karen is to him too often the predator and he the prey. In the end, Whalen never finds the right reader of his words, and becomes a writer without an audience.

Whalen's plight is a variation of those of the narrators of *The Painted Bird* and *Steps*, both of whom knew what power was but did not possess it. Whalen begins with potential power, but he does not know how to activate it. As a child dominated by a dynamic father, he thinks of himself as a victim; but as sole heir to the same dead father, he is powerful. Reversals such as these are perhaps summarized by the phenomenon of the devil tree. Whalen describes the cycle of this tree to an unsuspecting victim, his godfather, Walter Howmet. Whalen's explanation also appears separately as an epigraph to the novel itself:

The native calls the baobab 'the devil tree' because he claims that the devil, getting tangled in its branches, punished the tree by reversing it. To the native, the roots are branches now, and the branches are roots. To ensure that there would be no more baobabs, the devil destroyed all the young ones. That's why, the native says, there are only full-grown baobab trees left. (1)

The image of the baobab tree, with its implied clash between the generations (the "young ones" are destroyed, the "full-grown" survive), provides a link with *Being There* as well: in that book Benjamin Rand spoke to Chance about his impending death in terms of a tree with upturned roots. Rand sees himself about to be displaced by the younger Chance (Rand actually encourages Chance to think along these lines), whose youth and strength contrast sharply with Rand's own appearance. In *The Devil Tree*, shortly after his comment about the baobab tree, Whalen lures his godparents, Howmet and his wife Helen, to their deaths. The tree images in both books, then, represent the replacement of the weakened father by the stronger son. Both fathers, Rand and Howmet, use the mask of authority to hide vulnerability; both confront a surrogate son, whose youthful inexperience masks a vitality that will eventually supplant the father.

The reversal of branches and roots of the baobab tree also suggest Whalen's personal plight. He was once helpless, dominated by his father, whose power—imagined by Jonathan as a special language— he envied and abhorred. His fear of his father, Whalen says, "began in early childhood when I lay in bed and listened to my father rage" (36). He recalls watching helplessly as his father beat the young Whalen's dog. "I did not interfere. I simply watched, torn by pity for the dog, anger at my father and hatred for my own weakness" (36). These recollections of early childhood make up his past; now, as the book begins, Whalen is one week from his twenty-first birthday, when he will inherit his dead parents' estate. But he does not yet have the confidence in himself to play the role of master. He feels himself split between two generations. "I told her [Karen, his girlfriend] I had always wanted to conceal both portions of my personality: the manipulative, malevolent adult who deceives and destroys; and the child who craves acceptance and love" (23). Whalen knows very well the precarious nature of his personality. Only because both parents are dead, in fact, does he feel he exists at all.

Kosinski's interest in the child as victim reflects itself in all his novels before *The Devil Tree*; the child is victim either because the father is absent and powerless to help (*The Painted Bird* and *Steps*) or the father is present and domineering, such as the Old Man toward Chance. But *The Devil Tree* offers Kosinski's most extensive treatment of the father as victimizer of the child. In the book's first scene, Whalen has returned to the United States to accept his new role as heir to the Whalen estate. His father, Charles Sumner Whalen, died some time before from accidental drowning; his mother, more recently by suicide. But this is not the case of the father dead and the son triumphant. Whalen's identity is in a state of flux, still rooted in the role of son-victim and not yet assured the role of supplanter of his father. "As I become more and more aware of myself, I see myself divided. My most private, real self is violently antisocial—like a lunatic chained in a basement" (13). Above the basement the "respectable" family sits, "ignoring the tumult." The figure of the rebellious child locked in the basement represents the divided psyche of Whalen, who also desires the power and respectability of the family upstairs. "I don't know what to do about the family lunatic: destroy him, keep him locked in the cellar or set him free?" (13). As Whalen sees it, his identity is still unformed, subject to unpredictable and often violent changes of mood. Once, while engaged in the psychodrama of an encounter group, he summarizes his previous emotional state to himself. "The struggle within me was so great that I was sweating from the tension. It was as if a physical contest was going on between the two halves of myself. One moment I was speaking in a controlled voice, the next moment I was a child, screaming" (33).

Because Whalen lives in both the past and the present, between the existence of the lunatic in the basement and the respectable father overhead, he sees that he must map out a new identity, one that he himself creates rather than the one designed for him by his family and the wealth he has inherited. Like the narrator of *Steps*,

Whalen discovers that the creation of an identity often involves deception, a kind of trying on of masks. Deception can even help shape a style. "I have learned to be defensive. I have become a master of the art of concealment, of tailoring my reminiscence to the person I'm talking to" (31). Later, at an encounter session with Karen, Whalen tells her "in order to be honest I must always play a number of roles at once" (35). These forms of deception—role playing, masks, disguises—are necessary, Whalen claims, because "I have been continually watched. Because of my father, the Company and the money, people have always been employed to make sure of my existence" (34).Whalen is the antithesis of Chance, who could not prove his existence to the skeptical lawyer precisely because he lacked any papers of identification. Whalen's identity consists solely of such papers, legal documents, and the opinions of others. He wants to erase words, start a new page, write down his emotions instead of feeling them. "My depressions are no longer such natural urges as sex, sleep and hunger," he says. "Now they are completely calculated" (90). At an encounter session, Jonathan chooses control over confession: "But even with the protection of darkness I felt I must not give in to my emotions. I maintained my self-control and soon I was at ease" (94). His relationship with Karen reflects the same wariness at revelation and reluctance to be made vulnerable. Whalen does not have the control over Karen the way the narrator of *Steps* controlled his lover; but Whalen's continual analysis of his relationship with her functions in a similar way. He engages in a variety of sexual encounters in order to distill from those experiences both a sense of freedom from conventional restraint and an expansion of the self's awareness. Karen, however, is more than a match for Whalen. "My impulse is not to speak or write, but to remain elusive, to present Karen with cartoons of my fears and sexual desires rather than my real ones. But her own elusiveness makes this impossible: she intimidates me into talking frankly" (68). Whalen wants to control his lover, but she forces him to expose himself in words, making him vulnerable. He wants to control his emotions, but several times experiences severe depression ("During the last few days I have fallen back into self-hatred"). He wants to escape from his father's domination but also to replace his father and to dominate others, which implies mastering his father's language.

Whalen's search for an identity of his own making turns naturally to the wealth that is his inheritance. Kosinski's analysis of American wealth—especially inherited—is more pronounced in *The Devil Tree* than in *Steps* or *Being There*. Whalen is living on a trust but can trust no one, not even himself, and so breaks the trust between himself as a child and his parents' aspirations for him. He uses, for one thing, the fruits of his trust in a way that offends his parents. He drops out of Yale, wanders through Africa and Burma, becomes addicted to drugs, dresses in leather pants, and wears his hair long. After he returns to New York and accepts his inheritance, he spends his money on experiences that provide new perspectives of himself. He hires a helicopter to fly him around the city of New York. "Every-time I fly in a helicopter," he says to the pilot, "it reminds me of the model gyros I had when I was a kid. It's like being guided by remote control" (5). The helicopter ride gives Whalen the momentary feeling of being a child again—he is enclosed in a self-contained world and guided by another's will. But his perception of himself as a child is not satisfactory; he returns to the streets, oblivious to the crowds around him. "He was his own event" (9). Next he sheds his long hair and begins to plot his life as if it could be made predictable, which is always for Kosinski a form of self-deception. "I note all my appointments on my calendar, make lists of things to do and to buy and neatly cross off my accomplished chores" (46). But when Whalen rejects an offer to work for his father's company because "I don't want to fit myself into any kind of structure," he seems to be taking tentative steps toward determining his destiny. First he orders the Company to acquire a small apartment in Manhattan. Then, within close access to the apartment, he arranges private transportation in the form of a helicopter, a small speedboat, and a Ford with a "twelve-cylinder Italian-made engine . . . installed in place of the American one" (143). Whalen's new sense of power, of the freedom to manipulate technology for his own ends, surpasses even the power of the narrator of *Steps*, who "required" money to support the life-style he had chosen. Whalen has so much money that he does not know just what his requirements are. He buys the smallest tape recorder available, one made "to look exactly like a pack of American cigarettes." But he never uses it. He orders fifty books of poetry to be delivered to his apartment in the middle of the night, reads a few lines from several, then discards them. He seems engulfed by words—but cannot sort them out and impose a design on them. He returns to his father's closed-up mansion near Pittsburgh, and, in an act which he apparently sees as a defilement of his parents' house, he brings with him a black prostitute. They explore the rooms together, while Whalen reads old letters written to him by his parents, apparently still searching for the "hidden power" of his father's words.

Whalen's vaguely formed plans to free himself from his father— frenetic encounter sessions, sexual promiscuity, the break-in of his father's house—finally focuses on the figure of Walter Howmet. Charting two airplanes, he flies to Mombassa, Africa, with the Howmets as his guests. After guiding them to an empty sand bar far from land, he leaves them to the incoming tide. Their drowning duplicates the death of his own father, accidentally drowned offshore from his Rhode Island estate. But Whalen's vicarious triumph over his father brings him no peace. Shortly after experiencing elation at this ultimate prank ("deep within himself he could hear a child's laughter"), Whalen becomes mysteriously sick and is confined to a clinic in Geneva. "He did not know why he was in pain. He only wanted his mind turned off" (206). The book closes with Whalen watching the fog lift over Lake Geneva. He seems to have no more words to write.

Part of Whalen's failure to achieve freedom is his attitude toward language. Both the narrators of *The Painted Bird* and *Steps* knew that their own language marked them as victims and that they would have to master the language of their oppressor to survive. Whalen also engages himself in a search for a language. As a child he attributes Godlike power to his father's words. "I remember how, as a boy, I used to collect the cork tips of my father's cigarettes and stick them in my stamp albums. I believed they contained his unspoken words, which one day would explain everything'' (25). The spoken words of the father are few and unmemorable, so Whalen attributes the source of his father's obvious power to some deeper mode of language to which he has no access. As we have seen, he writes down his experience in Africa for Karen, but rejects his own written words as somehow false. His trust is still in that hidden language of his father. ''There's a place beyond words where experience first occurs to which I always want to return. I suspect that whenever I articulate my thoughts or translate my impulses into words, I am betraying the real thoughts and impulses which remain hidden'' (32). Whalen's distrust of his own words suggests an underlying uneasiness with the vitality of language, a reluctance to seize on language's potential power. Whalen's real wish is for a womblike existence, a place beyond words, something like Chance's garden. Recalling an experience in Nepal with a Tibetan refugee, Whalen again laments the limitations of his language: ''Tibetans have based an entire culture on death and the various states following it. They have symbols and a language that convey what it is like to die, and what one feels and thinks while being dead'' (157). But for Whalen the Tibetan language only underscores the inadequacy of his own. ''Our language has no words to express such alien concepts as the event of death or afterlife'' (158). He can only imagine mastery of his father's language; he cannot speak it. ''When I play my father [at an encounter session], I must speak in the voice that punishes me. Yet that condemning voice is also the voice which comforts me saying: 'Because you are my son, you are safe and better than others.' The roles overlap like a cover which protects a child but which may at the same time suffocate and destroy him'' (35).

Throughout the novel Whalen is suspended between the realization of his victimization and his attempts to dominate. He can never speak the language of power because he cannot separate the voice that punishes from the voice that comforts. Whalen on one occasion confesses that his fear of his father led him as a child to read biographies of great leaders. What pleased Whalen about these stories was that his heroes seemed—unlike himself—fatherless. "These men seemed to have been born without fathers; no wonder they had always been strong and powerful, able to mete out punishment whenever they pleased. They were born fathers" (37). But Whalen is a born son. His distrust of language marks his limitations as a person; it is as if the potential power of language were frozen within himself, never to be released. At the end of the book Whalen is still clinging to the cover that both protects and suffocates him.

Whalen Revised

Kosinski's fourth novel in eight years was his least satisfying to critics and reviewers up to that point in his career.[4] He himself described the book as a deliberate break from his previous work. While *The Painted Bird* and much of *Steps* articulated a world unfamiliar to most Americans, Kosinski attempted in *The Devil Tree* to examine a problem closer to his adopted home: the cultural disarray of the late sixties, especially the proliferation of drugs, pornography, clashes between the generations, and the effect on society of inordinate wealth and consumption. Whatever the motivation, Kosinski himself felt something had gone awry. "And so in many ways I feel that *The Devil Tree*, in terms of my old relation to my work, did something which puzzled me; I'm far more perplexed by *The Devil Tree* and by Jonathan and his environment, than by anything I have ever done in the past."[5] Kosinski's puzzlement perhaps stemmed from his ambiguous attitude toward his protagonist, Whalen, whom he conceived as a representative of certain trends in American life. Whalen is "frankly lost, like the majority of us, between his roots and his branches," says Kosinski. But the book reflects indecision as to whether Whalen is a representative of the ills of American society or a critic of them. Sometimes Whalen is so immersed in his memories of childhood that he is not a convincing observer of the social decay that surrounds him. Or, he is simply the silent listener to other voices, each of which exposes some evil in American society. One voice, for example, says, "You may think heroin-dealing is a dirty, vicious business, Mr. Whalen, but you yourself are in an equally corrupt enterprise. The fish caught near the outwash of one of your father's factories are unfit to eat because their flesh has been contaminated by nickel" (152). Another talks of a bank scam, another brags to Whalen about mechanics who sabotage foreign-made cars by slipping sugar cubes into gas tanks, another discusses how corporations make profits from ghetto housing, and so on. Because Kosinski chooses to exclude any response to these voices by Whalen, we do not know what Whalen thinks of it all. The voices appear as fragments, unattached either to a character or to Whalen's acknowledgment that he is interested, or even listening. "This country's culture is antiseptic," pronounces still another disembodied voice. "No one wants to talk about disease and lameness. People are terrified of malformation" (120). Thus the novel veers back and forth between acerbic observations on American culture that Whalen presumably hears but does not initiate and monologues in which Whalen analyzes his personality, frequently in a rather whining tone, such as when he wonders if Karen would fly as far to see him as she did to interview a ballerina for a magazine article.

Whalen as a character cannot sustain the role of critical intelligence that analyzes the wrongs of American society. And the many vignettes, although often interesting in themselves, do not resonate from within a convincing if bizarre intelligence, as they do with the complex and cunning narrator of *Steps*. Kosinski's perplexity prompted an extensive revision of the novel, which he published in 1981. The numerous alterations of the original text that he made reflect a later stage in Kosinski's developing attitude toward his own fiction, a stage characterized by defensiveness about his reputation as a writer, anxiety about possible failure of inspiration, and a seeming compulsive determination to explain directly attitudes toward writing that his earlier fiction only suggested or implied. He is also willing to insert playful autobiographical allusions, such as the scene in which a cook applies for employment to Whalen by bringing a reference from "Mary Hayward Weir."

Kosinski prefaces the 1981 revision of *The Devil Tree* with an explanation of why he felt the original required a revision. "When I wrote this novel initially, I felt restricted by the proximity of its story to the environment and events of my recent past decade. This might account for the cryptic tone of the novel's first version." Now, Kosinski continues, he feels "free to reinstate all the additional links that bound Jonathan James Whalen to those whom he loved." This preface is surprising for two reasons: he now sees the "cryptic tone" of the original as a source of weakness rather than the very quality that, I would suggest, characterizes *Steps*, his National Book Award winner. Secondly, he refers to the additional material as reinstatements, "links," that, having once been dropped, are now being restored. The function of these links is to tie Whalen with "those whom he loved." Aside from the fact that the original *The Devil Tree* demonstrated that Whalen loved no one (his relationship with Karen is too full of doubt and denials of commitment to merit the word love), the actual "links" consist primarily of statements similar to Kosinski's essays on American culture with a scattering of allusions to the novels he wrote after the publication of the first version. Whalen, for example, watches a TV show called *Blind Date* and visits a nightclub called "the Cockpit."

The problem—in the first version—of Whalen's detachment from the vignettes that criticize different aspects of American culture Kosinski solves in the revised version by letting Whalen articulate these criticisms himself, often after first explaining in rather tedious terms how he got the information. "My own situation," Whalen says, "is thus an extension of a larger economic and social disproportion. The company's researcher, who collected for me some newspaper clippings about the American superrich, came up with some interesting facts: over half a million Americans own assets worth a million or more dollars, and—I was amused to note—almost sixty thousand of them reside in New York" (34). When he runs out of company researchers, Whalen becomes an insufferable quoter of other texts. After recording a particularly long passage on economic life, he coyly adds, "I could have written it, but I did not. Karl Marx did" (107).

One character absent from the original version perhaps reflects the state of Kosinski's mind during the seven months he revised *The Devil Tree*: he is a fashion photographer and former writer. "In his mid-forties, widowed, he was an abrasive, restless, mean neurotic with the face of an angry hawk. . . . He had once been a writer, but his paranoically gruesome novels—sexual quid pro quos concerning industrial society—had failed to secure a niche for him in the intellectual market place. . ." (50). In this second version, then, Whalen the protowriter is afforded a glimpse of a fellow writer pinned wriggling to the wrong end of the spectrum between success and failure. Kosinski's image of the failed writer—at once parody and coy inversion of himself (Kosinski turned from photography to writing) marks some of the changes Kosinski lived through between the writing of the original version of *The Devil Tree*, a time when his work had generated highly favorable reviews, and the writing of the 1981 version of *The Devil Tree*, when his recent critical reception of *Passion Play* was fresh in his memory.

The final difference between the two versions is Kosinski's determination to tone down the repulsive but often intriguing side of Whalen in order to grant more authority to his pronouncements about the ills of American society. The result is a new Whalen, a trifle more admirable but less interesting as a person. Here are contrasting versions of the same scene in which Whalen leaves a lover, Barbara, who is suffering from the withdrawal pains of opium:

> The next day Barbara and I moved to a small hotel. A few days later, while I was still sick, she left me.
> When I returned to Rangoon after my cure, I found her in a hospital, receding under the grey sheet that was drawn tight across her shoulders, separating her head from her body.
> She told me she wanted to be committed, to lie in a bed and be put to sleep. She loved the idea of death, of taking a needle and plunging it into her heart or of jumping from a skyscaper. (22)

The reader never learns the fate of Barbara, or if Whalen even cared. Here is the second version:

Back in the hotel, I was cold and sweaty. My heart fluttered and my pulse slowed. My body itched. I trembled. I oscillated between diarrhea and vomiting. Barbara's face was flushed, her pupils dilated; moistness blanketed her body. Her touch left my skin cold and damp. When we kissed, her tongue seemed swollen. Like me, she was ill. I was confused, not organized enough to summon help at first.

A few days later I called the hospital and asked for the ambulance to take us there.

After I was disintoxicated and released from the hospital, Barbara remained there, steadily receding under a sheet that was drawn tight across her shoulders, looking as though her head were separated from her body. (17)

Whalen here not only initiates the hospitalization and visits Barbara, he pays her bills and attends her funeral. There, he listens soberly to the minister's words which he feels probe at the meaning of his own life:

For reasons obscure to me, I have failed to extract from my Protestant heritage its only prophetic and creative truths: that for as long as I live and in every situation, I must protest against the sin of distortion and the limitations of human existence, including the distortion and limitations of my own life and nature; that such protest contains both the hope of my spirtual rebirth and moral resurrection and the peril of uncertainty and personal confusion. Until now I've betrayed my sacred calling. (18)

The gains of the second version of *The Devil Tree* in clarity and consistency for Whalen's character do not overcome the obvious losses of the indirect, open, and "cryptic" implications the reader must cope with in the first version.

three

The Wheelgame of Words
Cockpit and *Blind Date*

Kosinski frames his fifth novel, *Cockpit*, between two quotations from other books which, taken together, underline the tension between control and revelation, between restraint and release, that drives not only the central character, Tarden, but surely every writer. The first quotation, the epigraph for *Cockpit*, is taken from Antoine de Saint-Exupéry's book, *Flight to Arras*. The second, placed at the novel's conclusion, is from Dostoyevski's *The Possessed*. Saint-Exupéry's words comment on Kosinski's own title and his increasingly obsessive theme—the individual's need to control his life, and, by implication, the writer's need to control his characters: "But I dwell now well in the making of the future. Little by little, time is kneading me into shape. A child is not frightened at the thought of being patiently turned into an old man. I too play my games. I count the dials, the levers, the buttons, the knobs of my kingdom."

The "kingdom," of course, is Saint-Exupéry's cockpit. The time is 1940, and he is flying over his own country, France, which is rapidly collapsing under the German invasion. His reconnaissance mission over German-occupied Arras is so dangerous that he and his crew are not expected to return. Thus if the cockpit is a kingdom, it is a fragile one, held together by the will power and imagination of the pilot, who is also a writer. By making the future himself, Saint-Exupéry escapes being made a prisoner of time, a passive victim. He defeats the thought of aging and death by actively controlling his flight, which he sees as his life. And this control is gamelike; by concentrating on the buttons and knobs of the game, he becomes both ruler and child.

The second quotation focuses on an antithetical psychological need—the compulsion to confess, to reveal, to record. It is taken from the scene in *The Possessed* in which Stavrogin presents his written confession—he has defiled a young girl and driven her to suicide—to a monk famous for his holiness, Father Tihon: "Tihon began coming straight to the point: 'Legally you are well-nigh invulnerable—that is what people will say first of all—with sarcasm. Some will be puzzled. Who will understand the true reasons for the confession?' "

Although Tihon is fascinated by what he reads, he wonders if Stavrogin is more interested in gaining an audience for his words than repentance for his deed. Tihon's doubts about the "true reasons," together with Stavrogin's rapt absorption in Tihon as he reads the confession, forces readers of *The Possessed* to reflect on the deceptive nature of the writer. For readers of *Cockpit*, the excerpts from Dostoyevski and Saint-Exupéry alert us to the twin obsessions of the main character, Tarden, who often sees himself pulled in opposite directions: he desires to make the future by confronting the random nature of experience and imposing some form of rule over it, while he simultaneously wants to withdraw from life in order to record his impressions, to make, in short, a "confession" that can be experienced by another. How to look at one's experience doubly, as something to be lived, but also as something that might also be written about, is Tarden's dilemma.

Tarden, at the moment he begins his narration, which is both confession and game, is a former member of an American spy network he calls the "Service." He once belonged to a special unit in the Service called "the hummingbirds," agents who are so "valuable," Tarden says, "that to protect their covers no central file is kept on them and their identities are seldom divulged to fellow agents" (100). Because Tarden has defected from the Service some time be-

fore, he is subject to "elimination" by one of the hummingbirds who
have been pursuing him. But thus far, Tarden says, he has eluded
them. "To date, I know of only one man who has never been tracked
down: myself" (100). Tarden, then, resembles the Boy in *The
Painted Bird.* By becoming a hummingbird, he once joined a select
flock, but by defecting he brings on the wrath of the other hummingbirds who now pursue him, although for the present, unsuc-
cessfully. The unique characteristic of the actual bird after which the
unit is named reflects the dual nature of Tarden: just as the hummingbird can hover in the air or fly like other birds, Tarden is
capable of either observing human life or participating fully in it.
This rhythm between observation and participation, detachment
and involvement, aptly summarizes Tarden's status as a person and a
writer.

Tarden, like Saint-Exupéry playing with the knobs of his cockpit,
wants to control the present by embracing its unpredictable nature,
by thrusting himself into a variety of situations with strangers in
order to dominate them—anything to "make" the future rather than
be passively shaped by circumstance. But Tarden, like Stavrogin in
The Possessed, also wants to narrate a record, a fiction, an imaginative
act which can be experienced by another—even if as a game—after
he himself is dead. And so the annihilation of Tarden's memory
threatens him more than does actual death. He thinks of his possible
fate, for example, should a prostitute discover him dead in his apartment. "I saw it all: the girl would come out of the bathroom and find
me sprawled on the floor. . . . It wasn't the thought of dying that
disturbed me, but that I might die without leaving a trace" (3).
Tarden's compulsion to lead a life without record, yet to create a
vicarious life through confession that will ensure he leaves a "trace,"
results in the long letter to an unnamed woman that becomes Tarden's book.[1]

Tarden begins his book by addressing this woman whom he
knows in ways of which she is unaware. He has entered her bedroom,
he tells her, in her absence, examining her clothing, her checkbook,
her closets, and her prescription drugs. "For some reason," he tells

her, "learning these details increased my desire to know you" (2).
For, he now confesses, "I did not want to just tell you about my past.
I wanted you to relive it" (2). Thus the woman—and the reader—re-
lives the life of Tarden by means of the trace of the words he leaves
behind him.

We never know what the woman thinks of all this, or even if she in
fact reads it; but for us, the readers of *Cockpit*, Tarden's long letter
reveals him to be—among other things—the most cunning and re-
sourceful of Kosinski's line of picaro figures who are also writers.[2]
Tarden has the will power of the narrator of *Steps* and some of the
financial power of Jonathan Whalen; his zest for technological devices that confer on him power over others is unsurpassed by any of
his predecessors. Tarden resembles certain aspects of Chance as
well. Chance had no identity and sought none; but Tarden consciously creates the anonymity that was Chance's birthright by
sustaining multiple identities, each one as difficult to trace as
Chance's own was. "I have stored my important documents in vaults
I rent under assumed names in residential hotels, banks and post
office boxes," he tells the woman. "If I need to leave the country
suddenly I can do so without having to return to any place that might
be identified as my home" (3). While Whalen tries to free himself
from a predictable identity as son of a wealthy father, Tarden's
multiple identities allow him freedom to discard or assume whatever
role he wishes. His former life as a hummingbird in the Service once
provided Tarden with a "shield for the self I wanted to hide" (64).
But having defected from the Service, he takes up a new vocation—
he transforms people into characters, bids them live under his
authorial control in plots he invents for and against them.

For one girlfriend, Valerie, Tarden offers an "unconditional trust
fund" as a lure to free herself from the drudgery of her profession
and live with him. She objects at first but then is attracted to the idea
simply to "see if she could become emotionally or physically involved and still retain her independence" (6). Control is a dimension of creativity, a temporary redemption from the void. By offering to arrange Valerie's life—to probe and channel her energies

multiple identities

control

—Tarden discloses the writer's need to assert his existence by controlling his characters. Hidden within a tiny workroom in his own apartment, he discovers she is unfaithful to him. He "frames" her: first with his camera, which is really Tarden's perspective of her place in the plot, the outer edges of which he cannot yet trace. "I captured Valerie's breast resting near her lover's shoulder, her leg brushing his, his elbow touching her belly" (9). But he captures only *not quite accurate* pieces of her. The totality of her personality eludes him. He tries to frame her (in the slang sense) by revealing to her the incriminating photographs; she walks out of this frame too. Valerie's autonomy threatens Tarden because what he cannot control loses the capacity *control + existence* to exist at all for him. Valerie's free will, her ability to elude his plot, reminds him of his inevitable disintegration as a consciousness. Even his own body is not under his control. As a youth, he recalls, he was revolted by the behavior of his own blood cells. Exposed to air, they would coagulate. "I hated the sense of an autonomous force in my body, determining what would happen to me" (13). He picks at scabs, angered at the sight of his blood asserting itself against his will. Valerie, like many of Tarden's characters, behaves like his blood cells; she escapes the plot.

Yet Tarden has many successes, and each portrays the writer in the act of writing. Years before his life in the West, Tarden, an unwilling citizen of an unnamed East European "State," plots his escape by words. Working alone in a photography darkroom, a kind of sanctuary for his inner thoughts, he invents fictional members of the "Academy" of that State. He stores his fabricated credentials of the members "in boxes of photographic paper whose labels warned that the contents would be damaged if exposed to light" (20). The members are still sketches, slowly taking form in the dark recesses of his psyche. His plot to escape the State, if exposed to the light of its representatives, would destroy him. Only when the sketches are carefully revised are they ready for the reader, the State's gatekeepers, who dutifully write confidential letters about Tarden to the fictional Academy members. Tarden reads them all, selecting those which support his application for a visa. Years later, Tarden's first written characters lie silent in a New York bank vault, turned into Gogol's "Dead Souls" (38), a phrase Tarden uses to describe them to a former professor of the State, now expelled from his country. This professor had written a condemning letter about Tarden to one of the Dead Souls. Thus the professor betrayed his student. But this is not the last time that a teacher turns against the apprentice Tarden. When Tarden reaches New York, years before his career as a hummingbird, he rooms with Robert, who teaches him English. "He continually corrected my speech, checked my term papers for grammatical mistakes and often helped me rewrite them" (40). Robert is a writer, sending concisely composed analyses of the young Tarden to Tarden's parents, still living in the State. "They were letters about me written by a man who understood my character and my roots intimately" (41). But Robert is also psychotic; with sudden unpredictability, Robert attacks Tarden with a knife, vowing to cut off his head. Years after this betrayal, Robert still teaches his former student. "In a sense, Robert continues to be a close friend, reminding me from time to time of the estrangement that may lie beneath apparent mutual understanding" (49). These betraying writers—first the professor, then Robert—warn Tarden that he himself may be drawn into a writer's plot, reduced to the impotence of a mere character.

Tarden's attempts to control his life—by Kosinski's fifth novel a hallmark of his work—represent more than the sheer determination to survive that motivated earlier protowriters. The way Tarden controls the unnamed woman's reliving of Tarden's experiences suggests the techniques and discipline of the novelist. In one recollection, Tarden calls from his past an image of himself as a child playing with an old bicycle wheel he feels "was animated by a powerful spirit." Running beside his wheel, he says, he would whip the wavering wheel "back to life" with a stick. "The wind whipped my face and chilled my fingers, but I felt nothing. I was conscious only of vaulting through space" (148). As a boy, Tarden controlled the motion and the direction of his game, but the wheel also compelled him to run, controlling him as well. Whipping the wheel meant exhilaration and escape from stasis. "Whenever I rested and the wheel lay still, I felt impatient and guilty. Its very shape demanded movement, and soon I would leap up and send it on its way again" (147). This rhythm between resting and running, stasis and dynamic flow, resembles the rhythm of the writer, who often is exhilarated when writing, guilty when resting. The wheel is the work of art in the process of being created; the writer escapes the tedium of his own life by escaping into the flow of the wheel, which seems at times to the writer more real than his own life. "The life of my wheel was superior to the lives of men and beasts," Tarden muses (147).

The wheel game of the young Tarden becomes transformed into another kind of game by Tarden the adult. The flow of individual lives around him in the city "inspires" him with "that same sense of vaulting" he knew in his youthful game: "Each person is a wheel to follow, and at any moment my manner, my language, my being, like the stick I used as a boy, will drive the wheel where I urge it to go" (148). Tarden's "wheel game" provides, as he reveals to the woman, "the human associations my current life style prohibits." He chooses one life of the hundreds of anonymous ones around him and enters it "unobserved," directing, manipulating, controlling that life by means of his "language." Tarden's wheel games with strangers force them into the same kind of unforeseen intimate relationships with him that the woman to whom he is writing is forced into should she read his words. And this relationship (Tarden calls his strangers "pseudo-family members") also reflects that of the reader and the writer described by Kosinski on more than one occasion: "Fiction assaults the reader directly, as if saying: It is about you. You are actually creating the situation when you are reading about it; in a way you are staging it in your own life."[3]

Tarden is the embodiment of the subversive and aggressive nature of the writer. In *The Devil Tree* Whalen is a writer whose journal, he says, attempts to "show [Karen] something tangible from my past to make her understand it" (31). Tarden, too, writes to a woman, acutely aware of his own mastery of the art of deception. Within the pages of his long letter, Tarden reveals a series of deceptions against others, many of them exposing the deceptions of writers. In one case, to test his powers of memory he speed-reads every work by a specific living writer. He becomes the reader as flyer, gliding over the exposed topography of the writer's words below:

> Surrounded by the man's collected works, I began reading. Soon my mind took off, soaring above the jumble of words, expressions and notions, which slowly became abstracted into predictable patterns, just as rough farm fields seen from the air look like a neatly sown quilt of velvet smooth patches. As I read, I dictated brief bursts of thoughts into a tape recorder. Only when I finished scanning everything the writer had produced, did I become aware how flat and unchallenging the topography of his work was. (92)

Tarden reading resembles a pilot in the cockpit of his fighter plane. His "brief bursts" of words, like gunfire, are meant to destroy. After Tarden turns over the results of his analysis to a friend who is a scholar studying the works of that writer, his amazed friend remarks that "if used indiscriminately, the map [Tarden] supplied could not only discredit the author's work to date but might cripple his self-confidence and stifle his desire to write" (92). The "map" Tarden drew of the writer can penetrate the labyrinth of deception that surrounds him. Kosinski thus sets up some complex analogies between writing and reading. If writing is a masking, reading can be an unmasking. Since every writer is also a reader, no one is more qualified or apt to expose one writer's mask than another writer. As a counterpart to Tarden's mapping of the writer-deceiver, Kosinski shows Tarden exposing a reader-deceiver, a professional critic. While working for the Service, Tarden discovers a critic who plagiarizes criticism previously published in a foreign-language journal: "I selected several of the critic's recent reviews, then looked up the original criticism of the same works. As I had expected, some of his opinions and turns of phrase were crudely disguised piratings of earlier foreign reviews" (93). Tarden then passes on this information to his Service chief, who recognizes that the Service can blackmail the critic into cooperating. Again, one writer's deception is exposed by another writer, and this time the "map" is used to blackmail. The writer, Tarden suggests, can be both oppressor and victim.

Kosinski's most extensive treatment of this notion of the writer who both deceives and risks exposure is Tarden's unmasking of the "best-selling author," Anthony Duncan, who is a popular "espionage writer."[4] Tarden had been insulted by Duncan's editor, Richard Lasker, so Tarden's act of vengeance is the appropriate response for the picaro figure that he is. But the episode goes beyond mere retribution. Tarden looks through the record of Duncan's biography searching for the "map" that will expose him: "As I read on, I learned that of Duncan's four novels only his first had become a big best seller in both hardcover and paperback. . . . His second novel had been a best seller, but not nearly as successful as the first. The third sold rather poorly. Now Duncan's disappearance [he is rumored to be a prisoner in East Germany] was generating new interest in both the man and his fiction" (163). This final point, the connection between the life of the writer and the public perception of his fiction, is the opening that Tarden—himself a deceptive writer but without a public identity—decides to exploit for his revenge against Duncan's editor, Lasker. After an "investigation" of Duncan's files, Tarden locates by phone the missing Duncan in a Danish fishing village. Duncan answers the phone, expecting to hear the voice of Lasker, who is directing the disappearance ruse; but Tarden identifies himself to Duncan as "a protagonist from someone else's novel" (166). Tarden, in his moment of triumph, supplants Duncan's role as author. Now Tarden will control the plot, arranging Duncan's life as if Duncan were a character in a novel. After ordering Duncan to travel to another town and remain silent, Tarden confronts Lasker, his original antagonist. Like Duncan, Lasker has become part of Tarden's "novel." "Now I'm in charge of the plot. It's my novel," Tarden tells Lasker, threatening to expose the ploy unless Lasker "tells the truth" on television. But the plot is more unpredictable than even Tarden has planned. Duncan is discovered dead—an apparent suicide—by the Danish police shortly after Lasker has announced in a television interview that Duncan had phoned, is safe, and unaware of the uproar over his disappearance. Tarden's revenge is—by chance—more complete than the one he had arranged as part of his "novel."

Tarden seeks to impose the discipline and control of the artist on the turbulence and isolation of his life. He recognizes that language holds possibilities of either imprisonment or escape, and that the tale-teller, the writer, imposes control over his reader through deception. Kosinski's parables of a writer's manipulation of his readers make up a good portion of *Cockpit*. In one, Tarden, at the time a young ski instructor employed in Switzerland, lives with a couple and becomes friends with their ten-year-old daughter. The two recognize each other as loners: "We agreed that I despised my work as much as she hated school" (49). His power as a teller of tales of escape soon enthralls her; she becomes a prisoner of his words, a listener turned captive. "She hung on every word as I described the strange animals we would see in the jungles and the parties we would attend on the roof-top terraces of skyscrapers. As we talked, she would pull at my parka, demanding that we escape right away" (49). But when it is time for Tarden to depart, the girl is determined to accompany him. Tarden tries to explain to her that "our trip had been make-believe," but she threatens to jump from a roof if he does not conjure up the power of his words to transform the stifling reality of her life. Her inability to distinguish between Tarden's "make-believe" world of words and her actual life is both unpredictable and nearly fatal; she jumps from the roof, is severely injured, and her subsequent paralysis epitomizes her status as a victim of Tarden's words. The episode underscores Kosinski's belief in the unpredictable nature of the reader's experience. In one sense the reader of *Cockpit* is controlled, hanging on every word like the young girl; in another, the reader is free to respond in a way as unpredictable as Duncan's suicide or the girl's plunge from the roof. Tarden conceives of the writer's special power as a dynamic flow back and forth between two poles, reader and writer. The writer controls the reader yet provokes in him or her an unpredictable response. The catalyst between writer and reader, is, of course, language. Duncan the writer is destroyed by being transformed into a character in another's novel; the girl leaps from the roof when she sees Tarden's words cannot remake her reality. Each is manipulated by Tarden's words, but each defies his control, slips outside the plot. The two incidents clarify for us Kosinski's insistence that the writer-reader relation is by no means passive, but one that entails an imaginative act on each side, and which results, often enough, in a response that resembles life as Kosinski believes it ought to be lived: imaginative, intense, unpredictable.

Tarden's obsession with transforming autonomous people into characters confined within the scope of a story he hopes to control is evident as far back as his childhood years, when he plays a game to celebrate the arrival of the "Thule," a term Tarden uses to personify the remorseless power of winter. He and some other rather cold-blooded children place captured animals in a nearly frozen pond and wait for them to be imprisoned in the ice. "Throughout the winter, they sat in the frozen pond like frosted glass sculptures from the church fair. On our way to the slopes, we often stopped to stare but never touched them. The animals belonged to the Thule, which had transformed them into creatures from another world" (120). The trapped animals are also transformed into a kind of art. Process has been extracted; though dead, they live briefly in the mind of the observer, who sees "their heads cocked to one side as though listening, their eyes frozen open" (120). Tarden's adult career can be seen as a relentless effort to force other people into the congealing form of his plots; some like Valerie break out and reach the shore. Others like Veronika do not.

Tarden is an inveterate reader of texts, often with the purpose of borrowing ideas, stimulating inspiration. "Inspired by the story" of a sabotage, he injects harmless dye into food samples, provoking a public panic. In Europe, he works as a translator, reads "local literary journals and magazines"; in New York he takes on jobs that give him access to letters, personal files, publishing contracts, anything in print. He is a word thief, a magpie of words filched to build his nests. He finds new directions for his life in randomly encountered literary plots. Contemplating a stay in a rented mansion by the sea, he sizes up the prospects for a gothic romance. "The grounds were as unkempt as the road; weeds choked the flower beds, bushes had grown into huge grotesque shapes completely obscuring the windows of the house" (189). He rents the property called "the Park" and devises plays using local residents as characters. He is Prospero, waving his magic wand, controlling hapless trespassers who stumble into the dunes of the Park from the sea. His Ariel is a set of directional microphones that evoke "ghostly voices from the depths" (194). Ferdinand and Miranda are replaced by two lesbian lovers, Linda and Alex, whom he invites to the Park for a stay. Instead of scrutinizing the chastity of two lovers, this Prospero encourages their sexual abandon in order to, as he says to them, "learn things about myself" (201). Tarden then changes the plot; his feigned deaths of Alex and Linda leave an audience of townspeople convinced Tarden is a murderer. But they can do nothing with this knowledge, for, like Stephano and Trinculo, they are aware of only part of the plot. Even Prospero does not know how it will turn out.

Tarden's most complex invention is his creation of Veronika. At first she is compliant, completely dependent on him. He reinvents her life, choosing a new name for her, surrounding her with new words that affirm the legitimacy of her identity—passports, credit cards, financial statements. He arranges her training as a skier and matches her with a ski-loving rich bachelor, whom she soon marries. His plot is successful. Veronika has a wealthy husband, and Tarden can look forward to regular trysts with Veronika as payment. But Veronika displays more autonomy than Tarden had bargained for. Eventually she resists further sexual installments and assumes the status of a rival writer. "She disclosed in a TV interview that she was working on an autobiographical novel" (219). As she increases her distance from her creator, Veronika threatens to turn Tarden himself into a character. She boasts to him that even if she were accused of murdering her husband she would never be convicted. This new

Veronika—a character turned author—expounds to Tarden how she would "exploit the trial, monopolizing the media and exciting the world's imagination" (229). Veronika's ultimatum is to write about him, "create a scandal" (227), and expose him to an unseen audience.

Tarden knows that rival writers can be destroyed only by words. He reads aerospace magazines, screening articles for a possible candidate for a new character in his ever-widening circle of plot. He finds a test pilot short of cash, bribes him to bathe Veronika with deadly radiation from a plane's radar system. Here is Tarden in his true cockpit—that of a jet fighter aptly named "Snipe," both a long-billed bird and a secretive mode of attack. Like Saint-Exupéry, Tarden is at home in this cockpit, counting the dials and knobs of his kingdom, delighted with the game of revenge. The image of Veronika coalesces on the radar screen like "rapidly multiplying cells." Unlike his own blood cells from years past, these obey him. He writes his character out of the plot, turns her into something like the ghostly "Ono," a patient he once saw wandering through the halls of a nursing home, condemned to haunt the healthy from behind a shroud of cancer bandages.

Like Proust's persona "Marcel," Tarden is struck by the power of his memory, and the revelation of this power to make another relive what he remembers becomes the form of his narration. Kosinski frames *Cockpit* between two writers, Saint-Exupéry and Dostoyevski, but it is Tarden himself who conjures up the presence of Proust, during a liaison in Paris between himself and a beautiful married woman.[5] His anticipation of experiencing the woman's beauty is described in terms of Proustian irony—the actual experience always falls short of the imagined one. Tarden is so awe-struck by her unexpected willingness to meet him that he fears his sexual performance will suffer. When they finally rendezvous in an elegant Paris hotel, the woman first invokes Proust. "Proust says, 'Leave pretty women to men without imagination.' Do you disagree with him?" (81). Tarden gallantly replies that "your beauty can be fully appreciated and defined only by a man with imagination" (81). They drive together to Combray, further emphasizing the Proustian parallel, but Tarden's gallantry cannot sustain his sexual potency, and the liaison quickly deteriorates into comic reversal. The next day, when they part, the woman calls up once more the presence of Proust: "God spare beautiful women from men with imagination" (85). A chagrined Tarden leaves Paris and drives to northern Italy. Looking for a prostitute there, he discovers that none will allow Tarden to penetrate her. All are determined to preserve their hymens for future Italian husbands. "No inside," they say to Tarden, who remains as sexually thwarted here as with the woman in the Paris hotel. Yet the two incidents remain in Tarden's memory "vividly": "Though I wish now I could forget the Paris incident, and wonder why I remember the whores so clearly, I can't free myself from either memory" (90). Just as for Proust, whose memories of his childhood were so vivid that they sometimes existed more intensely in his imagination than the real events of his present, so too Tarden's memory acts—almost without his will—to recapture the past.[6]

Memory for Tarden, as well as for Proust, supplies not only the structure of the narration but some of the themes as well. The nature of memory, especially its relation to the powers of sleep, is just as fascinating to Tarden as it was for Proust. When Tarden's capacity to recall images is tested in the "State," he discovers he possesses a photographic memory. "I began to experiment with my memory. I found that it automatically intensified while I slept. If I misplaced something, such as a set of keys, I took a nap. It was as if I were dreaming a film about losing the keys that was being run backward in slow motion. By the time I woke up, I recalled where I had left them" (91). Still another link between Proust and Tarden is the increased perception of reality that illness sometimes affords. Tarden is in "uncertain health" (104), and his blood pressure is so low that when he falls asleep he barely breathes. "My sensitivity," he writes, "to the slightest change in my environment, and my craving for unusual psychological pressure have made me aware how little other people are aware of their surroundings, how little they know of themselves and how little they notice me" (105).

Tarden's memory—the source of his inspiration to write his book —possesses the vivid quality that Proust's persona described. Tarden claims that "If I evoke a single memory picture, others will spring up automatically to join it and soon the montage of a past self will emerge. It's an autonomous process, and the fact that I have no control over it excites me" (13). Tarden's narration is shaped by the same autonomous principle: one memory leads to another, one anecdote to the next, until Tarden's original audience—the unnamed woman—seems to disappear from our view. Tarden in fact does not refer to her again, but lets the process of his memory create montages of past selves, each of which links sections of the narration.

If Tarden's tales seem to form no particular pattern beyond sheer association (his anecdote about a large dog he owned, for example, reminds him of a small dog he trained to set off a bomb beneath a car), certain themes of Kosinski's previous novels reappear in new forms: the son's vengeance on the father, the need to escape cultural repression, and the sophisticated pranks played by the picaro (who is also a writer) on his enemies. All of these are variations of the central theme, the need for the individual to create and control his own identity through writing.

Rivalry between father and son is as deadly in *Cockpit* as it was in *The Devil Tree*, and, to a lesser extent, in *Being There*. Whalen lacks the confidence and guile to seize his father's language except through the fantasy of a cigarette butt collection. Tarden takes action. At the age of twelve he overhears his father being bullied on the telephone by a bureaucrat from the State. He decides on the spot to strike back both at the State and his father. He telephones random citizens, mimics the voice of that same bureaucrat, and orders dozens of strangers to make hurried visits to imaginary government offices. They become characters in a spontaneous play directed by Tarden. As Tarden says, "If, like my father, they had abjectly surrendered their rights, they deserved to be punished" (113). Eventually the phone calls are traced, and Tarden's parents are arrested. Confronted by the tape recording of his own voice, Tarden briefly relishes his successful impersonations. "Until that moment, I hadn't realized how perfect my imitations were" (116). By mastering the voice of authority, the young Tarden had already spoken the language of power. But his role as punisher is brief; the voice is only an imitation, and he is released to the custody of his chastened and baffled parents. Tarden's act of vengeance strikes at his biological father, but not at the system that victimizes Tarden's life. Eventually he senses his father is only another victim, not a punisher. So Tarden takes on the State, which possesses qualities that Tarden identifies with the concept of fatherhood—power to punish, authority to control. "The State was a vicious enemy. Whether I escaped abroad or committed suicide, it would punish those who had known of my plans" (16). His escape from the control of the State is more elaborate than the telephone plot, but involves the same principle. Tarden becomes, in effect, a writer. As we have seen, he invents four academic figures, complete with their own official stationery. "I started by giving each of them a name, a title, and a unique, yet plausible, bureaucratic assignment" (19). Thus for Tarden, and for Kosinski, the act of writing is also a declaration of personal freedom, a challenge to the dominant cultural power. Tarden's first readers— government bureaucrats—are deceived; his passport is granted, plane tickets are delivered, and he promptly escapes two fathers at once.

Deception and desire for freedom are the twin powers of the picaro, and *Cockpit* provides Kosinski's most elaborate tricks, pranks, and deceptions which collectively define the nature of the freedom that so elates Tarden. Tarden's pranks range from harmless to savage, but each says something about authorial control, the character as victim, and the necessary deception of the audience. His disguise is "never simply a deception or a hoax," explains Tarden, but rather "an attempt to expand the range of another's perception" (130). Deception increases the control of the writer over his readers. "Confronted with my camouflage," says Tarden of his victims, "it is the witness who deceives himself, allowing his eyes to give my new character credibility and authenticity. I do not fool him; he either accepts or rejects my altered truth" (130).

One prank shows Tarden as a sexual picaro, imposing a deception on his lover. As a teenager, he invites a girl to his parents' house while they are away. He wears a "plastic-edged metal clamp" over his "member," explaining to the shocked girl that he was wounded in the war and is incapable of normal intercourse. Her fears of pregnancy soothed, she becomes aggressive in her lovemaking, which is of course what Tarden had planned. But as she loses her control—and this is another power relationship between victim and oppressor—Tarden plays his prank: "I surreptitiously removed the clamp and shot into her without warning" (129). After the girl's initial anger at being deceived subsides, Tarden says, "she finally admitted that being aggressive with me had released her in a pleasurable way" (129). The deception was "a small price to pay for her new-found freedom, her new sexual identity" (129).

Tarden's victims find their perceptions of themselves expanded by his altered truths, and Tarden creates a grab bag of imaginative roles that compensate for his need to lead a solitary existence. Each prank renews Tarden's sense of himself as a writer who provides material for his imagination by forcing random and unpredictable contacts with other people. In a typical prank, he dresses as a mailman and steals letters. "Many of the letters are like pages torn at random from novels: they reveal a lot, but never enough. I feel cheated and disappointed. Often I endow the writers with voices, with gestures and facial expressions" (155). His theft of the mail suggests Tarden's method as a writer. The initial effect of reading the secret writing of strangers is to provide material for the unexpected, to force inspiration instead of waiting passively for it. But reading is not enough to create art; only the more conscious effort, the laborious creation of fictional voices, will result in the narration he writes for the unnamed woman. To endow the fragments with voices, gestures, is the craft that Tarden works at with more dedication than his spy craft. The search for new material for his writing is devious and dangerous. Tarden is, after all, breaking the law when he steals the mail. But it is his own craft—the control by Tarden over his words—that redeems the randomness and meaninglessness of raw experience.

Tarden's wheel games represent some of Kosinski's most imaginative depictions of the paradoxical nature of the writer thus far: Tarden's plight is to endure unpredictable reversals of his role. He is both predator and prey, victim and oppressor, writer and reader. *Cockpit* exposes the naïveté of the Boy's notion of the writer as "great man," surrounded by readers as loyal and forceful as Gavrila's fellow officers. Tarden's experiences suggest that the writer collects enemies in proportion to his acquisition of power and that his words inevitably assume the configuration of maps that can be read by readers who choose to track him to his lair and tear off his necessary mask. Kosinski's next novel, *Blind Date*, places the writer in the context of just the sort of public fame dreamed of by the Boy. This writer, Levanter, aware that his art requires the cool detachment personified by Tarden, nevertheless tries to formulate an ethical code more commensurate with conventional notions of moral behavior.

Words and Wind

The levanter is a wind that originates in the East and blows west across the Mediterranean basin. A seasonal phenomenon, the levanter signals change and is an apt name for George Levanter, whose drift from East to West is charted by Kosinski's sixth novel, *Blind Date*. The word for wind and breath in Latin is the same—spiritus—and the wind of the levanter also suggests breath itself, the flow of air that gives life to human speech. The levanter brings to mind flight as well, in both the sense of flying and fleeing. High above the Mediterranean Sea, this westerly flow of air recalls for us not only the individual flights of George Levanter but the plane flights of other Kosinski protagonists, such as the narrator of *Steps* and Tarden. In this way *Blind Date* assesses the themes and attitudes of previous Kosinski novels; it examines—sometimes self-consciously—the dilemma of a writer who has achieved celebrity status by creating protagonists who defy the very cultural and economic conditions that support the phenomenon of celebrity.

One scene in *Blind Date*, for example, not only comments on Ko-sinski's previous fiction but also suggests the complex connection between writing and flight that permeates the book. George Levanter is in Switzerland dining with Charles Lindberg, who is at once a writer, an aviator, and a victim of fame ("one of the world's most hounded public figures"). Levanter is writing a book which he describes later to Lindberg as "a study of individuals who through chance accidents have been propelled into national prominence and become important investors" (91). Levanter's book is a "pilot study," and its themes, especially its analysis of the role of chance and individual fame, anticipate those of *Blind Date* itself. Levanter discovers that he has left the only copy of the manuscript in a hotel lobby, so Lindberg graciously drives Levanter there through a driv-ing snowstorm. "The car, engulfed in a blanket of moving snow, was like an airplane lost to everyone but its pilot" (91). Lindberg—good pilot that he is—guides Levanter to the lost manuscript, but Lind-berg himself, in the mind of Levanter, embodies the attitude that once encouraged the rise of Nazi Germany and the subsequent hor-rors of the Holocaust, of which Levanter himself is a victim. Before the war Lindberg had flown to Russia from Nazi Germany, passing over the very land where Levanter lived as a child. "A few years later," Levanter tells Lindberg, "during the war, when I was six, I was separated from my family and wandered alone through the same villages you saw from your plane" (88). Lindberg's complacency about the nature of Germany before the war resembles the attitude of the pensioners in the hotel—also in Switzerland—which Kosinski claimed prompted him to write *The Painted Bird*.[7] Thus Levanter's assessment of Lindberg is ambivalent; Lindberg rescues Levanter's "pilot study," but earlier in his life he had failed to pilot a moral course. "He thought of the German state as an airplane and of its racial hatred, persecution, and aggression in the early thirties, as a temporary flight aberration caused by the pilot's misreading of the plane's control panel" (90). Levanter and Lindberg represent rival readings of the text of the history of Nazi Germany; Levanter had read accurately the direction of the flight of the German state, while Lindberg had misread it. "Chance accidents" have propelled the writer Lindberg from fame to victimization; similar chance events have propelled the writer Levanter from victim to the status of one who dines with the likes of Charles Lindberg. In such ways does Levanter's name call up for us the clash between word and wind, language and flight, conscious will and random event that animates the pages of *Blind Date.*

Blind Date is strikingly different in both tone and format from Kosinski's previous novel, *Cockpit.* "The modern character George Levanter," Kosinski says, "is engaged in the Socratic quest—one's obligation to examine and assume responsibility for *one's own* actions regardless of the societal framework in which they occur. Whereas in *Cockpit* Tarden is preoccupied with the impact of his own camouflage on others who either accept or reject his altered truth (and so does *Cockpit* as a novel), in *Blind Date* George Levanter reveals his unfulfilled longing to be able to examine one single human being, one single truth at a time."[8] Levanter's "development of the soul," as Kosinski refers to it, contrasts with that of Tarden in the format of the novel as well. *Cockpit* is narrated by Tarden entirely, and as readers we are immersed in his voice, which draws us into the life he has lived. His narration imposes itself on the unnamed woman so that she—and the reader—can "relive" that life.[9] Tarden's voice acts as a kind of prison for us—there are no other viewpoints, no alternate ways of judging his words except by experiencing his subversive, obsessive vision. Tarden is the oppressor; his listeners, like the unknown woman whose privacy he invades, are the victims. *Blind Date,* on the other hand, is narrated in the third person, a technique which invites us to make judgments about Levanter's behavior, to chart the "development" of his "soul" against our own perception of moral standards. *Blind Date* stimulates moral reflection for its readers; Tarden's cool, detached voice consciously precludes moral consideration.

Levanter differs from Tarden in a number of other ways as well. While Tarden exhibits confidence and pride in his capacity to deceive, to live without an identity, and to impose his will on random people, Levanter—at least the mature Levanter of the opening scene in Switzerland—exhibits more conventional drives and aspirations: he desires to belong to a social unit larger than himself, to seek an intimate relationship with another person, to foster a network of attachments with friends and business acquaintances. Levanter is involved first of all in the search for an authentic moral vision, one that would take into account what he has learned from his own experience—the unpredictability of human life, the integrity of the individual, and the recognition that any destiny for mankind, whether political, national, or religious, is an illusion. These concerns have surfaced in all of Kosinski's previous books, but *Blind Date* attempts to codify this vision, to assemble its separate components under a more coherent statement. Levanter's credo—if it could be called that—takes much of its inspiration from a single book, Jacques Monod's *Chance and Necessity* (1970), which makes its presence felt in *Blind Date* in several ways. Kosinski uses an excerpt from Monod's book as an epigraph to *Blind Date*: "But henceforth who is to define crime? Who shall decide what is good and what is evil? All the traditional systems have placed ethics and values beyond man's reach. Values did not belong to him; he belonged to them. He now knows that they are his and his alone. . . ." Before we are well into *Blind Date*, we sense that Levanter, like other Kosinski protagonists, believes ethics and values are his alone to create from experience. Jacques Monod, one of several real people who appear in *Blind Date*, sums up his own view of destiny in a conversation with Levanter about the latter's friend, Romarkin, who, as Monod says, still believes that "man's destiny is spelled out in the central plot of life" (86). Worse, continues Monod to Levanter, Romarkin believes in the "existence of an orderly, predetermined life scheme," and so "bypasses the drama of each unique instance of his own existence" (86). The reader is left with the clear impression that Monod's assessment of Romarkin coincides with Levanter's own "ethics and values." Although the connection between utilizing the moment and doing so in a moral way is often elusive in *Blind Date*, there is little doubt that Levanter has reached a level of compassion and social concern that Tarden consciously avoided. In one scene, Levanter is asked by his friend Romarkin if people in the West are "good" or at least "better than where you and I come from" (83). Levanter's answer seems worlds away from the wheel games of Tarden: "I have found people to be good every-where. . . . They turn bad only when they fall for little bits of power tossed to them by the state or by a political party, by a union or a company, or a wealthy mate. They forget that their power is nothing more than a temporary camouflage of mortality" (83).

On the surface, Levanter's statement to Romarkin is an unex-pected blend of Rousseau and Judeo-Christianity: all people are good (Rousseau) until they "fall" by embracing the temptation of power (the serpent's offer to Eve). Only after giving in to temptation do they "turn bad." But since power is offered in every society or political system, the task of avoiding temptation, of refusing to "fall" into power, demands a self-discipline and control that would rival that of Saint Anthony in a Bosch painting. When Levanter states his view of human nature to Romarkin early in the novel, we are not sure of the extent to which he himself has fallen, but it is clear that he includes himself in the judgment, that he regards his own past seizures of power as signals of his lapse from goodness. In fact, with the possible exception of Jacques Monod, very few of the characters in *Blind Date* have not fallen; after such knowledge, we might ask with T. S. Eliot, "What forgiveness"?

To continue the Judeo-Christian parallel for a moment, if "good" people surrender to the temptation of power and become "bad," can they redeem themselves? Can they ever be good again? The question is salient because if Levanter senses he himself has fallen—and as recently as the time he lived with a "wealthy mate"—has he reached the point in his own eyes of being good again? And if so, how did he do it? Does he look back to any of his own falls, his own roles of power, as regrettable, such as his rape of Nameless when he was fifteen, or his incestuous relationship with his mother, with its attending betrayal of his dying father? Or does he regard these actions in the same way he regards his efforts to free political prisoners or to execute an oppressive state's deputy minister, that is, as equally necessary assertions of his identity? One critic of *Blind Date* suggests that "Levanter can be a demon: an incestuous son, an arsonist, a murderer, an extortionist,"[10] but what is Levanter's own attitude toward his past actions?

At least in this scene with Romarkin in a Paris cafe, Levanter articulates a relatively conventional moral standard: all people are good by nature but become bad when they give in to the temptation to wield power. But the experiences that make up so much of *Blind Date*, especially those that have helped Levanter to articulate his moral standard, are precisely the actions he claims make people bad. The oppressor is bad because he enjoys power; the victim is bad if he tries to seize power. Perhaps this look at the logic of Levanter's statement to Romarkin strains the meaning of the passage, but the dilemma remains: how does Levanter feel he himself has lived up to the standard he articulates to Romarkin? If Levanter's reflections suggest he is disillusioned with himself, or regretful about some of his past actions, then we have moved far from the spirit of Tarden and from Tarden's prerogatives as a writer.

Levanter's rejection of the right to seek out power by any means in order to escape the role of victim is nowhere more evident than in the scene in ValPina, Switzerland, where Levanter poses as a Soviet ski instructor to intimidate three vacationing Soviet bureaucrats who, confident that he cannot understand Russian, have ridiculed his ski outfit. Levanter's revenge is as zestfully conceived a prank as any by Tarden. Levanter barks orders to the three in Russian, demands to see their papers, and promises a full investigation when they return to the Soviet Union. The bureaucrats are crushed. But Levanter is disturbed by his talent for revenge. "Then he felt ashamed and somehow unnerved by his deception. To his surprise, the short encounter with the Soviets had resurrected a part of himself he had believed to be buried, the enjoyment of having certifiable power" (21). This quest for power, which came so naturally to Tarden, Levanter sees as an impulse he needs to keep in check. Deception as a mode of life becomes shameful, a part of his past he has consciously tried to repress.

Tarden's insights about himself emerge from the process of his writing; his long letter to the unknown woman becomes the book we know as *Cockpit*. Levanter is engaged in reflecting on the text as written. His talk with Romarkin in the Paris cafe is really a reading of the text of his life. "It was and it was not" are for Levanter words that compel continual rereadings. Another difference between Tarden and Levanter, then, is their status as writers. Each is a writer confronting the meaning of his experience, discovering new aspects of his identity by exploring the richness of his memory. Unlike Tarden, Levanter is a writer who is experiencing the public rewards of his writing. While Tarden had to penetrate the world of publishing by deception and blackmail in order to transform randomly selected people (an editor, a spy novelist) into characters for his own imaginary "novel," Levanter's initial article, a study of investment and risk, was first published in *Investor's Quarterly* and then "condensed and reprinted by various newspapers and magazines" (206). The success of Levanter's article leads to contacts with influential people, including a wealthy widow, Mary Jane Kirkland, who eventually marries him. His reputation as an "investor" brings honors and influence: he teaches a course in "investment" at Princeton University, and becomes a prominent figure in Investors International, an investment group that also attempts to free political prisoners, especially writers, from oppressive regimes. He meets and becomes friends with several famous people, some of whom, like Jacques Monod, Charles Lindberg, and Leopold Senghor, are also writers. George Levanter, much more than Tarden, represents Kosinski's attempt to dramatize the tension of Kosinski's present life as a writer: the pressure of public recognition, the special freedom of wealth, the commitment to certain public institutions, the problem of viewing his own experience as possible material for future writing. When Levanter travels to Impton "looking for business," for instance, he is a writer seeking out an experience that may prove to be profitable as a subject for his fiction. Levanter's frenetic pace of life results from his conviction that writing and living nurture each other. Like Tarden, he initiates random contacts that might prove

fruitful investments of the imagination. The public state of Levanter's writing and the contacts with other writers and celebrated
figures that his writing has brought about place Levanter in a
position somewhat like that of his friend JP, the East European
fencing master, who sees his art and his life inextricably blended. JP
says to Levanter that because no one is as skillful a fencer as himself,
he uses no sparring partner. "I fence against my own reflection in a
specially constructed triple mirror" (152). Levanter also confronts
himself in mirrors. His perception of himself in the glass is not only
the subject of his art but also his antagonist, his opponent, the
standard by which he judges his own performance.

Levanter is a natural teller of tales, and he is willing to provoke a
variety of listeners to act out roles that imprison or liberate. *Blind
Date* abounds in complex transformations of identities, each
brought about by the power of a teller's language to both capture and
release a listener. When we first see Levanter at ValPina, he impro-
vises a game with a five-year old girl whose mother is reclining on a
deck chair nearby. He insists that the girl, Olivia, is really a boy.
"Don't be ashamed—you're Oliver, a handsome boy" (3). The girl
at first resists this unexpected transformation, but then relents,
accepts her new identity as "Oliver," and challenges Levanter to
continue the game. But he is unprepared for what happens: an older
professor appears at his side with a young woman "half his age,
wearing a blouse which revealed her plump breasts" (3). The little
girl, taking her cue from Levanter's game, ridicules this January-May
union by insisting the professor is a "Madame." "Even if you think
you're a man, you're really a woman," she says, and glances at the
uneasy Levanter for confirmation. Levanter's game is out of control;
liberated from her own sense of being a child, Olivia unknowingly
transforms herself into an aggressor, forcing the professor into a role
he does not want to play—public defender of his masculinity.

When Levanter plays a similar game with two young daughters of
an attractive blond pianist, he does so to draw the mother into a
more complex game. After he describes to them an imaginary scene,
he coaxes the older girl to play the role of his wife, who must inform

him that his dog Frecky has died. Each child assumes the role of wife
and renders a convincing scene in which both become emotionally
involved. Levanter congratulates them on their acting performance
and then reveals the goal of the game: "Let's see whether you are
good storytellers. Tell me about your mother" (7). Levanter's game
and tales with the girls initiate a complex relationship between
Levanter and Pauline, the girls' mother. Pauline appears at the
opening and conclusion of *Blind Date*, and Levanter's final intimacy
with her, begun and sustained by storytelling, results in a transformation for both of them, a release into a new sense of self, and an
escape from the weight of past guilt and repression.

Levanter takes Pauline for a boat ride in an underground lake near
ValPina. As they float together in near darkness, the cave seems
carved by a giant sculptor, nature. "Levanter had the sense of
intruding in the domain of an artist who worked hidden from the
world" (11). Levanter and Pauline are artists themselves, one of
words and the other of music, and each in different ways is hidden
from the world, and from each other. Levanter, the artist of words,
begins to tell Pauline a story about a baseball player and his lover,
whom he kills after she rejects him. "This is how we get close to one
another," Levanter tells her. The story of the baseball player's
desperate desire to impose his will on his former lover is Levanter's
emotional investment in Pauline. He hopes she will keep alive the
memory of his story should they meet again. The scene in the cave
shows Levanter using language not so much to imprison as to form a
tentative union. When Levanter meets Pauline again, his investment
in words reaps unexpected dividends. The complex nature of their
final encounter we will return to later. Here, in the cave near
ValPina, Levanter's tale to Pauline of a baseball player who transforms himself into a star while his lover, a waitress, transforms
herself into a prostitute, serves as a fragile bond between this
storyteller and listener until the time when a more powerful one can
be formed.

Levanter's first stories were in his native tongue. As a student
assigned by the state university to give lectures to peasants working

on a collective farm, Levanter and other students compete with one another on a train in the game of capturing the peasant passengers by words. "A student who was a good storyteller would begin a tale; as the train approached the market station, the drama would mount, with the narrator piling incident upon incident of comedy and tragedy, of betrayal and passion, of happy reunions and incurable illnesses" (187). The peasants, completely absorbed in the tale, would forget to leave the train at their market station. But the peasants are grateful, willing prisoners of the tales. "The farmers' market would always be where it was, they said, but a storyteller took their minds to places where they could not travel" (188). Imprisoning the peasants is for Levanter both a word game and an artist's performance, but it is also an act of liberation for the listeners. For a time the peasants are free from the mental restrictions of their lives, moving through places beyond the reach of a railroad timetable.

One of Levanter's lovers, Serena, reacts to his storytelling in the same way. When she comes to his apartment, she says she is aroused by "listening to a man talk" (186). "She insisted he tell her things about himself, stories that would break the routine of her life." Levanter obliges, and Serena is a "good listener." She sits "spellbound" by his words, which have the effect of not only "binding" her within a net of words but liberating Levanter from the routine of his own busy life. "Only with strangers like you," he says to Serena, "am I what I really feel myself to be" (187). When he finally discovers that she is a prostitute, the power of the teller shifts from Levanter to Serena, and it is Levanter's turn to be captivated. She tells him how she electrocuted an unwanted customer in a whirlpool bath, how a strange old man's eye popped out onto her face. She tells him that she came back to Levanter because "I liked your act: your stories and games" (203). But the roles are reversed. Her words make him feel "powerless." Although she has been transformed into a formidable tale-teller, her tales lead only to the discovery that he can never be more than a passive listener. The relationship ends.

Only one other time in Levanter's life was he made the captive of another's words, and the consequence reverberates throughout the book. At the age of fifteen, he falls under the spell of Oscar, a rapist of women and, in a sense, a rapist of language as well. Levanter meets Oscar at a summer camp in East Europe after Oscar jumps under a stopped train in order to recover Levanter's suitcase. Levanter is attracted to the daring Oscar. If he "could have magically changed his appearance, he would have wanted to look exactly like Oscar" (60). Levanter's willingness to undergo such a transformation makes him especially vulnerable to Oscar's tale-telling ability. Oscar, Levanter learns, is not only a rapist, but an inventor of words for his deeds. "Breaking the eye was what he called rape" (60). By describing so graphically his rapes to Levanter, Oscar holds out to Levanter the possibility of a more daring transformation than Levanter had first wished. "Levanter was captivated. What his friend envisaged was to him an adventure, a thrilling game of hide-and-seek" (64).

Oscar extends his vocabulary of rape to every part of the female body he intends to violate. "Along with these bits of terminology, Oscar had developed a whole sex vocabulary. A female's head was a melon, her mouth a lock, hands were grabbers, the back a sun deck, breasts points, nipples contacts, and her belly a plate; her legs were sticks, the groin the cut, and her buttocks pillows, divided by the narrows" (61). The domestically neutral plates and pillows help to reduce for Oscar the felt reality of his violations. The mouth is a lock so as to imprison the emotional power of words as well as the victim's cries. After Oscar coaches him in the new language, Levanter sees a teenage girl at the camp who attracts him. He decides to call her "Nameless," a phrase which effectively rapes her of her identity, her presence as a real person. Just as Oscar's language turns rape into "breaking the eye" and rape victims into "blind dates," so Levanter unnames the girl in order to prepare himself to violate her. Once she is "Nameless" he is free to imagine her as an object. "If she were a thing," Levanter muses, "one day he could own her" (67). The episode begins with the sentence, "It was when he was fifteen . . . . What "it" was—the rape of Nameless—marks the low point of Levanter's gradual rise to the perception of a moral standard that he exhibits when he rescues, many years later, a woman on a ski slope in the "name" of "simple humanity." At the age of fifteen he is an unnamer.[11]

Like the wind his name evokes, Levanter never loses his sense of originating in the East. His own identity is an improvisation, his speech a blend of the Russian of his childhood and the English he has acquired as an adult. His bilingualism also bifurcates his character— a single unexpected phrase in Russian can jolt buried memories, underlining once again the provisional nature of his identity. Since, like Novak, he views his time in the East as a form of imprisonment, the Russian language evokes for him images of containment, even repression. Once, while thinking of what seductive phrase to use on a Russian woman he encounters in New York, he discovers that his "mother tongue had turned into an uninvited chaperone, guarding his passion from getting out of hand" (59). He sees in his childhood language the speech of victim, subject to oppressors in many forms. In Russian, "he regressed to memories of parents and school teachers, to early emotions of shame, fear, and guilt" (58). Even as an adult in the United States, to speak Russian is for Levanter a return to powerlessness. Not only does Russian—as chaperone—inhibit the kind of sexual terms he would like to speak, but it reestablishes the bond between victim and oppressor he severed years before. When he rents a house in Princeton in order to lecture at the university on the art of investing, he discovers that Stalin's daughter lives next door. "The thought of her proximity to Stalin paralyzed him" (78). It is as if the world's most powerful writer had reached out to claim Levanter as a character. "Her name alone, even over the telephone, was enough to call up visions of his Moscow past, and for him she became a direct link to the awesome power that Joseph Stalin had wielded" (78). Only with his friend from university days, Romarkin, does Levanter feel that he can speak Russian comfortably —because Romarkin himself has escaped from the East. "Their reminiscences seemed to justify the break both of them had had to make with the very past that held them together" (83). Each saw early that the social system within which he found himself would

110 Words in Search of Victims

destroy his identity; each was a subversive. Romarkin, the more impulsive, openly defies the system by asking in a university class the one question that unmasks as a fraud the state's most celebrated new writer on Marxism and linguistics—Stalin. "Would you, Comrade, [the professor at the dais] tell us when and for how long Comrade Stalin studied linguistics?" (44). Romarkin is promptly sent to Siberia; Levanter, into the army. They are written into a new text. For in the Russia of their youth Stalin is the only tale-teller. All others are his listeners and prisoners.

If Levanter was once a prisoner of Stalin's words, he is now free to write his own. Such freedom requires surges of energy that need to be renewed, and *Blind Date* offers Kosinski's most extensive analysis of the complex relationship between creative language and sexual union. Levanter's sequence of often bizarre sexual encounters teach him to look deeper at his feelings; and these feelings in turn need words to express them. Levanter's sexual experiences become fables of the life-giving power of narration itself. When he first sees Pauline, for instance, he is "awed" by her beauty, but "his feelings seemed to be triggered by something he could not define" (4). What triggers the feeling—we learn shortly—is a sexual relation with his mother, who resembles Pauline in startling ways. Pauline and his mother are concert pianists taught by a Russian master who was also the lover of each, years apart. But Pauline touches far deeper feelings. Levanter has also been the lover of his mother, something he obliquely suggests to Pauline in one of their first exchanges:

> "If he [the Russian who taught both Pauline and his mother] were my lover too, would I be linked to your mother?"
> "Yes, and if I had been my mother's lover," said Levanter, "I then would be linked to you." (8)

Although Levanter and his mother remain lovers for years, their relationship is surrounded by a self-imposed silence, a mutual agreement to exclude speech from the dark side of their lives they have discovered together. Even lips are taboo: "She never allowed him to kiss her on the mouth. . . . He never talked with his mother about

116 (serena)

their lovemaking. Her bed was like a silent, physical confession:
what happened between them there was never talked about" (10).
The feelings mother and son arouse in each other are too dangerous
for speech.

As she plays the same piece of music his mother played, Pauline
awakens the buried feelings of Levanter toward his mother. When
Levanter later leads Pauline into the underground lake, they journey
into a darkness toward some new discovery about themselves as artists, tied not to the past, but to the future. For the moment, their
union—at least here in the cave—consists of words alone. Pauline
wonders aloud what would happen if the mountainside should fall
down, sealing them up inside the cave. Levanter replies that they
would talk "about ourselves. . . . Possibly for the last time." Thus
their journey toward each other, like any into the hidden recesses of
the self, is potentially dangerous, and could end in death—but not
before they discovered each other's true self, as hidden from them as
the entrance of the cave itself was until recently. "Still," Levanter
says, "this cave has brought us close to each other" (12). Although
the cave is cold, in other ways it resembles a womb: Pauline and
Levanter are suspended in water, surrounded by darkness. Levanter's desire to enter this surrogate womb with Pauline is a way he can
redeem himself from the psychological burden of those years of entering his own mother's womb, the act for which Oedipus blinded
himself.

The two encounters with Pauline function as a kind of frame for
Blind Date: the first, at the opening of the novel, suggests that
Levanter needs to come to terms with the buried sexual encounters
of his past. The last meeting, just before his death on a mountainside
in Switzerland, shows the extent to which he believes his union with
Pauline can redeem him. In between we see Levanter engaged in a
round robin of sexual encounters, each one a discrete unit in the
narrative, a fixed point on the grid of Levanter's life, and each
representing a gesture—often a failed one—that attempts to explain
some part of himself or to free himself from the burden of memory.
What he seeks in these encounters, as he says to Pauline, is a

"sensation that isn't just a ricocheted memory" (228). In all of them, Levanter tests out the precarious but often liberating relationship between sexual union and speech.

With the exception of his relationship with Pauline, his sexual experiences are flawed by the imbalance between the rival powers of speech and flesh. Levanter's earliest sexual initiations—sleeping with his mother and raping Nameless—occur about the same time in his life: the first when he was in high school, the second when he was fifteen. Although it cannot be determined from the text which came first or how each experience shaped the other, both of Levanter's acts are such radical distortions of conventional behavior that speech itself is banned. Levanter utters no words either during his rape of Nameless or his lovemaking with his mother; tongue and lips, words and kisses—all are banned. It is as if Levanter were trying to sever the humane connection between language and sex. The presence of speech would name the sexual act, exposing it to a sudden influx of feeling. Somehow Levanter hoped that silence would control feeling. Thus a private taboo is respected, even as Levanter defies a public one. What he and his mother are doing will not be put into words by either; what he does to Nameless will be uttered only in a surrogate language, the vocabulary of eye-breaking and blind dates. This severance of language and sex is Levanter's self-inflicted psychic wound. Only when he opens himself to the humanizing force of speech, nurturing the relationship between speech and sex instead of severing it, can he experience the sense of being "wanted instead of remembered," as he says to Pauline.

Levanter learns early that sex detached from speech can transform a person into a thing. When he sees Nameless before the rape, he is already dispossessing her of her personhood, turning her into an object to be used. He does not speak to her before or during the rape, because speech would not only name his act but restore Nameless's name. Levanter has been carefully coached by Oscar about the main obstacle in the game of eye-breaking—the power of the tongue. Oscar's dream about losing his tongue to one of his blind dates effectively warns Levanter of the danger of permitting his own tongue

—both literally and figuratively—from intruding into the domain of eye-breaking. We have seen how speech formed into compelling tale-telling can captivate listeners ranging from peasants on trains to Levanter himself within the prison of Oscar's language of rape. In such cases the relationship of speech to hearer turns into that of oppressor and victim. On the other extreme, deliberate silence can also enforce the oppressor-victim relationship, as in Levanter's wordless rape of Nameless, or Levanter and Romarkin's renaming of the Chinese girl, "Robot." Romarkin and Levanter, in this last case, meet the Robot at a Communist convention. Since the girl cannot speak their language, her capacity to sustain her own identity is diminished, and she becomes their willing captive, "a person in a trance, her body almost immobile, her face impenetrable" (43). Although she has been conditioned to obey all orders by a repressive system, once deprived of speech she can only be a victim and "submit obediently" to the whims of Romarkin and Levanter, who test her relentlessly for signs of "emotion or hints of feeling." Only when they return her to the Chinese delegation days later does the Robot reveal that she does have feelings. "Suddenly she began to embrace and kiss both men, clinging to their chests, necks, thighs, crying and sobbing quietly like a hurt and disappointed child" (43). In a sense, the Robot is tongueless; her silence releases in Levanter all restraint, and she becomes for him the "thing" that he once wished for in Nameless. Years later, when he is living in America he becomes attracted to a former Russian actress and he finds it is the spoken word—their common Russian—that acts to restrain him. Only in English, which she cannot speak well, can Levanter "name the nature of his desires." The situation is like that of Oscar's years before: a new language—in Levanter's case, English—needs to be learned in order to express the turbulent nature of his sexual desire.

Levanter's next three lovers—Jolene, Foxy Lady, and Serena—teach him new insights about the complex communion between words and flesh, but each leaves Levanter a victim, nursing emotional wounds, his search for the hidden nature of his desire unfulfilled. Levanter meets Jolene in her hometown, Impton, an

American town, content in its provincialism and complacency, whose citizens cannot distinguish between a Communist and a Nazi, and who, as Jolene says, never "notice anything." At first, Jolene seems an appropriate partner for Levanter. She too thrives on random and unpredictable encounters in order to escape boredom and seek freedom outside conventional behavior. She is an outsider consciously revolting against the cultural and moral standards of Impton. Like Levanter, Jolene sees the relationship between memory and desire as problematic: she perceives her life as a series of passionate moments preserved by her from the erosion of time, like so many photographs. Her sexual liaisons measure the meaning of her life. "O.K.," she tells Levanter, "Snapshots from Jolene's album. Womanhood begins in grade school, age twelve. Jolene loses her virginity to a high school varsity basketball player, who also loses his. More dates. Click. Jolene discovers the orgasm. Click. High school. Meets Greg, law student. Local rich boy. Click. Going steady and bedding steady with Greg. Click. No orgasms with Greg. Click. Orgasms alone" (104). Isolated from the values of her community, Jolene taught herself the cult of subversion. Her revenge against the conformity Impton represents is masturbation, a conscious withdrawal from intimacy with another. The tight circle she draws around herself excludes the risk of real human contact. Her "grope suit" becomes her sexual partner, and she makes love to herself in a way that reminds us of a scene in *Steps* in which the dying woman in the tuberculosis hospital makes love with the narrator in a mirror: both acts represent deliberate refusals to take on the risk of a genuine encounter. When Levanter and Jolene become lovers in the hotel, their violent coupling echoes the rape of Nameless. "Without warning, he grabbed her by the waist and forced her down onto the floor" (107). It is the intensity of Levanter's assault that shakes Jolene's complacent reluctance to love anyone but herself. The next day she confides to him, "For years, I've been hiding in my private maze, cut off and isolated. I didn't even know who I was anymore" (110). But after the disruptive experience of their lovemaking, Jolene feels she is somehow free from the constraint and inhibition she has imposed on herself. "I'm myself—it's the ultimate risk" (110).

For Jolene, then, their encounter has been fruitful, but Levanter, gradually realizing Jolene's deceptive nature, feels trapped. He learns too late that she is married to Impton's most powerful man and is involved in a steamy divorce trial for which Impton—in the person of the chief of police—will require him to be a witness against her. Levanter's new knowledge of his partner destroys their relationship. He has been forced into a plot not of his own devising, in which she is the tale-teller and he another "click" in her tale.

Levanter's relationship with Foxy Lady endures much longer than that with Jolene because Foxy Lady is a better tale-teller. Foxy Lady meets Levanter between the border of Switzerland and France, a "no man's land" that hints at the tentative nature of her sexual identity. Her physical beauty enchants him in a way that he cannot understand, so Levanter continues the relationship in order to discover for himself "the view of the world and of himself" he wants from her (150). Somewhat like Jolene, Foxy Lady is her own best lover, so pleased with her own beauty that her need of Levanter is limited to his role as a mirror. "Caring for her body and her appearance," Levanter realizes, "constituted her only sense of herself" (142). But Levanter is captivated by her tale-telling as well. "Foxy Lady would spin out the stories of her encounters one after the other and Levanter would listen, trying not to feel threatened by her erotic exploits with others" (141). Another Scheherazade devising tales in order to prolong life, Foxy Lady knows that her final revelation will terminate her relationship with Levanter. In their lovemaking, she manages to maintain a mysterious control over him, to penetrate his identity without revealing her own. "Then it was she who was the instrument of his satiation and he who was her slave" (142). When he discovers she is a transsexual, Levanter feels "cheated," but her words continue to engage him as she narrates for him her final story: she is a lost prince, fated to lose rather than gain a kingdom. "In a matter of days," she tells an astonished Levanter, "my transformation was complete. Once a man, I was now a woman. Once rich, I was rich no more. Along with my manhood I had lost both my father and my country" (148). It is Foxy Lady's final metamorphosis and last tale. Levanter knows she can no longer aid him in the discovery of his deepest self, so he breaks with her.

Sometime later—in Los Angeles—looking for a "chance" encounter, he sees a young woman in a bookstore, scanning paperback titles in the manner of a typical university student. Serena eventually becomes his lover but reveals nothing of her identity to him other than that first glimpse of her as a reader. Their relationship is sustained—as it was with Foxy Lady—by his fascination with her unknowable self and her role as captive of his tales. Levanter, we have seen, woos Serena with words. "She loved to be aroused by listening to a man talk, she claimed, and she knew that her arousal would then excite him" (186). With Serena, Levanter also engages in a series of couplings that test the relationship between language and desire. "For Serena, just as passion was expressed by gesture, desire was expressed by language" (188). She is a lover who uses words to define the nature of desire. "Each time they were together, she kept demanding that he tell her what it was that made him want her so much" (188). But Levanter, at least in his own mind, cannot determine the nature of his attraction to her. When he first meets her, he says he is trying to find out the "source" of his need for her. Later he reveals obliquely to her that this source is linked to a prior sexual experience—what we know is his rape of Nameless. "You remind me of a girl I made a pass at in a summer camp once" (185). With Nameless, Levanter's blind date precluded speech; a year or so later, his identity as her rapist was revealed to Nameless when he licked her neck with his tongue. The relationship is reversed with Serena. She knows him, but he does not know her, and he uses his tongue not as a device to expose her identity but as a means to turn desire into words. Unconsciously, Levanter seems to be working out some sort of expiation for his rape of Nameless by his frenetic coupling with the mysterious Serena, whose verbalization of desire while they make love parallels the kind of question the young Levanter wanted to ask of Nameless as he raped her—but dared not. Serena's vitality

*source of
Serena's
attraction*

releases speech, frees the tongue, and charges the air with startling questions about the nature of desire, but ultimately Serena cannot help Levanter discover the source of his need. When he learns that she is really a prostitute, he feels cheated again. It was her mystery that intrigued him and sustained him, her resemblance to a "girlish" university student that evoked the lost Nameless. Serena, he reflects, is "a lover pretending to be a stranger," and this role—so painfully reminiscent of his own when he had pretended to be a stranger to Nameless a year after his rape of her—destroys Levanter's interest in Serena without resolving the mysterious "source" of his need for her.

Levanter's most enduring relationship with a woman is with his wife, Mary Jane Kirkland, and it too begins with a disparity of knowledge between lovers. When they first meet, she knows he is "a small investor," but he thinks she is "Madeline," a private secretary for the wealthy Mrs. Kirkland. "Madeline" is, of course, Mrs. Kirkland herself, some twenty years Levanter's senior. She keeps up the pretense until she reveals her identity to him at a cocktail party in the Kirkland Park Avenue triplex. Later that night they are alone in her bedroom, and she becomes "open to him, all frontiers gone" (220). Although they marry, their relationship is based not on passion but on mutual freedom. The Kirkland wealth once freed Mary Jane from her own limited background, and now, as Levanter's wife, Mary Jane seems determined to bestow on Levanter the opportunity to create. Her yacht, *Nostromo*, and her plane, *The Night Flight*, represent not only the freedom to travel but the time to create, in the manner of the authors, Conrad and Saint-Exupéry, whose names they evoke. When Mary Jane learns that she is dying of cancer, she affirms to Levanter that her wish in their marriage was "to expand his freedom." As he looks at her photograph, he knows his real inheritance from her death is, in the end, only words: "the words 'it was and it was not' returned to him" (225).

Levanter's final encounter—and final insight about language and sex—is with Pauline. He meets her in New York after her performance in Carnegie Hall, completing a circle that began in ValPina.

The link between that time and this is not only music (again, her playing reminds him of his mother's) but words. Pauline asks him about the story of the baseball player, and Levanter acknowledges that he told the story so that she would remember the teller. When he says to her that he wants her because "I'm afraid of losing you" (227), he unconsciously repeats the phrase he once spoke to Nameless, before she discovered he was the one who had raped her. "The sound of his words brought him a faint memory, so faint that he dismissed it" (227). Levanter's meeting with Pauline revitalizes for him the tension between the confines of the past and the open nature of the present moment, between language and desire. Levanter links language with memory. Words encapsulate the present, making the present disappear into the past. Words more than ever seem prisons—they act as barriers to understanding what it is that disturbs him about himself. His hidden nature seems encumbered by those words, "It was and was not." To escape the past he needs more than language; he must exploit the present in a wordless, passionate way. His desire for Pauline is more desperate than lust. The chance encounter of her face on a Carnegie Hall billboard comes to mean to Levanter an opportunity to experience an emotional intensity unburdened by his subconscious memories of guilt, by the long string of words that reduces his life to tense changes in the verb "to be." Pauline's conversation with Levanter in the Carnegie Hall dressing room tests his knowledge of himself. "How do you want to be remembered?" she says to him.

> "As a memory with feelings," he said.
> "Without the magic of the spontaneous?" (227)

The phrase had come up a moment before when they were discussing her performance. With her concert over, the "magic of the spontaneous" is lost; but now Levanter invites her to reenter the spontaneous in another kind of performance. It is at this point that he finally defines his desire—for her and himself. Pauline, he says, is his last chance to be "wanted, rather than remembered. To have a fresh emotion, a sensation that isn't just a ricocheted memory. To be part of that spontaneous magic" (227). It is also his last chance to free himself of the memory of those early sexual encounters that did psychic violence to himself and to another, violence which he has never named—incest and rape. In his apartment with Pauline, he unlocks the secret self he has repressed since adolescence. Just as Pauline unlocks Levanter's apartment (she comes "to his rescue" by freeing the door lock) making love to Levanter unlocks a repressed side of herself as well. For Levanter, their intense lovemaking recapitulates the two sexual acts of his adolescence. Pauline and Levanter make love wordlessly, but unlike his union with his mother and Nameless, Pauline kisses him. "When he felt her tongue upon his, he realized that it was the first time Pauline had kissed him" (229). Pauline and Levanter re-create the master-slave relationship (he is a "bird of prey"; she is tied to the bed) but in a way that brings freedom to both—Levanter from the memories of sexual violation, Pauline from her own inner repression. Her body "softened, freed from its own bondage, no longer struggling against any restraints" (231).

Levanter's end comes when he misjudges the power of still another wind—a spring storm rising out of the valley of ValPina, where he is skiing alone. "The wind, pumped by invisible bellows, lifted him, then pushed him against the fall line, throwing him to the ground. He understood that he was caught in one of those spring storms that might end in hours or last for days" (233). This is the wind that bears Levanter on his final flight, away from cages, words, life itself. "I must keep climbing, he thought." But the invisible bellows literally take his breath away, dividing his sense of self from his capacity to articulate that sense. " 'I' was still here, on this steep slope blanketed with fog; 'must' was drifting away with the wind" (233). The pronoun "I" remains grounded; the auxiliary verb "must" rises into air. Bereft of speech, the dying Levanter is nevertheless not despairing. Collapsing onto the snow, he manages to assess the "game" he has made of life. "The game was good to him, made him want to play it, yet even a solitary player needs his rest"

(235). Levanter's life ends in the midst of his achievement as gamester and storyteller; in fact, his story and his life end in midsentence, as he remembers a story he once wanted to tell to a boy on a hot summer beach. Perhaps only such a flight can ensure escape from Kafka's cage: Levanter's tryst with Pauline released him from the cage of oppressive memories from his past; alone above ValPina, the invisible wind lifts him clear of life's cage.

Kosinski's next book, *Passion Play*, asks, among other questions, What if Levanter's killing wind were postponed and the writer-protagonist were made to endure the knowledge that his game was going badly?

four

The Sacred Flame Flickers
Passion Play and *Pinball*

When Fabian, the polo-playing protagonist of *Passion Play*[1] reflects on the mythical properties of the horse through human history, he touches on a metaphor of his own life: "Man astride his mount—even that first man, his horse at a full run, its hoofs cleaving soil and space—had been the original passenger through air, the traveler borne by winds" (6). Like Levanter in *Blind Date*, who was borne by other winds, Fabian sees himself engaged in an endless quest to sustain the personal freedom needed to be a writer. He moves from experience to experience, each one as independent an event as his skillful polo shots, not astride a mount but encased within the aluminum skin of his "VanHome," which is where he writes his books. Fabian, says the narrator, is a "nomad of the highway" on a "voyage without destination" (5). But if the destination of Fabian's voyage is open-ended, what drives him to keep a ribbon of highway unwinding behind him is his obsession with escaping the ravages of time. What he learns at the end of the novel is that only through writing can he transcend physical decay, his own annihilation. "At the wheel of his VanHome, Fabian tracked in the mirror above the dashboard—the mirror no longer ready to be bribed by vanity—the changes nature had worked in his face" (10). Angled to reflect the past ground he has already covered, the mirror yields up an image of himself in decay, a kind of death's head of his own future. "Frame by frame, the documentary of aging unreeled in his imagination: the bad faith of the balding patch, the descent of graying hair, the betrayal of the lashless eye, the juiceless eyeball, the waxless ear, the dry, freckling skin; the snares of pus in sputum, of bile in urine, of mucus in feces; the reflection that debauched the spirit" (11). His body, Fabian muses, "once only the expression of his spirit, had become a form for aging, nature's own expression" (12), and this expression Fabian feels he must express. He is a writer jotting notes on his own changes even as they occur. Fabian is his only subject, and the cage is himself.

Against the steady depletion of his physical resources, Fabian drives himself to renew his spirit, his will to live and to narrate. Even as the death's head grins in the mirror, Fabian guides his VanHome into the heart of still another nameless city, which is for Fabian a "place of deliverance," the "habitat of sex," and the source of the writing that will redeem him. In these unfamiliar streets where "flesh was only feet away from flesh," the death's head in the mirror can be temporarily ignored, and he can permit his sexual desire to romp and play, somewhat the way he frees his two polo ponies from the confines of their stalls in the VanHome for exercise and training. Human sex, especially exotic contacts with pubescent girls, transsexuals, and "partners as transient and avid as himself," renews Fabian's belief in not only his sexual potency but his capacity to create his own destiny, which is to write it into existence. Sexual expression Fabian sees as directly related to the vitality of his own sense of language. "Sex liberated him, giving language to an urgent vocabulary of need, mood, signal, gesture, glance, a language truly human, universally available" (7). The language of sex invigorates the language of Fabian's art, but only for a time. The face in the mirror returns, aged even more, and Fabian reaches for his pen.

Fabian's vocation is polo playing. It is his "sacred flame," at once his "only art" and "only craft" (25). Crouched over his horse at full gallop, his polo stick a "lance," Fabian resembles both a knight (epigraphs from *Don Quixote* and *Moby-Dick* bring to mind a knight-errant pursuing a symbolic enemy with a lance) and an outlaw. As a player, he resists the notion of team play, and sees the game as "essentially a one-on-one contest" (30). Gradually he becomes a "menace to the collective soul of the game," and is dropped pointedly from one team after another, slipping gradually into the "notoriety of isolation, a maverick" (31). Fabian sees polo as a form of dueling. His victims are not only his mastered ponies and his mounted team opponents but his own team members as well. The hard wooden ball is a weapon, an instrument of his personal vengeance. In one match Fabian imagines a former lover, Alexandra, who once betrayed him, being hit by the ball he is about to strike with his mallet. "Then he saw the ball pounding into Alexandra's head, leveling her ear, the ruptured veins spurting blood, her jaw fallen away" (86). These are only words; he does not hit Alexandra. But the description acts as a vicarious killing. Fabian's polo ball is a weapon, and so are his words.

Not only is Fabian a polo player, he is also a writer on "equestrian art," and the two activities are really indistinguishable parts of his sacred flame. Fabian is rider and writer, and what he writes about, he confides to one woman, is "what it means to be a rider." The Van-Home contains not only his polo ponies, but his writing desk, with a saddle for a seat, surrounded by "large windows opaque to the world outside but transparent to the traveler within" (5). Alone inside his VanHome, Fabian reminds us of that other writer, Tarden, observing his victims from within the hidden workroom of his apartment. The VanHome itself is protected by portable signs composed by Fabian to victimize curious readers. Phrases like "SELF REACTOR: AUTHORIZED PERSONNEL ONLY" and "QUARANTINED" help deceive, according to Fabian, "the lawless and the lawful." Even the readers of Fabian's books on equestrian art sense they are victims. The books have been rejected by the public, the narrator says, dismissed as a "brutal excess of case histories that passed the bounds of credibility" (178). Although Fabian's first book was a "novelty in its time," he watches with "sorrow" as interest in his books dwindles over the years. "Fabian's books failed as mass-market tributes to the pleasures and rewards of riding" (177). One former lover, Stella, suggests to him that the reason his books do not sell is that his readers "get upset by what you write about riding" (176). "Still," Fabian replies to Stella, "what I know about riding is the only truth I feel I must share" (176), so he can only aim at another book.

Fabian's problematic status as a writer continues Kosinski's portraits of writers begun with *The Painted Bird*. If Tarden was the novelist as beginner, his work a seemingly random account of his bizarre and complex life, and Levanter the writer as celebrity, his work on investments bringing dividends in public recognition and influential friends and acquaintances, Fabian is the beleaguered writer who has maintained a consistent but unpopular vision and has paid the price—dwindling sales and readership, a growing defensiveness about his books, and the pain of isolation and self-doubt. How can he write himself out of this cage, wonders Fabian. Should he write for a different media, such as television, with its lavish financial rewards? Fabian is a writer in a special state of crisis. His past writing directs the shape of his future writing, and so these prior texts act to confine him. The text of *Passion Play*, moreover, forces us to reflect on what Kosinski considers his own stature as a writer. The many parallels between Fabian and Kosinski—especially the public accept-ance of their past books—are urged on the reader to the point of self-indulgence.[2] Here is the narrator summing up Fabian's first two books:

> *The Runaway*, Fabian's first book, concentrated on the trauma an accident had on riders, and it won particular praise, even though it disturbed many critics and book reviewers by what they labeled as Fabian's mistrust of the established principles of horsemanship. *Obsta-cles* was his second work, a detached rehearsal of the still more complex variety of potential mishaps that might ensue within the riding arena. The audacity of its technique was widely acclaimed, and even though *Obsta-cles* was singled out for the prestigious National Horse Lovers Award, the book further alienated a large number of critics, who chose to ignore the wisdom of its warnings to unseasoned riders, electing instead to warn unseasoned riders of the unwisdom of exposing themselves to such a pessimistic book. (178)

The overt allusions to *The Painted Bird* and *Steps* and the self-righteous and defensive tone ("the wisdom of its warnings") distract us from consideration of Fabian as a character in proportion as they lead us to speculate about Kosinski's perceptions of his past work. These allusions are risky in still another way: Kosinski invites us to witness his attempt to restore a vision of himself as a writer by means of the pages of *Passion Play*. The burden is too great for the novel, which simultaneously confesses doubt and brims with confidence and self-justification.

Whether or not the restoration of a flagging vision was on Kosinski's mind as he composed *Passion Play*, certainly Fabian himself, as the book opens, is aware that his psychic energy is in need of a recharge. In the novel's first scene, Fabian has his hair cut by a young woman in a fashionable salon. She is physically attractive, but he feels only a "languor of senses," a mere substitute for desire. In his routine conversation with her, he senses the "poverty of language" that forces him to obliterate his "true state of being" with the "soiled currency of 'thank you' and the worn coinage of 'fine' " (1). Both Fabian's sexual drive and vitality of language are drained. As he drives through the streets of the city looking for a revival of his spirit, what the narrator calls a "deliverance," he turns the decline of his body into sentences. "He kept a log of the steady remolding of his face, particularly when fatigue set in, the folds in the eyelids thickening, the overpliant chin sagging with flesh" (12). When "Latin Hustle," a Hispanic con man Fabian meets, offers him the chance to procure a young girl under the guise of a legal adoption, Fabian considers the photograph of a sultry fourteen-year-old and is tempted "to embark on the road of fatherhood" (22). But he dismisses the notion, acknowledging to himself that "he had neither the energy nor the means to follow through" (22). Fabian's deliverance from a sense of exhaustion and deterioration will have to come from another source.

As the book opens, then, the knight Fabian ponders his stalled quest, the many false paths, such as the road to "fatherhood," leading in different directions. His confidence in his art—both riding and writing—is undermined, his sexual energy listless. As he moves from one encounter to the next, we see him faced with the need to distinguish between genuine psychic renewal and mere self-indulgence, between acts that confirm his own integrity and those that dissipate it. Fabian the knight errant, his "lance" a writer's pen, is surrounded by temptations to abandon his quest, by trials testing his aging body, by siren calls of technology to woo him away from his self-imposed code of independence. And facing him always is the rearview mirror that displays the past he cannot repeat, the words he has already written.

One temptation, a familiar one by this point in Kosinski's fiction, is the lure of high technology, especially the electronic media. Fabian believes that television, for example, is as mentally debilitating as Kosinski claimed it was in his essay "Packaged Passion."[3] Fabian is befriended in Florida by a nameless young woman who watches television incessantly, and he marvels at how completely she has surrendered her sense of herself to the "deafening sound and turbulent images" of television. "Fabian saw her as television's faithful babysitter, standing watch over a child that never offered her an unruly face, never encroached on her world, never imposed on her energy" (145). But if television watching is easy for Fabian to dismiss, the temptation to reap the lavish rewards for the privileged few who write or perform for television is a strong one. When Fabian arrives at a polo tournament held by the wealthy Stanhope family, he is urged by Michael Stockley, a representative of "Grail Industries," which is owned by the Stanhopes, to become a host for a projected television series on the game of polo. "Who could be better?" asked Stockley of Fabian. "You wrote books about polo" (47). But Fabian puts Stockley off. He is a word man, not an image man, after all. Fabian, moreover, possesses little of Tarden's fascination with technology for the sake of promoting pranks or vengeance. Despite his pleasure at the gadgetry of his VanHome, "an ingenious hybrid of truck and trailer," Fabian senses that technology represents for him more of a temptation to surrender his imagination than a salvation of his spirit.

Another temptation that threatens to lure Fabian from his quest is the phenomenon of celebrity status. Although his reputation has fallen, he was once a celebrity himself, and his memories of his former life as a guest in the homes of the wealthy seem particularly poignant as he cruises alone along the highway, in search of a one-on-one polo match, only a few hundred dollars to his name. He recalls his first visit to the Eugene Stanhope estate. "Installed in a guesthouse at the millionaire's sprawling estate, Fabian succumbed readily to luxury" (145). His books, popular then, gave him ready access to this "seductive atmosphere of easy acclaim." Friends, prospective lovers, writers line up beside the pool waiting for a chance to speak to him. His books prompt invitations to teach at various exclusive riding schools; like the successful writer Levanter, Fabian accepts an offer to "conduct a seminar at an Ivy League university," which he calls "Riding Through Life" (189). He even uses his book *Prone to Fall* to talk his way past a ticket booth at a Madison Square Garden horse show. When his books are first translated into Spanish, he is soon invited into the "sealed world" of Falsalfa, a Caribbean dictator who hires Fabian to play polo with him in order to sustain the illusion that the aging Falsalfa is an athletic, "macho sportsman." But Fabian's most unsettling temptation is a gift of a one-million-dollar check from the woman he loves, Vanessa Stanhope, niece of his former friend, Eugene Stanhope. Fabian, practically broke at the time of the announcement of the gift by a Florida banker, imagines the check as "an agent of transformation," one that would restore his lost status as a celebrity. "He saw himself a resident at Palm Beach, the lavish spaciousness of a Wellington duplex the successor to his VanHome. There he would be, the celebrated polo player again, the renowned author" (249). Fabian resists the temptation to accept the check because such a gift would ensure that "his own life's every moment was no longer of his own devising" (249), and this removal of himself as the primary designer of his own life is the one concession he cannot make to anyone, even to his lover. He will write, unrenowned.

A third temptation that challenges Fabian the knight-errant is the darker side of his own sexual code. His belief that sexual congress will regenerate his creative impulse and liberate the self is counter-balanced by a tendency toward sheer self-indulgence that some-times leaves him listless, bored, or courting sexual exploitation. Fabian articulates his dilemma as he thinks about the desirability of a married woman, Elena, who, with her husband, a prominent jour-nalist, is accompanying Fabian on a horseback trip through the jungle of Falsalfa's island. Fabian's attraction to Elena is a form of sexual revenge: he wants her because she wants her husband. "He was aware that, even though he did not intend to pursue her in any way, he was drawn to her nonetheless, and the source of that attrac-tion was the visible force of the devotion she exhibited toward her husband" (97). He fantasizes about Elena, imagining them at "an adult sex entertainment center," each on opposite sides of a glass wall inside a private booth. The scope of his fantasies show Fabian drawn to the need to degrade Elena rather than to liberate her with a new understanding of herself. "Would he be coarse and carnal with her to the brink of abasement, and would he enjoy the spectacle of a charming, sensitive woman incited, driven to language and action so lewd that they seemed to violate the mouth and body that offered them? Would the presence of that glass partition urge him to excess or restraint?" (98). Fabian's fantasies about Elena eventually cul-minate in tragedy. Her husband is killed by a tarantula (apparently placed there by Falsafa's bodyguard), Elena is drugged and defiled, and Fabian appalled at the damage he subconsciously desired.

Fabian's sense of himself as a knight on a quest for personal liberation but tempted by side excursions into self-indulgence is best illustrated by his attitude toward Dream Exchange, a private club that offered "the next stage for the exploration—and exploitation—of the new [sexual] intimacy" (210). Fabian was "among the first to accept the offer" to explore this new area. But is it a dead end, a wandering off from the true path toward self-liberation? Fabian's attitude is ambivalent. He realizes that Dream Exchange is exploitive, yet he is drawn to the sexual excess that the place seems to promise, the "covert knowledge" of each partner of the other, the "knowl-edge of sensation alone" (211). Fabian leads his lover, Vanessa, through the steamy group sex scenes of Dream Exchange, uncertain of his own intentions, or even what he wants from Vanessa. "The intensity of his emotion bewildered him." He stands before the diverging paths of excess and restraint, surrounded by writhing figures, wondering which one leads to insight and which to exploitation. Fabian then pronounces judgment on the other members from a superior critical stand that he has not actually earned. "They're consumers of passion," he tells Vanessa, "in search of bargains." But as one of the first to accept the offer of places like the Dream Exchange, he is implicated in this same search for bargains. Fabian leads Vanessa through a "zone of cubicles," each resonating with "whispers, chuckling, the slap of flesh on flesh, a body thudding against the floor, the moan of a woman, a man whimpering, broken words and phrases stillborn" (218). Against this backdrop of frantic bargain hunting, Fabian the knight chooses to disclose his love for his lady. "I've loved you all along, Vanessa" (221). Even at the moment of his declaration he is at a loss to see how their own sexual union differs from those pulsing around them. Exploration or exploitation? The reader is left wondering if Fabian is capable of discerning the distinction.

Fabian's love affair with Vanessa turns out to be still another path straying from the true one. As he sees it, the commitment of love between two people is itself a design that narrows both the openness and the unpredictability of experience. Love, in short, removes control of his destiny. "Now," he thinks, "when she was willing to resume what he had initiated so long ago, to receive the finality of his mark, to embrace the long arc of his design for her, he saw himself caught in that design" (221). Vanessa's love is no less a cage than the aluminum railing and knobs that surrounded a paralyzed polo player Fabian once knew. His love for Vanessa, especially their lovemaking in Dream Exchange, has made her "free of him, free of herself" (225). It has also left Fabian free to return to his nomadic life, to continue the quest for the true flame, which is his art.

Fabian's writing desk, enclosed behind darkened Plexiglas, represents a perspective on experience that has its origins in Fabian's East

Fabi's fantasies of transforming himself— as in PB

European childhood on a farm of a peasant who sheltered him from the disruption of war in exchange for labor. Here the young Fabian, a "refugee from the city," parentless, learns about life—its cycle of birth, pain, and death—from the horses he feeds and cares for. Motherless himself, he watches a mare give birth and imagines himself placed within the safety of the mare's womb. Inside this refuge, the boy Fabian is "free to peek out at the hostile world merely by lifting the mare's tail, a curtain he might raise or lower on an uncertain stage" (131). The world outside Fabian's Plexiglas window is also an uncertain stage, but from the safety of his writing desk he can record life's drama unfolding while simultaneously remaining detached from it. Outside the window is life, something that needs to be kept free of design, unpredictable and random. Inside the window, Fabian imposes the design of art on life. The duality of his past continues into his present life. His life is divided between polo playing, with its intense but random moments of challenge, and observing his play, which becomes the writing of his riding. This tension between the simultaneous need to live life and to write about it, so keenly felt by Levanter, presents to Fabian a painful dilemma. Living and writing are really separate zones of experience; success in one need not necessarily bring success in the other. "Yet, confusing progress toward that goal with progress through life, he believed that he had simplified the maze of life. He would, however, soon lose himself in one of the traps which composed that maze . . . and so become the prey of his own facility, a parody of prowess and technique" (29). Fabian wonders if his writing will deteriorate, become a parody of his former power, an empty technique without the vision that once gave it life. Like other Kosinski protagonists, such as the Boy in *The Painted Bird*, Fabian has fantasies of transforming himself into someone with power or youth or the freedom of action that he does not possess. This "adolescent urge to escape his own shape" is Fabian's subconscious recognition that life is by nature a prison, that the death's head will always be in the mirror, and that he, enclosed within the shape of his aging body, can only escape by nurturing his art, which is not polo playing, but writing. The VanHome provides Fabian with the illusion of freedom, but writing is the "private trailer for his mind," and, like the experience of reading one of the novels he collects for his VanHome book shelf, his writing permits him to travel "to a reality outside the dominion of nature . . . a weightless passing through time and place and thought, coasting with a freedom unmatched by any spaceship" (127).

Fabian is a reader, not a writer, of novels, but Kosinski is both, and his veiled comments on the state of the novel in America seem gratuitous, bouncing around in some corner of the VanHome with Fabian's horse tack. We have seen how Fabian's books "failed as mass-market tributes to the pleasure and rewards of riding"; now Fabian cannot make his living from the sale of his books. Bookstore owners tell him that the general public, hooked on "how to" books, seems to want riding portrayed as "an easy diversion, as fun" (177). Fabian, moreover, does not permit pictorial illustration in his work. "He suspected that to submit to that [pictorial] vision would be to clog the active play of images that were fluent and mobile within each person, fantasy and emotion that written language alone could quicken" (178). Such reservations about pictures are appropriate for Kosinski the novelist, committed as he is to the written language, but it is hard to see how Fabian's books on polo could be so seriously compromised by the presence of illustrations of horses. We are forced to look away from the fictional character for the moment in order to ponder another parallel between character and author: once again Kosinski reminds us that he views himself a beleaguered novelist surrounded by hostile critics who disown his conception of "equestrian art" as too bleak, "a brutal excess of case histories that passed the bounds of credulity." Even Fabian's boyhood success in hitting a ball on horseback with a rake handle implausibly parallels Kosinski's early commercial success as a writer (his first four books, *The Future Is Ours, Comrade* to *Steps*, were "strikes" by any measure). "Fabian had discovered his aim as a boy, playing a peasant game, astride a farm horse at full gallop: with a rake handle, he had sent a ball the size of an apple, twenty yards across a meadow, hitting a target no larger than a pumpkin. It had been his first strike; he hit the target a second time, then a third, finally a fourth" (29). Since that fourth success, it was not Fabian who shaped his "faultless stroke";

the stroke shaped him. His talent, Fabian implies, designs his fate, or, to put it another way, the success of his art shapes the contours of his life. Fabian's final paradox is that his art has made him a prisoner, reducing his freedom. To practice his art he must enter a chicken wire cage, sit on a dummy horse, and fire shots at the walls of his cage. Ultimately, he can only be the one who once hit four targets in a row. Thus Fabian the knight must also tilt his lance against a remembered image of himself, resulting in an inevitable psychic wounding, perhaps symbolized by Fabian's self-mutilation—the loss of his finger tip—which hampers his grip not only on the polo mallet but on his pen as well. Just as Fabian was forced to measure the contradictory impulses of his character, the tendency toward restraint or excess, so too must he face the possibility that his art, the capacity to make faultless strokes, might deteriorate into a "parody of prowess and technique."

As Kosinski composed *Passion Play*, his seventh novel, he must have taken into account the risk that his work might be perceived as a parody of his former novels, especially the earlier ones that had formed his reputation. His determination to find a new context for each of his novels, shifting from a spy on the run in *Cockpit*, to a lone-wolf investor in *Blind Date*, and now to a shunned maverick polo player, has its counterpart in the style of *Passion Play* as well. *Steps*, and *Being There*, and parts of *The Painted Bird* were characterized by a starkness of style, a sparse vocabulary, a conscious restraint. Here in *Passion Play* the style is lush, lyrical, the vocabulary elaborate and decorative, peppered with words like "pupfish," "borax," "trefoil," "quillwort," "mayapple," and "liverwort." Especially in scenes involving sexual release or descriptions of nature is Kosinski's style so much more ornate than in these earlier books. Here is a scene in which Fabian, making love to Stella in the Van-Home, sees the clutter of horse tack seemingly turn into living things:

> Near her feet, a welter of nosebands and reins spilled and jutted like the roots, suddenly bare, of a huge, stricken tree. Above her, trays mounted the wall, their overflow a shimmer of bits and metal equipage, snaffles,

curbs, rein loops and mouthpieces, alien jewelry of stud and mare. From hooks on another wall, stirrup straps and girths, collars, breastplates, martingales and halters were coiled like snakes frozen in their twining. (169)

The exotic vocabulary here seems a necessary element in the scene: lifeless objects are transformed by the play of passion into animate beings—reins and nosebands into the roots of trees, halters and martingales into snakes. Another scene seems to veer into excess; here Fabian and Vanessa dismount from their horses to make love in the woods.

The heart of the woods, a chapel of silence, was invaded only by the scuttling flurry of the tender creatures of the ground, the chaste quiver of a fawn. Spent, drained of desire by the exhilaration of the chase, Fabian and Vanessa would dismount and lie down enfolding each other, brother and sister now, leaves of the same branch. (197)

The metamorphosis is familiar—lovers into siblings, flesh into leaves, but the passage descends into sentimentality. The chapel of silence, the tender creatures, the chaste quiver of a fawn seem cloying and strained. If Kosinski in *Passion Play* often gives in to this kind of verbal excess, there are also a number of passages in which he records what Fabian sees with power and conviction, such as this scene in which Fabian rides his horse to the brink of a trench filled with dead and dying wild horses, all shot by ranch hands to save grassland for their cattle.

Cramped in heaps in the narrow furrows of the mass graves, most of the animals were dead; some twitched, a last flicker of life. Settled at the brink of the spilling trough, Fabian saw the mound of dead and dying mustangs as an infernal creation: meshed and intersecting heads, shoulders, hocks, erupting muzzles, ribs, and tails, twisting coils of a monstrous snake that burrowed greedily through the stony ground of the valley, its scattered eyes blinking, its venomous mouth open, ready to strike, indicting earth and sky. (135)

Here the transformation of the dead horses into an enormous

snake aptly conjures up the sense of human cruelty and exploitation of nature without direct commentary or the more distracting and immediately recognizable parallel to Kosinski as a writer.

We have seen how Fabian, confronted with his strongest temptation, to accept Vanessa's love, wealth, and life-style, breaks with her in order to preserve his, and her, freedom. Alone once more, he reflects on the life ahead of him, bereft of his design of love that at least had offered a temporary refuge from his awareness of the flow of time. "Time would no longer be the span that had passed since they had been together, and no more would he be the architect of time, devising a form to arrest its ceaseless motion" (268). Despairing at the emptiness he must now face, Fabian falls back on his richest resource, his art as a tale-teller. Only his writing can save him. He recalls how he had often stopped his VanHome to visit a hospital or a "home for the aged and abandoned" in order to tell stories to lonely sleepless patients inside who were "like him, traveling, but merely on a different path" (269). The stories he tells on these occasions redeem his listeners from confinement in a dying body.[4] His words permit his hearers to call on—at least for a moment—the only power left to them: "Always careful to keep his fantasy in check, so as to release the imagination of his listener, Fabian might explain the art of horsemanship, talk of strategies of combat to one for whom victory was beyond reach, chronicle the embraces of lovers to one who would embrace no more" (270). One by one the dying patients, connected to Fabian by words alone, take flight, soar above a welter of oxygen tanks and kidney machines. Fabian, who has been in and out of many cages, knows well how the "careful language" of art, to go back to a phrase from *The Painted Bird*, can offer an exit.

Language without an Accent

If *Blind Date* dramatizes the life of the writer who has reached the top—Levanter dining with Lindberg or introducing his friend Jacques Monod to hangers-on at the Cannes Film Festival—Patrick

Domostroy of *Pinball* represents the writer who has hit bottom, although, as the narrator says, he is "comfortable sitting on it" (9).[5] "He had no friends. Most of the people who had been his friends when he was on top assumed that success and failure ran parallel and were therefore not supposed to cross paths, and because he had once felt the same way himself, he could hardly burden them now with an explanation of his failure, making them feel guilty of their own success or uncertain of their own talents" (9). Domostroy is a composer of a special language—a music that enlarges "his spiritual world by demolishing boundaries of time and space" (10)—but when we see him in the first scene, lugging a dead battery to a service station for a recharge, he is no longer composing, and in fact resembles the dead battery he is carrying. His banishment from former celebrity status brings him, paradoxically, a new sense of personal freedom. "Freed as he was from the deceptive security of accumulated wealth and the chimera of success—his freedom a useful by-product of his composer's block—he rejoiced at being able to live his life as he pleased" (9). Domostroy is not completely resigned to failure, however. Two hopes sustain him: that his music, regarded at the time of composition as "original" and "experimental," might someday be more appreciated, and that his will to compose, presently lost in "the prime of his life," might return. Driving alone in his aging car through streets that resemble "lines of music stripped of notes," Domostroy waits for a revival of his talent for marking notes on empty lines. "He would park in a deserted street where no sound broke the silence and sit and imagine that one day the well of his music, now as empty and soundless as the avenues of the huge city, would fill up again" (9).

From Levanter to Fabian to Domostroy the gradual decline of the writer from a peak of renown and success to failure and obscurity rounds out Kosinski's dramatization of the complex relationship between the writer and his writing, between the flux of the writer's experience and the stasis of the words that describe the experience. In each of Kosinski's novels the writer-protagonist has sought to express himself in a new language, one that would transform him into a figure of power by captivating an audience. In *Pinball*, Kosinski continues his analysis of the tension between writer and reader, the book as predator, the reader as prey. Domostroy, however, embodies the inverse of this relationship: his composing once created an audience that now has turned against him. His listeners are no longer captivated by his music, and so he avoids contact even with former fans, knowing that their roles have changed. He has ceased to control through his art their response to him. Domostroy plays an organ at Kreutzer's, a rather garish nightclub in the Bronx complete with pinball games and a bevy of call girls. He works as an accompanist only, preferring not to play alone because "it made the break with his past—as a solo performer —clean and complete" (8). Domostroy's playing at Kreutzer's parallels prior compositions: Beethoven's *Kreutzer* Sonata and Tolstoy's *The Kreutzer Sonata* (1889). Tolstoy's book addresses itself to the power of music and its relation to human sexuality. The main character, Pozdnyshev, relates his long tale of sexual anguish, marital hypocrisy, and eventual wife-murdering to a sympathetic fellow passenger on a train ride. At a crucial moment in his marriage, Pozdnyshev recalls, a musician he had suspected of having an affair with his wife began playing the *Kreutzer* Sonata. Pozdnyshev was so moved by the music that he now (at the time of his telling) feels that the music bewitched him, duping him into thinking his wife was faithful. His feverish attack on the power of music is a reflection of his revulsion at the related power of sexuality:

> "They were playing the Kreutzer Sonata by Beethoven," he continued. "Do you know the first presto? You do?" he exclaimed. "Ugh! Ugh! That sonata is a terrible thing, particularly that part of it. Music, in general, is a terrible thing. I cannot understand what it is. What is music? What does it do? And why does it do that which it does? They say that music acts upon the soul by elevating it,—nonsense, a lie! It acts, acts terribly,—I am speaking for myself,—but not at all by elevating. It neither elevates nor humbles the soul,—it irritates it. How shall I tell it to you? Music makes me forget myself and my real condition; it transfers me to another, not my own condition: it seems to me that under the influence of music I feel that which I really do not feel, that I understand that which I do not understand, that I can do that which I cannot do."[6]

Both music and sex are terrible things to Pozdnyshev precisely because they "transfer" the self, as he says, into another condition, another perspective. Pozdnyshev resumes his tale with an attack on marriage, claiming that human sexuality has been unnaturally stimulated by modern society. Marriage is a hypocritical arrangement, a trap. Pozdnyshev's outbursts against men's lust, women's entrapments, and current moral standards are played off in Tolstoy's book against "The Domostroy," a sixteenth-century Russian treatise on moral behavior which revered marriage as a "mystery." Thus one moral code, if rigid and old-fashioned, has been replaced by a modern one: marriage, according to Pozdnyshev, is a "sale. An innocent girl is sold to a libertine, and the sale is surrounded with certain formalities" (339). The discarding of "The Domostroy" by modern Russian society and Pozdnyshev's frantic search for a moral code that confronts honestly the reality of human sexuality are themes from Tolstoy's novel that reverberate in *Pinball*. Like "The Domostroy," Patrick Domostroy has been discarded, made to seem old-fashioned; like Pozdnyshev, Domostroy understands that social conventions surrounding human sexuality are often hypocritical. Domostroy's solution, however, is poles away from Pozdnyshev's, who argues for continence before marriage and self-restraint during it. Domostroy seeks out the very qualities of consciousness which horrified Pozdnyshev: unpredictable transformations of himself by means of the powers of sex and music. As he says to Donna, who is about to play Chopin for him, music is meant to give pleasure, "to make us [the audience] feel something that, without you [the artist] we might never be able to feel" (247).

For all his insights into the power of art, Domostroy himself must play the role of the writer as victim. Only composing could rescue him from his fallen state, his devolution into powerlessness, but he can no longer rely on his art to redeem his life. He is in a cage of his own making. Ten years before, Domostroy had pronounced in an interview published as "Life's Scores" that "composing is the essence of my life. Whatever else I do provokes in me a single question: Can I—would I—should I—use it in my next score? . . . My music is my sole accomplishment, my only spiritual cast of mind" (11).[7]

Whatever else Domostroy has been doing in the intervening years, he has been unable to transfer the random experience of his life into disciplined compositions. As a writer, he has come to doubt that his experience as a person can be transformed into the language of his art.

From the reader's point of view, Domostroy's role as the failed writer cannot be separated from that of Domostroy's antithesis and alter ego, Goddard, the sensationally successful but mysterious composer of a different music, rock. The two rival composers, one publicly known and failed, the other hidden and successful, stand in dynamic relationship to one another. For Kosinski, they are really two sides of the same concept: the writer-protagonist bedeviled by the simultaneous need for privacy and public exposure, secrecy and publicity, independence and public support. Both Domostroy and Goddard represent for Kosinski forms of artistic achievement. Each working alone has accomplished something lasting. Domostroy has chosen to master a language in which his own identity, and thus his vulnerability as an outsider, a refugee from Poland, cannot be revealed by the language itself. As Domostroy says, "Accents don't show up in music," and so his own identity remains hidden within his achievement, which, to the public, consists of eight individual recordings of his compositions. His art disguises his identity, while that art penetrates the secret life of his listeners. For those listeners, such music might "untangle something within oneself," as one character, Leila Salem, describes her own response to listening to Goddard's music. But the music will not expose the composer.

Pinball is Kosinski's first book in which there are two main characters, rather than one character dominating many lesser ones. The book is divided into four parts or movements, each of which brings the reader closer to a complex unmasking as he watches Domostroy seek out the identity of his rival artist, who is in fact the missing half of his own creative force. In the first part, we see Domostroy urged on by a voluptuous blonde Juilliard drama student, Andrea Gwynplaine, to play the game that will entrap Goddard and expose his real identity. As in *Cockpit*, a writer is about to be

unmasked by another writer. Domostroy begins by composing letters to Goddard in the voice of a woman who knows his music. As
Goddard reads these letters, which are written on stolen White
House stationery, his relationship to Domostroy is unknowingly
established—prey to predator.

The second part of the book reveals that Goddard is Jimmy Osten,
an unremarkable youth whose public image is that of a literature
student but who secretly writes and records the best-selling songs of
Goddard. Osten's hiding place, the counterpart to Domostroy's
own (an abandoned ballroom in the South Bronx called "Old
Glory") is his ranch in California which he calls "The New Atlantis." Here, in the seclusion of his state-of-the-art recording center,
his "House of Sound," he composes his music "safe and secure."
Soon Domostroy's letters penetrate Osten's House of Sound, draw-
ing Osten into the plot that the writer Domostroy has written for
him. In the novel's third part, Domostroy becomes involved with
Osten's former girlfriend, Donna Downes, a black pianist also
studying at the Juilliard School. Domostroy eventually succeeds
Osten as Donna's lover, forming still another tie between Domostroy and Goddard. In the fourth and final part, predator and prey
finally meet in a bizarre shootout in the empty ballroom of the Old
Glory. Here, with the burned-out South Bronx as a backdrop,
Domostroy finds that he is a victim of a larger plot hatched by
Andrea and her boyfriend, Chick Mercurio, a disgruntled and failed
rock star. When the smoke clears, only Domostroy and Osten, now
allied in their status as victims, survive. Each has come to know the
other's true identity, and each has been given a singular glimpse into
the other's wellspring of creativity. After he learns that Domostroy
has been duped by the dead Andrea and is thus innocent of intending
any real harm to himself, Osten says to Domostroy, "You have
understood me, and my music, better than anyone else ever has"
(277). The two depart, Osten back to his life as Goddard, Domostroy to brood over his inability to compose. But Osten's parting
words seem to suggest hope for Domostroy. Sales of Domostroy's
previous eight records are increasing, says Osten (his father owns the

company), and his status as a composer for Etude Classics is an honored one: "Your records are still the pride of their contemporary Classics list" (278).

Domostroy and Osten are the most important characters in *Pinball* in that they embody the plight of the writer faced with the problem of continuing to create. Each has a series of affairs with women, and these relationships suggest something about how Kosinski views the role of sex in artistic creation. Both Andrea and Donna become involved in turn with Domostroy and Osten, so all four characters pair off in different combinations, each new pairing exploring a different dimension of the relationship between emotional experience and the inspiration that drives the artist to objectify that experience through art.

Although Osten is the mysterious Goddard and thus is experiencing the peak of his success as a composer, he is not without doubts about his ability to sustain his inspiration, to produce more and more rock compositions. Staring out at the desert that surrounds his ranch, Osten can readily picture a time when his inspiration will fail him. "Here, where no sound broke the quiet, he would stand and imagine that one day the well of his music might become as dry and as soundless as this desert. Until then, he knew, he had to search his inner life for traces of any spring that had so far eluded him" (139). His inner life has so far brought forth only one inspiring relationship with a woman, Leila Salem, the wife of the Lebanese ambassador to Mexico. Yet his brief affair with her managed to fuse the "ideal" aspect of his creativity with the "physical" nature of experience. The result is a new spurt of creativity. He writes innovative compositions based on some of the Mexican folk songs that Leila has come to love, and the record sales surpass even his previous successes. Here is the narrator describing Osten's need to base his inspiration on the passion of experience:

> The mind, he reflected, was like an ideal musical instrument—invisible, portable, capable of synthesizing all sounds—yet powerless in itself; it was also flawed because it required its listener, the body, to exercise leverage on physical matter. This prompting, this necessary transfer of

power from the mind to the body was for him one of the deepest mysteries of life. (133)

The affair with Leila, the only meaningful one of his life, has been
over for two years, and Osten feels he needs the contact of human
love in order to continue creating. His first thought when he receives
Domostroy's unsigned letter is that Leila herself has written to him.
When he reads the letter further, he realizes that the writer is too
knowledgeable about music to be Leila, and a "sense of entrapment
came over him" (167). Osten's recollection of the inspiring love of
Leila and his present sense that he is drifting as a composer and needs
another infusion of love is what attracts Osten to take the bait. Osten
then begins to track down the mysterious "White House woman"
because he thinks knowing her will help him to write. When he eventually becomes involved with Andrea, unaware that she is the model
for the character Domostroy invented, he already thinks of her as a
partner with whom he could share not only his life as Jimmy Osten
but as Goddard himself. He fantasizes how he would drive her to his
ranch, pretending he was lost. "He would stop at the main house,
and they would get out, and as if he had never been there before, he
would open the door for her—to the New Atlantis and to his entire
past" (268). By winning Andrea, whom he regards as "natural" as
Leila, Osten believes he can recapture the emotional intensity of his
past love affair with Leila. Andrea, he thinks, will make "the perfect
partner to share his creative secret" (269). The way out of the cage
for this writer is to let someone else in.

For all his success as the artist Goddard, the real Jimmy Osten is as
alone as his counterpart, Domostroy. Reading his first letter from
Domostroy makes Osten feel that his life of mystery is "a prison
with no exit" (92). Both face the same dilemma: creativity is
enhanced by a stimulating partner but endangered as well. When he
discovers who the White House woman really is—a fictional version
of Andrea—his vision of a partnership in passion is shattered, his
tongue nearly torn out (as if Oscar's nightmare in Blind Date of
losing his tongue were to come true), and his life is threatened.

The relationship between Osten and Andrea is based on an illusion; each thinks the other is victim, but only Osten is. But the affair between Donna and Domostroy does result in a new surge of creativity for one of the partners. We first see Donna initially dating Osten. When she plays Chopin at a party attended by Domostroy, she finds herself attracted to him. In the rather wooden dialogue that characterizes so much of *Pinball*, she tells Osten what Domostroy told her about herself, namely, that she has "Chopin's Żal," which is, as she says, "A spiritual enigma—pain and rage smothered by melancholy—an emotional trademark of Poles, or any people oppressed for long periods of time. Żal permeates all of Chopin's work. Domostroy said that because I'm black, Żal will probably color all of mine as well" (109). Domostroy sees in Donna a version of himself as an artist: both are spiritual exiles, practicing their art in an alien language. Donna's father was a jazz pianist, but by choosing to perform classical music she cuts herself off from the tradition of black music she inherited. Her art challenges and competes with the European musicians whose inheritance is the classical tradition. Aside from the obvious analogies between Donna and Kosinski, who also chose to write in an alien language, Donna's voluptuous presence at the keyboard makes her seem to Domostroy more than merely a promising student. "As he listened to her, he came to see that the state of his mind and the pattern of his life would be arbitrary from this point on unless he could go on being replenished by her" (220). Once again, the writer's lover is food; sexual energy can be converted into words.

Osten once fell in love with Leila and produced a successful rock composition; now Domostroy hopes to recover belief in himself by falling in love with Donna. Donna, it turns out, is more than a willing student. When she was Osten's lover, for instance, the intensity of her playing seemed to arouse her sexually. "Her eyes would shine then, her cheeks would burn, and, as if she were starved and sex were an act of nutrition, she would spell out the kind of lovemaking she wanted" (124). Osten was not prepared to supply such acts of nutrition. When, "after practicing the piano in front of him, she would suddenly fall on him and attempt to impale herself'' (125), Osten would, perhaps not surprisingly, practically flee the apartment. But Domostroy is searching for precisely the kind of passion that once delayed Chopin's tuberculosis, allowing him to continue composing masterpieces. Osten recounts Domostroy's ideas on the subject to Andrea: "Genius and chaos can somehow be reconciled only through sex, and that sexual promiscuity, by combating isolation, timidity, and emotional routine can actually engender creativity" (263). Whatever Osten thinks of Domostroy's theory, in the final scene between Donna and Domostroy, when the two of them are alone in the ballroom of Old Glory, she playing Chopin on the grand piano, he lurking behind her, teacher and now lover, it is clear that the reader is supposed to see that their union, first on the piano bench, then on the ballroom floor, brings to them both a surge of creativity. "At length, with one last plunge into her beautiful young body, he finally found, in a realization as swift as sound, the certainty of his own wholeness" (253). Their lovemaking engenders in Donna a confident spirit that eventually assures her first place in the War-saw competition. She also becomes the only one of the three artists to protect the integrity of her own identity from the pressure of pub-lic recognition of her accomplishment, the one balancing act neither Domostroy nor Osten could manage.

Three of the major characters, Domostroy, Osten, and Donna— embody versions of the artist. Each seems caught between the need to compose in private and the need to perform in public; each is burdened by the dilemma that Gerhard Osten articulates to his son: "In today's world, in music, as in everything else, it is success, unfortunately, that determines value" (115). Each asks variations of the same question: How can the artist know he is good? If he is spurned by the public as is Domostroy, is he a failure? Or is his own vision superior to the opinion of the critics?

Kosinski insists that the reader reflect on these concerns about the complex of aesthetics and commerce not only in terms of the char-acter Domostroy but also in terms of Kosinski's own career as a novelist. The parallels between Kosinski and his main protagonist,

Domostroy, are even more overt and persistent than those between Kosinski and Fabian; sections of *Pinball*, in fact, resemble a resume of Kosinski as a writer.[8] Here is Domostroy, for example, explaining to Andrea why he called his first composition, written twenty years before, *The Bird of Quintain*:

> In the Middle Ages . . . a quintain was a practice jousting post with a revolving crosspiece at the top. At one end of the crosspiece was a painted wooden bird and at the other a sandbag. A knight on horseback had to hit the painted bird with his lance and then spur his horse and duck under the crosspiece before the heavy sandbag could swing around and unseat him. I thought the bird of quintain was an apt metaphor for my work—and for my life as well. (25)

Domostroy's description evokes not only Fabian on horseback but *The Painted Bird*; the passage also reminds us of Kosinski's notion of writing as a challenge to the self, a game in which one might score a "hit," such as the success of *The Painted Bird*, or be unseated by failure, in the form of negative criticism or one's own self-doubt. Domostroy expounds on the meaning of the phrase "the bird of quintain" while his lover Andrea is playing "all eight of Domostroy's records," stacked on the turntable the way Kosinski's eight novels (including *Pinball*) might be lined up on a library shelf. One of these records, we recall, is called *Octaves*, which won the "National Music Award." Domostroy later recalls how he originally composed *Octaves*: "It would be a series of metamorphoses of a single melody broken up and punctuated, step by step, by frequent pauses, solo voices, and silences" (198). The obvious parallel to *Steps* Kosinski apparently feels needs to be stressed further. Kosinski even reworks an incident in which a writer submitted as a hoax a typed manuscript of *Steps* (changing the title) to a number of publishers, all of whom not only rejected the work as unpublishable but failed to recognize the manuscript as identical to Kosinski's *Steps*.[9] Donna's subsequent assessment of the hoax leaves no doubt how Kosinski evaluates his own novel, *Steps*. "The hoax indicated that even ten years after its publication *Octaves* was still ahead of its time, too original to be assessed objectively" (173). The defensiveness, the self-praise, and the coy allusions to past successes (like Kosinski—as well as the characters Levanter and Fabian—Domostroy has taught at an Ivy League school) create the impression that one role of *Pinball* is to provide a gloss for Kosinski's previous fiction. Kosinski even sets up a parallel between his 1981 revision of *The Devil Tree* and one of Domostroy's eight records, *The Baobab Concerto*, which, Andrea reminds Domostroy, "you rewrote because you said it wasn't good enough" (76). Kosinski's conception of Domostroy suggests how an artist can be made prisoner to his own successful past work. Domostroy is a composer who has encaged himself. "Because of his former celebrity as a performer and composer, [Domostroy] could never separate his life from his art" (279).

Obviously Domostroy is not Kosinski. Domostroy had ceased years before to compose, while Kosinski, with *Pinball*, has written ten books. But Domostroy clearly is an extreme version of some of the unique concerns that Kosinski seems to face as a writer. Osten, another extreme version, has managed to separate his life from his art; Domostroy represents the failure to discern exactly what in the writer's experience is useful for his art. As Domostroy phrases it, the events in his life constitute not only potential themes for his music but often the inspiration to compose at all. "Can I—would I—should I—use it in my next score?" (11). Such reliance on the unpredictable incidents in one's life to stimulate and even structure the work of art is both Domostroy's fate and a particular anxiety of Kosinski himself. On at least one occasion Kosinski has wondered in public if he is running out of material for writing novels.[10] Speculations about an author's psychological make-up on the basis of a published novel obviously risk shallow generalizations, but a look at certain scenes in *Pinball* does illuminate the direction of Kosinski's writing since the publication of *Blind Date*, which I regard as Kosinski's last significant work. In the 1981 version of *The Devil Tree*, new words rescue the old. Kosinski here is a revisionist, rewriting the prior text. In *Passion Play* and *Pinball*, old words prop up the new, and Kosinski becomes the devoted commentator, elucidating but not surpassing the prior text, whether code-named *Obstacles, Octaves,* or *The Bird of Quintain.*

We have seen how *Pinball* dramatizes the crisis of the writer as a public person. The book also reflects Kosinski's restlessness with the often frustrating nexus between the book as written by the writer and the book as perceived by the reader. Domostroy, like every artist, looks to art as a means to defeat time. During his early years as a composer, Domostroy thought of his music as a "shadow cast before him," creating "the means to outlive himself" (52). But this sense of outliving himself is thwarted by a fickle listening public and critics who "bombard" him "savagely." Domostroy's writing block is caused by a growing sense that only in the *process* of writing does he experience a sense of the "eternity" that another composer, Karlheinze Stockhausen, described in these terms: "A musical event . . . was neither a consequence of anything that preceded it nor a cause of anything to follow; it was eternity, attainable at any moment, not at the end of time" (279). Domostroy's eight records are so dependent on the unpredictable response of a particular audience that they cannot sustain for him the illusion that he will be outlived by his art. The art of writing, word by word, or in Domostroy's case, note by note, is by nature locked into the past of the writer, continually receding from his present. If Domostroy once felt a sense of eternity as he composed, he now feels banished from that world; his own music—he is listening to his records with Andrea—comes to him as isolated moments of memory rather than as ongoing creative acts of his will. "As always, when he listened to his records, he was surprised by his own music, by the sounds he had once been able to hear only with his inward ear" (13). The public cannot confer on Domostroy a sense of eternity, and the glimpse of eternity that Stockhausen defined cannot be sustained beyond the actual moment of composing.

A second scene reflects still another frustration that Kosinski apparently is experiencing in his own writing. If eternity can be glimpsed only in the process of writing, it quickly dissipates under the day-by-day pressure of revision, editing, negotiation for publication, and, finally, sorting through the inevitable, often unfriendly, reviews. Domostroy and Osten both resent the paradox of their art: while composing is a solitary, even lonely experience, the presentation of their work ordinarily demands collaboration with others— editors, publishers, lawyers. Andrea, for example, in her initial conversation with Domostroy about exposing the identity of Goddard, is convinced that no successful artist can work alone: "There must be a fair number of them—his family, relatives, friends, lovers, record company bigwigs, tax accountants, IRS agents, attorneys, clerks, secretaries, doctors, nurses, music technicians. No matter how great—or cunning or clever or rich—Goddard is, he could not have made it all alone!" (17). But Goddard, in the person of Jimmy Osten, has not only made it all alone, he is himself obsessed with simplifying the act of composition even further by marshaling technology to exclude collaborators. Osten, for example, argues with his lover Donna about the potential advantages for the artists of the electric synthesizer, which he sees as a "creative multi-use musical erector set" (122). This kind of technology, Osten proposes, would be "a boon to composers and performers; at the merest touch of a button, they could hear full arrangements, as well as endless variations on a single theme; they could compress or extend a phrase, slow it down or speed it up. All this seemed to him an invaluable enrichment of the musical tradition—as well as a means of transcending it" (122). Later Osten buys a Paganini, the "ultimate electone console," and brings it back to his House of Sound. Osten now "could instigate and control the whole creative process, from the initial source—his own songs and voice—to his arrangements for any of the electronic and non-electronic instruments he used to produce the Goddard sound" (138). Osten composing in his House of Sound is a vision of pure creativity, one which Kosinski knows can never be available to him. Not only does each manuscript Kosinski—or any novelist—writes need to pass through a series of revisions, editorial corrections, and further rewriting, but each book that is eventually published cannot escape the public's perception of his previous books. As *Pinball* illustrates, Domostroy is so troubled by the confining nature of his previous work that he no longer composes; writing ceases to free him, and the bars of the cage appear to grow stronger. Domostroy, like Kosinski, and indeed like the Boy who first experienced the power of writing in *The Painted Bird*, saw his first efforts as a young man in terms of keys to open a cage, the cage being the limiting circumstances of his life at the time. "In his composing days Domostroy thought of his music as a key that could open the door to the future. . . . When his music was widely known and he himself famous, he kept the lock and hinges of that door well oiled" (52). Now Domostroy confronts the world from behind a locked door, a prisoner both of the public's assessment of his previous work and the necessarily collaborative circumstances of his art.

Domostroy is not the only composer in *Pinball* who has experienced what it is to be caged. Another composer, a "prisoner at Leavenworth," also used his musical writings to free himself, and, with the help of some "music luminaries," he is paroled. Once free, he does not remain the "gentle prisoner of the keyboard" as his supporters had hoped. Instead his true nature asserts itself, and he murders someone. He disappears from public view to become a kind of musical picaro, composing songs under another name and then "tipping off the newspapers to who he was" (46). The real life model for this episode, Jack Abbott, actually was later caught, tried, and returned to prison.[11] But Kosinski's version of the writer who wrote himself out of one cage only to enter another seems to epitomize *Pinball*'s obsession with the confining power not so much of the act of writing but of its consequences—all the stages from revision to reviewing.

Kosinski's predicament is that he can rely only on more words to open the cage his own words have constructed. In *Passion Play*, the metaphors of polo playing evoke for us a character, Fabian, whose early successful writings have been neglected; *Passion Play* then shifts the blame from Fabian to his readers, who are blind to the originality of Fabian's vision. *Pinball* in turn needs to be seen both as a novel in its own right and as still another attempt to gloss, justify, and defend

Pinball's immediate predecessors. In the revised version of *The Devil Tree*, by apologizing for the "cryptic tone" of the original, Kosinski seemed unwilling to trust the reader to "fill in the spaces"; in *Pinball* there are no spaces to fill in. Wordy explanations by the omniscient narrator crowd out the chance for anything resembling the reader's "implication" in the fiction. Here is the narrator describing Osten's emotional response at watching a young girl suddenly die of an overdose in his hotel room. "Osten panicked. How could death step between them this way—without warning, cutting off the girl's life as if it didn't matter at all, as if it were a crude synthesizer suddenly unplugged from the source of energy!" (95). The trite prose describing Osten's feeling of death compares badly with any number of scenes in *The Painted Bird* or *Steps* or even *Blind Date*, all of which rely on the reader to make her or his own inferences about the unexpected intrusions of death into the affairs of the characters. With *Pinball*, and to a lesser extent, with *Passion Play*, Kosinski has lost his former tight control of the reader. The book's vitality no longer mimics the tension between predator and prey; now the reader has become the predator, capable of turning on the book, destroying it. And yet Kosinski can turn only to more words to keep this kind of reader at bay.

Conclusion

Kosinski's published writings since *Pinball* mark time, literally, between that novel and his next. They are glances over his shoulder at his work. As the novels which won for him public acclaim recede further into his past, it seems he requires newer accounts of their genesis, freshly perceived relationships between them. Part self-promotion and part explication, these essays probe the ironies of his celebrity status while they labor to ensure its continuation. A piece called "A Passion for Polo," appearing in the magazine *Polo* some six years after the publication of *Passion Play*, reveals one characteristic that is often present in his fiction—a narrative scene which is also a paradigm of the art of writing. Ostensibly about polo, the essay visualizes the polo field as his "writing page," the action of the players as "the writer's paragraphs."[1] The riders colliding with one another on the polo field are both players and stress points in the contentious activity of writing sentences. The puns and pairings of words remind us of the verbal exuberance of passages from *Passion Play*. "I once wrote a novel about Fabian, a polo knight-errant who also errs at polo." He recalls his first polo lesson, in which he "moved from past tense to future present, from rapture to rupture." Galloping across the field of play, he imagines himself both ball and hitter. "Not only am I looking down at the ball, but somehow I am in the ball, looking up at myself, at the same time." He is writer and rider again, at once target and weapon, as if his most passionate effort to free himself—whether on horseback or in sentences—could only result in enclosing him. The green field turns into white paper, and the flow of energy from the game becomes indistinguishable from placing words on a page. "In my mind, the action becomes even more detailed, broken down into separate moments—as if they were the writer's paragraphs, sentences, words, punctuation."[2]

The analogy seems strained, and one wonders what regular readers of *Polo* thought of the game they enjoyed when they found it turned into words and commas before their eyes. But the piece is a lively tour de force and displays Kosinski's resourcefulness in seeking out exotic metaphors for what is a twenty-year concern for him—writing about writing.

Two other essays deserve a closer look: a brief interview in the *Paris Review* and a photo-essay in *Esquire* describing the last days of Jacques Monod, the Nobel Prize-winning biologist and friend of Kosinski. The first, entitled "Exegetics," asserts the confluence of Kosinski's life and writing: he is an escapee; his writing opened one cage of his life; he is in a new cage crowded with other writers, one of whom is occupying his writing desk. "Exegetics" explicates photographs of other writers (Stalin, Philip Roth), not written texts, but the exegeses are glimpses of the writer transformed by his writing. The first photograph shows Kosinski as a student at the University of Lodz in 1950. The photographer, identified as a "Stalinist Party hack," is Kosinski's enemy; the photograph is the cage in which the hack wants to enclose the young Kosinski, who is caught late for a Party meeting. But Kosinski escapes—he says—by quickly positioning himself in front of a photo of Stalin, the ultimate writer of plots. "There, posing patiently, I gave Stalin the eye." Two more photographs locate Kosinski in 1973 at the height of his fame—he is president of P.E.N. in one, and host to some well-known writers in another. "Carlos Fuentes and Arthur Miller have just usurped a place behind my desk—a sacrilege. No wonder I am talking to Philip Roth, who is on the right side of the desk."[3] All are chatting amiably in Kosinski's apartment, but they are rival writers, and if they once offered praise of his work they represent—in "Exegetics"—standards of excellence against which Kosinski's must be measured. So there is risk here, not just nostalgia for a pleasant evening.

"Death in Cannes," the essay on Monod, Kosinski describes as "autofiction," a "literary genre, generous enough to let the author adopt the nature of his fictional protagonist—not the other way around."[4] I take this to mean that the author, Kosinski, imagines himself inside the dying Monod in order to reopen a dialogue between Monod and the present and older Kosinski. Perhaps the dialogue had been closed since Levanter last talked with Monod in *Blind Date*. Monod's words, continues Konsinski (the essay is arranged in question-answer form), are quoted in "autolingua—the inner language of the storyteller," and here the term means that the words of Monod are not remembered quotes so much as they are the words Monod ought to have said then, or, even, the words he ought to have said *now* to a Kosinski ten years older and, paradoxically, even closer to Monod. First, Kosinski's pun-filled prose directs the reader's attention to a series of photographs of Monod, some with Kosinski standing next to him. "Now, with no pictures to assist you, picture a sprawling villa situated high above Cannes (and well above most people's situation). Outside picture a stream of limos and stream-lined sports cars. Inside picture a motion-picture crowd—all in motion." The crowd swirls around Monod, appreciative of his tanned good looks, ignorant of his identity and of the fact that he is a dying man. Later, at Monod's home, Kosinski lingers over a last glimpse of the author of *Chance and Necessity*, whose words Kosinski once quoted in *Blind Date*. "His smile is as radiant as the sun. It is a smile of Sisyphus who, staring death in the face, sees nothing but the sun." "Death in Cannes" is a meditation on closures—of stories, of earlier writers, of a writer's life. Only words can postpone endings, defer the silence of death. "Bet on the worth of a word," says Kosinski to his readers. Monod, dying, makes this bet. He speaks to Kosinski of other writers who have died—Maupassant, Camus, Balzac. "Don't you find touching," says Monod, "that when the fifty-one-year old Balzac was about to die he called for Bianchon [a fictional doctor created by Balzac] screaming, 'If Bianchon were here, he would save me!' '' Bianchon, made only of words, possessed a saving grace for Balzac. In a similar way, Kosinski's words labor to preserve an image of Monod, already dead ten years as Kosinski writes, which is itself a kind of closure, an assertion of an ending redeemed—if only for the time it takes to read it—by words. "One must imagine Sisyphus happy," Kosinski concludes by weaving still another text into his text, this one by Camus.[5]

Kosinski's retrospective writings take on a new twist with a piece published in 1982, an interview, in which he explicates his fiction in religious terms. He sees his writing shaped by three religious perspectives—Jewish, Catholic, and Protestant. "First, as a Jew, I saw literature as part of the literary, and religious, tradition that values *the word*—the tradition of storytelling—more than any other vocation."[6] The storyteller in Jewish tradition, he continues, is "holy, . . . entrusted with the spiritual mission of spreading the Word— *the tale of life*." *Steps*, *The Devil Tree*, and *Passion Play*, he says, "reflect this attitude most directly." Though born a Jew, Kosinski says he not only was "brought up as a Catholic" but "embraced Catholicism as a creative force." Catholicism, he continues, "gave my fiction the notion of the human condition as beneficially revealed by confession." In confession, the storyteller is the sinner, the priest a silent reader. "And that's why, I guess, I wrote *The Painted Bird* and *Cockpit* as confessional tales." Finally, Protestantism, particularly the ideas of Paul Tillich, "became yet another creative source for all my books."[7]

What are we to make of this belated location of the genesis of his fiction in the religious traditions of the West? Kosinski had insisted on the moral dimension of his work as far back as his analysis of *The Painted Bird* in 1967, but his appraisal then dwelled on the aloneness of the individual in the world, the need for hatred to keep alive a sense of avenging justice. "To possess hate," Kosinski said then, "is to possess great power."[8] In the novel itself, the Boy defends Mitka the Cuckoo's use of that power. "If he could not revenge his friends, what was the use of all those days of training in the sniper's art? . . ." (206). Jack Hicks claims that "to Kosinski, to be alone is man's precarious and basic state on earth."[9] If he is right, then religion—which at its minimal level asserts that man is *not* alone on earth—seems to fall outside the felt experience of Kosinski's art. My own reservations about religious sensibilities behind Kosinski's fiction is that the actual reading of his best work leads to a rejection of religion because of its conformist nature. In fact, without Kosinski's artful and intriguing gloss it would be unlikely for a reader to infer that *Cockpit*, say, explores "the human condition beneficially revealed by confession," or that the power of Tarden's tale stems from the "creative force" of Catholicism. Forgiveness is never an issue for Tarden, as it is in the short quotation from Dostoyevski's *The Possessed* that ends the novel. In that excerpt, we recall, Stavrogin is not really seeking forgiveness, but appropriating the notion of confession for his own purposes, such as testing his tale-telling art on a listener. Perhaps this scene epitomizes my point about Kosinski and religion. Clearly he uses a variety of religious images in his fiction, especially in his early books. We think of the priest in *Steps*, his bony white hands kissed by a peasant woman after confession, the Boy stumbling backward under the weight of the missal in *The Painted Bird*, or the minister's sermon at the funeral of Jonathan Whalen's girlfriend (1981 edition). But to declare as he does that "the novels I have written, from *The Painted Bird* to *Pinball* are, in a sense, a reflection of and meditation upon those various spiritual sources"[10] seems to downplay the energy that motivates the protagonists of the actual books, who are wary of commitment to anyone outside the self, skeptical of community or authority as a source of moral insight, in fact in certain novels skeptical of the existence of any moral code beyond the right to avenge an offender.

Forgiveness, love, community, family, religion—these are for other novelists. Kosinski's characters are survivors, not saving remnants, and his books are not meditations but tests of wills, flare-ups of energy between oppressor and victim, writer and reader. Kosinski's only faith is in words. "Bet on the worth of a word," he says. His whole career is that bet, no less risky now for having achieved success and celebrity status. In Poland once he risked all to write; now he sees the struggle changing—new betrayals, negative reviews. The bars of his cage take up another configuration. These recent writings are not mere provocative recastings of his previous work as he would have us see them. They are proclamations of the joys and risks of writing, as well as glimpses into one writer's recurring bad dream that the words he has written may go unread. Together they signal significant shifts of development in Kosinski over the years, in his sense of himself both as a writer with a moral vision and as a stylist.

Frederick R. Karl recently characterized the Kosinski protagonist as "roaming a neutral universe, controlling everything carefully, allowing himself all weapons, defining no moral or ethical area." These same protagonists, Karl continues, "judge authenticity only for themselves, never for their partners, mates, woman friends. Authenticity becomes a closed-circuit narcissism, with space only for one."[11] Karl's description—on target for *Steps* and *Cockpit*—seems less apt for the two most recent protagonists, Fabian and Domostroy, who know their ability to control is in decline and who allow space for another—Fabian for Vanessa and Domostroy for Donna, although the space is admittedly temporary. But whatever gains these books make in the direction of sharing authenticity with another are offset by the slackening of their verbal energy. If Fabian and Domostroy have moved away from Tarden's single-minded code of vengeance, Tarden's voice has devolved into a prose diffusive and explanatory. This broadening of a moral vision in the later fiction is precisely what some earlier critics of *The Painted Bird* and *Steps* once wished would happen. Irving Howe, troubled by the detachment of *Steps*, felt the moral point was "unclear or invisible." He turned to a more identifiable moral code outside the narration itself—the book's epigraph from the *Bhagavad Gita*. Howe asked, "Where are we to find the steps that take men from the moral universe of the novel to the moral universe suggested by the sentence from the Bhagavad Gita?"[12] Years later, William Kennedy, himself a novelist, was encouraged by *Passion Play* because Kosinski had toned down the obsession with revenge that dominated his earlier books. The irony is that as similar hopes for a more conventional moral code in Kosinski's fiction were gradually realized, the narrative power diminished. *Blind Date* is a transitional book in this trend: it manages to hold in balance these two aspects of Kosinski's skill—his ability to evoke a state of aloneness combined with a powerful will that knows how to survive and his ability to render a moral code in the act of being formulated by an experience that, however bizarre or cruel, is intriguing. In *Blind Date* we can trace the moral development of a character. The rapist that is the young Levanter transforms himself into the lover of Pauline by an act of will not located in self-interest. Levanter directs his vengeance against publicly recognized evil, such as a dictator's secret police, and he brings no retribution against former girlfriends, even helping down an inexperienced skier from a dangerous mountain. Fabian and Domostroy are more controlled than controllers, their loss of power made manifest by ridicule (one falls from a horse to the jeers of some wealthy people at a party) or nostalgia (the other broods over the scores of his previous music, unable to compose more). Neither is a threatening figure. But neither plunges us into an imaginary world of obsession, compulsion, and paranoia the way Tarden does.

Despite the decline of quality of the last two books, Kosinski's achievement is firmly fixed. If we accept that *The Painted Bird* is the core of that achievement, the following passage from that book is representative of his style at its most convincing.

> We halted at the edge of the pit. Its brown, wrinkled surface steamed with fetor like horrible skin on the surface of a cup of hot buckwheat soup. Over this surface swarmed a myriad of small white caterpillars, about as long as a fingernail. Above circled clouds of flies, buzzing monotonously, with beautiful blue and violet bodies glittering in the sun, colliding, falling toward the pit for a moment, and soaring into the air again (139).

Here is human existence conceived as a *place*, a pit, a set of boundaries that tempt and threaten the potential transgressor for any crossing over, any puncturing of the wrinkled skin. The narrator is positioned at the edge, staring at the surface which is also a face staring back. Beneath the surface lurks his own death, but in his imagination he can still look up at the life-giving sun. Burial below, escape above. The brown surface divides twin worlds. The flies are "beautiful"—how the word jars for being in its precise context—because they can brush against the surface then soar toward the sun, which is just what the Boy cannot do. Only two words are overtly evaluative, and they are antithetical: "beautiful" and "horrible" name for us the extremities of human life. Other words work to increase the complexity of the design. The repetition of "surface," the delicate similes (caterpillars as fingernails), the Greek "myriad," the Latin "fetor," the Anglo-Saxon "buckwheat"—all combine to draw us to one unwelcome crossover after another—human waste as a soup steaming heartily the way soup should. The passage's many violations of boundaries are replicated throughout the narration—the Boy moves from speech to muteness, Jew to Gentile, is a trespasser of farms and villages, enters and is expelled from peasant homes, partisan territory, German and then Soviet occupation zones. And these crossovers epitomize Kosinski's career—from mother to stepmother tongue, Lodz to New York City, social scientist to novelist. Like the Boy in the passage, and like Monod looking up at the sun, Kosinski is still positioned at the edge.

To the achievement that this passage represents we can add many more scenes: the Boy savoring his voice, determined to prevent it from flying like a bird through an open door; a cage in a peasant's barn enclosing a crazed woman; Tarden in the cockpit of the Snipe firing invisible shots of radiation; the Crabs of Sunset scuttling through Hollywood hills; Levanter's death in the snow; and the trench of dead and dying mustangs in the American desert, to end with another pit. Perhaps the intensity of such scenes could not be sustained in book after book, but Kosinski's fiction at its best takes us into nightmare—historical, in the case of the Holocaust, personal in the case of the Manson murders—while it hints at every writer's self-strictures, compulsions, fears, all the risks taken to write it down in a way that will be remembered. Bet on the worth of a word, he says, from inside his cage.

Appendix
The *Village Voice*
Controversy

On June 22, 1982, the *Village Voice* published a front-page essay by Geoffrey Stokes with Eliot Fremont-Smith called "The Tainted Words of Jerzy Kosinski."[1] The essay attacked Kosinski's veracity and compositional methods, prompting an immediate response from a number of Kosinski's supporters in the form of letters to the *Village Voice*.[2] Within weeks, accounts of the essay and some refutations of the charges began appearing in newspaper columns across the country.[3] On November 7, 1982, a defense of Kosinski entitled "A Case History: Seventeen Years of Ideological Attack on a Cultural Target," written by John Corry, appeared in the *New York Times*. This essay sparked a spate of articles in *Newsweek*, the *Nation*, the *New Republic*, the *Village Voice*, and the *Washington Post*, most of them suggesting that the unusually lengthy defense in the *New York Times* was explained by Kosinski's friendship with Arthur Gelb and A. M. Rosenthal, both prominent editors of the *New York Times*.[4] Sally Johns, summing up the whole affair in *The Dictionary of Literary Biography Yearbook*, refers only to one essay written in Kosinski's defense, Corry's piece in the *New York Times*. Johns reports that Corry painstakingly "recounts the details of the charges and with equal exactitude refutes them," but suggests that the refutation was not a "direct" one, because it concentrated more on the political nature of Kosinski's previous—and primarily Polish—detractors.[5]

I would like here to outline the charges made by the *Village Voice*, examining Kosinski's answers to them, some of which are found in a diversity of newspaper articles. I will then examine earlier statements Kosinski made about his compositional methods and the state of his English. But first, the charges by the *Village Voice*.

1. Kosinski has told conflicting tales about his past, specifically about the trauma of losing his speech: "Yet even though he, like many children of the Holocaust, is the sole source for our knowledge of that time in his life, there is more than one story about how the trauma occurred."[6] Because of conflicting statements like this one, his veracity is in doubt.

2. Kosinski's first two books, *The Future Is Ours, Comrade*, and *No Third Path*, were written with the assistance (especially editorial) of the Central Intelligence Agency. "He evidently grew used to this mode of work during the late 1950s when, under the pen name of Joseph Novak, he published the first of two anti-Communist tracts in which the Central Intelligence Agency apparently played a clandestine role."[7]

3. Kosinski originally wrote *The Painted Bird* in Polish, and used an unacknowledged and as yet unidentified translator or translators. An advertisement for just such a translator appeared in the March 7, 1964, *Saturday Review*. Helen Bastianello claims to have answered the advertisement, met with Kosinski in his apartment, and looked at a Polish manuscript of *The Painted Bird*. She said to Stokes and Fremont-Smith that she refused to undertake the translation because Kosinski would not agree to acknowledge her contribution.

4. Kosinski hired people to write his books. "For almost 10 years now, Jerzy Kosinski has been treating his art as though it were just another commodity, a widjit to be assembled by anonymous hired hands."[8] Three former assistants Kosinski hired are quoted for support: Barbara Mackey, John Hackett, and Richard Hayes.

The first charge: Kosinski encourages conflicting stories about his past. This allegation by Stokes and Fremont-Smith is both the least serious and the only one that can be refuted without relying on personal testimony. The "more than one story" about the manner in which the young Kosinski lost his speech—differences Stokes and Fremont-Smith discovered in Barbara Gelb's *New York Times Magazine* article and an interview Kosinski gave to Barbara Leaming of *Penthouse*—can be resolved simply by reading the relevant passages of *The Painted Bird* (pages 138–41), in which both accounts are dramatized as part of a single scene. Although the scene is fictional and hence cannot be used to assert anything about the biography of the author, nevertheless, when this passage from the novel was pointed out to them by columnist Jan Herman, Stokes and Fremont-Smith expressed chagrin: " 'This is news to me,' said Fremont-Smith, 'I'm going to have to rush to the book.' He did and moments later came back on the line. 'All I can say is that I'm deeply embarrassed.' "[9] One serious mistake does not discount any of Stokes's and Fremont-Smith's other allegations. Nevertheless, this anecdote was placed early in their essay as an example of the untrustworthiness of Kosinski: "The point here is not to question which (if either) version is true, but to note that Kosinski encourages the conflicting stories which surround him, that he denies the notion of truth."[10]

The second charge: Kosinski received help from the Central Intelligence Agency for the publication of his first book. This allegation is the most damaging to Kosinski's international reputation as a writer and the least documented. As Kosinski phrased it to Jan Herman of the *Chicago Sun-Times*, "The CIA issue is crucial because it ruins me with my European publishers. The thought that I would be run by the CIA for 20 years, according to Mr. Stokes, is very damaging. I have been staunchly anti-Communist for many years because I personally believe it. They make it seem as if I were ordered to be anti-Communist. And if I were to try to get a job as a teacher again, do you think any faculty would welcome me now?"[11] Stokes and Fremont-Smith begin by rejecting Kosinski's account of his contacting a Roger Shaw at Doubleday while enrolled in the doctoral program of social science at Columbia University. "First of all, Doubleday's personnel files for the period show no record whatsoever of any employee named Roger Shaw. Second, the Doubleday editor who *did* handle the book never met Kosinski. Adam Yarmolinsky, at that point Doubleday's public affairs editor, says he was told the author's identity needed to be protected and recalls that 'all the work on the book was handled through an intermediary.'" Stokes and Fremont-Smith then claim that Frank Gibney, an individual who worked with the CIA in publishing *The Penkovski Papers*, was the intermediary, even while stating that "Gibney has denied both to us and to Yarmolinsky that he was the conduit for this book."[12] The details of Gibney's denial appeared about a month later in Dave Smith's article, "Kosinski Whodunit: Who Ghost There If Not Jerzy?" Gibney denied to Smith that he had ever been in the employ of the CIA, nor had he heard of Novak-Kosinski at the time he was working on *The Penkovski Papers*. "The only connection I ever had with the CIA was in getting access to papers in their possession. I was a *Life* correspondent and I did *The Penkovski Papers* and later I worked on the papers of Peter Deriabin, a Soviet defector, and that later became a book. I also looked at the papers of a Polish defector, Pavel Monat, but I didn't work on them. But that was my only CIA connection, getting access to those papers, which was difficult, and only in my capacity as a *Life* writer."[13] Gibney also denied working with Yarmolinsky, claiming only to know him socially. As for Yarmolinsky, he denied knowledge of CIA connections with the Novak book. "The point is, I showed the Novak manuscript to several friends at the time, and it never occurred to me that the CIA might have been involved." Stokes and Fremont-Smith discount the denials of each, relegating their statements to typical CIA cover stories.

Five months later—after the Corry essay was published—*Voice* editor David Schneiderman defended the Stokes article, but added no new details to the charges of CIA assistance, and did not refer to Gibney or Yarmolinsky. "Stokes and Fremont-Smith also explored the possibility that Kosinski's first two books, written under the pseudonym Joseph Novak, may have been published with CIA assistance."[14] Alexander Cockburn, writing in the same issue of the

Voice, did not refer to CIA assistance at all. The Stokes essay, he said, "suggested that Kosinski had told lies about events in his life and about help in writing his books."[15] Both Schneiderman and Cockburn were more interested in the charges by Stokes that the Corry essay seemed to sidestep: the assistance Kosinski arranged during the writing of his more recent fiction, specifically *Cockpit* and *Passion Play*. But the impression remains that Stokes's charge that Kosinski received assistance from the CIA did not gain strength after the denials of Gibney and Yarmolinsky.

The third charge: Kosinski originally wrote *The Painted Bird* in Polish, and used an unacknowledged translator. The case against Kosinski rests on the assumption that *The Painted Bird* could be translated from Polish into the level of English found in the 1965 edition within an extraordinarily short period of time. For if it is true that March 7, 1964 (the date of the appearance of the advertisement in *Saturday Review*), is, as Stokes and Fremont-Smith assert, "more than a year before *The Painted Bird* was published," it is also true that the manuscript was submitted in September 1964 to Houghton Mifflin and that still another manuscript in English was submitted to Farrar, Straus and Giroux less than two months after "Bastianello says she met with Kosinski."[16] If Bastianello answered the advertisement, read the manuscript, and then refused to begin work because Kosinski would not give her credit as the translator, we can assume that at least a week transpired. With her refusal (around March 15, 1964), Kosinski was faced with selecting another respondent to the advertisement, now more than one week old. The earliest that another translator could read the manuscript and agree to begin would be the third week of March, leaving something like five or six weeks between the start of the translation and the mailing of the complete manuscript in English to Farrar, Straus and Giroux in mid-May of 1964. Austin Olney, the editor in chief of Houghton Mifflin, claims that a translation of a work the length and nature of *The Painted Bird* could not be completed in six months, much less six weeks. "It would have to be a genius of a translator," Olney told Dave Smith of the *Chicago Sun-Times*.[17] One translator of Polish into English, Professor Maurice Friedberg, chairman of the department of Slavic languages and literature at the University of Illinois, dismisses the idea of a genius translator. "When the Slavic languages are translated, certain seams always show. They don't show in *The Painted Bird* and Kosinski's images are not Polish. The book was written in English."[18]

Both Olney and Friedberg could be incorrect; a talented translator could have been found who disguised the "seams" and rendered Kosinski's Polish images into English ones. But without the discovery of this person, the charge seems a dead end. Neither Cockburn nor Schneiderman of the *Voice*, responding to Corry's essay, reiterates Stokes's original charge that Kosinski "probably wrote [*The Painted Bird*] in Polish."

The fourth charge: Kosinski hired people to help write his books. This allegation is the most serious because it attacks not his political views but his integrity as an artist. No novelist, say Stokes and Fremont-Smith, "with any claim to seriousness, can hire people to do without acknowledgment the sort of *composition* that we usually call writing. To purchase another's words is to cheat the reader, to trash the tradition. For almost 10 years now, Jerzy Kosinski has been treating his art as though it were just another commodity, a widgit to be assembled by anonymous hired hands." Some of the differences between Stokes and Kosinski center on what constitutes a manuscript; Kosinski acknowledges that he hired editors to correct galleys and that galleys often were turned back into new typescripts. Stokes and Fremont-Smith provided this account of Kosinski's use of assistants: "He hires free lancers to collate corrections, check galleys against retyped manuscript, and watch for errors (e.g., a word used too many times, an action inadvertently repeated)." But Stokes and Fremont-Smith insist that some of these assistants worked on manuscripts, not just on galleys.[19] They then proceed to demonstrate how certain of these individuals actually became the "hired hands" who assembled the widgits of Kosinski's books. Three names are cited by Stokes and Fremont-Smith: John Hackett, Barbara Mackey, and Richard Hayes.

John Hackett: Although Stokes and Fremont-Smith report that Hackett insisted to them that "his work for Kosinski had been strictly editorial," they claim that not only did Hackett work on manuscripts, as opposed to galleys, but his work with Kosinski constituted "joint efforts." Proof that the work of Hackett was with manuscripts, Stokes and Fremont-Smith argue, is that the manuscript of Cockpit was not received at Houghton Mifflin until October 10, 1974. But if Hackett entered the scene at this late a date (the summer of 1974) with something like two months to go before submission of the manuscript, Hackett must have been working on a manuscript already considerably revised. Barbara Mackey had worked on Cockpit at an earlier point.[20] Whatever the state of the text Hackett eventually saw, his involvement was confined to a short period of time. As Kosinski said to Publishers Weekly, "Actually Hackett only worked on it three half-weekends. He drove down from Middleton, Conn., on Saturday, got to New York in the afternoon, and left Sunday. The book took three years to write. How could they call it a joint effort?"[21] John Corry chose to focus on Hackett, concentrating on the charge that Kosinski maligned his former assistant by accusing him of using drugs.[22] But the drug issue obscures the fact that Hackett worked on Cockpit only a few weekends. When Dave Smith later reached Hackett by phone, Hackett asserted that he was "very disturbed" by the impression of his assistance to Kosinski conveyed by the Village Voice.[23]

Barbara Mackey: Stokes and Fremont-Smith describe Mackey's assistance to Kosinski in the preparation of The Devil Tree and parts of Cockpit by quoting her own explanations: " 'The ideas were all his—I think he is a brilliant thinker, central in the world and in American culture—but the words were often mine. The term "collaborator" isn't right. I shouldn't say that, anyway—it was more organizational. A collaborator would have a roughly equal input, but the intellectual notions are all his. If I had been a collaborator,' she added wryly, 'the book would have been very different—especially about women.' " Stokes and Fremont-Smith claim that Mackey reiterated that her "handwritten copy was typed up over night so that we could work on it again." All the ideas were Kosinski's, Mackey allegedly said, "all I did was put it into English."[24]

The quotes are obviously quite damaging, especially the remark about putting his ideas into English. But Mackey, in a lengthy letter to the *Village Voice*, denied the accuracy of these quotations, claiming instead that Stokes and Fremont-Smith "thoroughly misrepresented me, Jerzy Kosinski, and Mr. Kosinski's novels." Stating that she had taped her conversation with Stokes and Fremont-Smith when they telephoned her, Mackey says, "the fact that a tape exists is important only because it proves several times over that Mr. Stokes did not mishear me, did not misunderstand me, did not misinterpret my words and although he quotes me correctly as saying that 'the term collaborator isn't right,' he also attributes to me statements that are his own boiled-down, very free contractions of my comments on the editorial process, comments that were very different when explained, as I explained them, at length." Mackey goes on to cite specific quotations of her words in the *Village Voice* essay that she did not in fact say. "The resulting 'quotes' give a skewed vision of my role in that process. Stokes has me saying, for instance, that I 'crystallized Kosinski's ideas in a paragraph, a page, a chapter,' that 'the words were often mine,' that I 'put it into English.' Not only did I not say these things; they don't even sound like things I might have said, had I been interested in avoiding the truth." What she did say, Mackey asserts, is that the language she worked on was Kosinski's. "At another point I reminded Stokes that Kosinski's choice of words is very carefully considered, that Kosinski is 'precisely attuned to the English language. He has definite ideas of exactly what words he wants. I was simply editing . . . his language, his voice or the voice of his narrators.' At another point I said, 'I consider this editing, very clearly editing, because I was always working . . . with his language.' Finally, I said, 'it was not as though I was ever coming up with either his ideas or his language.' "[25] The rest of Mackey's letter disputes a matter of returned phone calls to Stokes.

Richard Hayes: Of the three assistants that Stokes and Fremont-

Smith cited, only the third, Richard Hayes, not only did not deny the accuracy of the *Village Voice* account, he amplified a bit his role in the composition of *Passion Play*. First, the account by Stokes and Fremont-Smith: Hayes "invariably worked from lengthy sheets of typing—'triple spaced and with wide margins, so there was room for my work.' Though he is emphatic that his work was *not* mere proof-reading, he too rejects the 'collaborator' title. 'I would say instead that I combed, fileted, elevated or amplified his language—that I invested it with a certain Latinate style which was sometimes more Hayes than Kosinski.' " When asked by Stokes the state of *Passion Play* if Hayes had *not* worked on it, Hayes replied, "That's really impossible to say, the initial manuscripts were so raw they could have led in many directions. All one can say for certain is that it would have been very, very different."[26] In a statement to John Mutter of *Publishers Weekly*, Kosinski downplayed the work done by Hayes, saying that Hayes did not work "in any systematic capacity" on *Passion Play*. Hayes told Mutter, however, that "my account [in the *Village Voice*] was absolutely scrupulous. I have done proof-reading, but it was not proofreading I did in this instance. I worked seven months from 9:30 to 4:30, six or seven days a week. I think that's systematic."[27] In a later interview with Dave Smith, Kosinski does not dispute the time Hayes worked for him, but asked Smith this question: If Hayes's contribution to *Passion Play* was as "exceedingly visible," as he told Stokes and Fremont-Smith, how could it also be "impossible to convey?" Kosinski also suggested to Mutter in *Publishers Weekly* to examine the style of *Passion Play* which, Kosinski claims, has "the same voices, the same tone, as any other book of mine. Read *The Painted Bird* and *Passion Play*. They're very much alike in tone because they're both about nature."[28] Although such a comparison would be inconclusive (one might con-cede similarities of style but claim that this resemblance is merely the result of Kosinski's final choices over words originally suggested by his assistants), the two books have, in fact, passages which resemble each other in tone and diction. Here is a passage from *The Painted Bird*:

In these dreams my artful hands induced wild passions in the village girls, turning them into wanton Ludmilas who chased me through flowery glades, lying with me on beds of wild thyme, among fields of goldenrod.

I clung to Ewka in my dreams, seizing her like a spider, entwining as many legs around her as a centipede has. I grew into her body like a small twig, grafted on a broad-limbed apple tree by a skillful gardener. . . . One part of my body grew rapidly into a monstrous shaft of incredible size, while the rest remained unchanged. I became a hideous freak; I was locked in a cage and people watched me through bars, laughing excitedly. (147)

This next passage comes from *Passion Play*:

He dreamed that although she seemed to be sprawled on the dirt floor next to him, her blouse open, boots discarded, her riding breeches pulled down, she was really behind a glass partition, lying next to another man; Fabian, from his exile in this hut was linked to her by thought only, his longing as translucent as the spill of a jungle cataract. . . . What he remembered at the last was a multitude of heads, nests and hives of faces he did not know, hovering over him, over Elena, intent on the two of them at love, as if witnessing the combat of insects locked in deadly embrace on the mud floor of the hut. (103)

Another possible point of comparison is a passage from *Passion Play* and a short essay entitled "Time to Spare" that Kosinski published in the *New York Times* in May 1979, a few months before the publication of *Passion Play*. Individual words, phrases, even whole sentences from the essay are duplicated in *Passion Play*. Again, the results are inconclusive: one could argue that Kosinski merely reworked a section from the as-yet unpublished manuscript of *Passion Play*, using sentences that Hayes already had "combed," "fileted," and made "Latinate." Here, at any event, are the two passages:

Once inside, I ask for the doctor in charge, the chief nurse, or the guard on duty. I introduce myself as a man in transit, still healthy, a sportsman even, but first and foremost a writer—a novelist, a teller of stories, stories about men and women, children and adults, tales I would read gladly or recount to the one who, at such a late hour, is lonely, or abandoned or ignored—anyone who cannot sleep and might care to listen.

From the pocket of my raincoat I take out the hard-cover jacket of my most recent book, the photograph of my face on its inside flap, the only meaningful passport I carry.[29]

Here is the corresponding passage from *Passion Play*:

Once inside such a place he would ask for the doctor in residence, a nurse in charge or a guard on duty. He would introduce himself as a man in transit, a horseman to be sure, but a writer too, a teller of tales, stories about people who ride horses, stories it would please him to give pleasure with, gladly tell to one who, at such a late hour, was lonely, could not sleep and was willing to listen. (269)

One explanation for the similarity of style between the essay and *Passion Play* might be that this is the way the person who wrote both actually writes. Still, by initially dismissing Hayes's seven-month efforts on *Passion Play* as not "systematic," Kosinski undermines somewhat his later claim that Hayes could not have contributed as much as he said he did because the voice of *Passion Play* is the same as that of *The Painted Bird*. The Corry essay is even less helpful on this point, choosing to discuss Hackett's contribution as if Hayes's statements to Stokes were not damaging: "The three editors quoted in the *Village Voice* did not say they had collaborated with Mr. Kosinski in the actual writing of his novels; two, in fact, [Mackey and Hayes] expressly denied it."[30] It is true that Hayes declined to be termed a collaborator, but he also stated that Kosinski asked him to "poeticize this sex," that is, rewrite a particular scene. Hayes later claimed that "Kosinski does not have the command of the written English exhibited in his books."[31] Dave Smith's conjecture that Hayes's statements "don't appear to hold up" also seems inconclusive;[32] a better approach might be to look at what Kosinski himself has said about his English over the years.

For a writer who enjoys a reputation as a person full of secrets—Barbara Gelb's widely read essay in the *New York Times Magazine* notes his penchant for hiding places and false identity cards—

Kosinski has from his earliest interviews been surprisingly candid about both the command of his adopted tongue, English, and the resourcefulness he has shown to make sure the final version of his published work is to his satisfaction. In an interview with Dick Schapp in 1965, shortly after the publication of *The Painted Bird*, Kosinski stated, "English is easy to learn, but almost impossible to master." Schapp then describes some of the writing methods Kosinski employed to ensure a voice as close as possible to his ideal of mastery. "He would recite three versions of a paragraph into a tape recorder, then listen to the replay for the one that sounded best to his ear. When he wondered whether he was getting his meaning across, he would call a telephone operator, explain his predicament, read her a passage and ask if she understood it."[33] Kosinski would also, Schapp reported, pass around multiple copies of drafts to a variety of people, each of whom was asked to mark any passage that might reveal less than mastery. Kosinski would then collate their suggestions and begin a new draft, eventually, Schapp says, "completely redoing even the first set of galleys." Kosinski made similar comments to George Plimpton in 1972 about the nature of the assistance he seeks in the revision process and the difficulty of English. Again, given the opportunity to downplay either editorial assistance or the continuing battle to master English, Kosinski did the opposite. Here is his reply to Plimpton's question about how long it took for Kosinski to learn English: "I am still learning. I think I will always be learning. My attitude towards the language is like my attitude towards a woman I love; she might leave me at any time. In other words, I shouldn't leave her alone for too long. When I travel abroad for a long period of time I get very insecure because I feel that I am forgetting English." Alluding to the many drafts of his manuscripts, Plimpton asked this of Kosinski: "Did you want to be sure that each word had exactly the power and meaning you intended, or was it a more general stylistic thing you were looking for?" Kosinski again stressed the tentative nature of his mastery of English. "In addition to the advantages I mentioned before, there are, of course, disadvantages to writing in an adopted language. The main one for me is that I am never certain whether my English prose is sufficiently clear. Also, I rarely allow myself to use English in a truly spontaneous way and therefore, I always have a sense of trembling—but so does a compass, after all."[34] In an earlier interview with Jerome Klinkowitz given in 1971, some thirteen years after entering the United States, Kosinski continued to stress the endless task of mastering English. "In terms of writing," Kosinski said of the time when he gained facility with English, "I would think about nine months after I arrived, but this has been a never-ending process. In terms of speaking, about a year and a half later, but I am still working at it. No prison is as impregnable as that of language."[35] He also elaborated on the kind of help he used for his Novak books, referring again to the technique he had mentioned to Dick Schapp in 1965 of dialing New York telephone operators late at night and asking them if particular passages sounded right. "This was the initial stage of my writing of the book. I looked for an ideal reader. I dialed 'O.' " But these clarifications, Kosinski pointed out, were not on the order of style. For style, he often relied on notes from his father sent from Poland: "I had access to all the grammars I wanted and to see all the dictionaries I needed, and I had maintained a very elaborate correspondence with my father which runs into almost 2,000 sheets, three letters a week, dealing only with the English usage. My father was a philologist—he knew English quite well."[36] Here, at least, Kosinski does not discuss his use of multiple readers of his drafts, nor does he mention Mary Haywood Weir's earlier "knowledgeable criticism in the preparation" of *The Future is Ours, Comrade.* Perhaps at this point in his career he could afford to hire professional readers. As recently as 1981 Kosinski described his experience with editors to Richard Rosen in *Horizon:* "Writing novels is the only thing in which I'm entirely responsible for what I do. It's entirely mine. This doesn't exclude the possibility of someone—like Les Pockell [his editor at St. Martin's Press for the revised edition of *The Devil Tree*]—making changes, if it's done in a very democratic fashion." As far as out-of-house copy editors, Kosinski said to Rosen, "Now, if the proofreader—whom, by the way, I hire myself because no one can afford to check these things carefully these days, they don't have time—says that 'Page 347 doesn't make much sense to me,' then I would take a good look at the page. But I think that writers are very vulnerable and to have a very powerful editor during the time of creation can sway negatively as well as positively."[37] The point of looking at all these comments by Kosinski, some made as far back as 1965, is to show that for the first ten years of his career as a writer he was willing to describe himself as "still learning" the language of his art, and that he frequently asked for advice from others on the clarity of his sentences. The transition from speaking to strangers on a telephone to handing around manuscripts to friends in the publishing world to hiring his own editors[38] may reflect more the rising personal fortunes of Kosinski than a machination to "cheat the reader," as Stokes and Fremont-Smith phrase it.

Since the publication of the *Voice* article and Hayes's later amplification of his opinion of Kosinski's mastery of English, Kosinski has emphasized more the relative facility with which he learned English rather than the inherent difficulty he described to Klinkowitz and Plimpton. He explained to Dave Smith, for instance, "What I had told someone years ago was that I arrived with a rudimentary knowledge of 'colloquial American idiom' and that got misreported as a 'rudimentary knowledge of English.' In fact, I had already studied English for seven years in Poland, got straight A's and was quite conversant with the language of the American sociological journals I studied. All I said was that my colloquial American idiom was not so good, but within three or four months I felt comfortable with that, too."[39] Although we will have to concede that a writer is as free to change his metaphors as he is to choose them, we are a long way from phrases like the "prison" of language and English as a woman to be loved.

Five years after the *Village Voice* article, critical interest in Kosinski has shifted from the nature of the assistance he has asked for in the past to the value of what he has written.

Notes

Introduction

1. Kosinski, referring to allegations made by the *Village Voice* about his writing, said, "They can make up a charge, and use it any way they want to. It's as if I'm out on bail. It's the old fear, the fear of a 6-year-old. The villagers are still after the little boy—the painted bird" (John Corry, "A Case History: Seventeen Years of Ideological Attack," *New York Times*, November 7, 1982, sec. 2, 29).

2. Jerzy Kosinski, *The Painted Bird* (Boston: Houghton Mifflin, 1965; revised, 1976); *Steps* (New York: Random House, 1968); *Being There* (New York: Harcourt Brace Jovanovich, 1971); *The Devil Tree* (New York: Harcourt Brace Jovanovich, 1973; revised, New York: St. Martin's Press, 1981); *Cockpit* (Boston: Houghton Mifflin, 1975), 9, 102; *Blind Date* (Boston: Houghton Mifflin, 1977), 230; *Passion Play* (New York: St. Martin's Press, 1979); *Pinball* (New York: Bantam Books, 1982). Subsequent page references are to these editions and appear in the text in parentheses.

3. George Plimpton and Rocco Landesman, "Jerzy Kosinski: The Art of Fiction," *Paris Review* 54 (Summer 1972): 189.

4. Plimpton, 192.

5. Jerome Klinkowitz, "Jerzy Kosinski: An Interview," in *The New Fiction: Interviews with Innovative American Writers*, ed. Joe David Bellamy (Urbana: University of Illinois Press, 1974), 165. This interview took place in 1971 and was originally published in *Fiction International* (Fall 1973). It should be noted that some of the statements made by Kosinski about his biography were later questioned by Klinkowitz in an essay, "Betrayed by Jerzy Kosinski," *The Missouri Review* 6, no. 3 (Summer 1983): 157–75. A few "betrayals" seem minor: Kosinski told Klinkowitz he would not permit his books to be filmed; later, *Being There* was filmed. Kosinski told Klinkowitz that Chance would be played by an unknown actor; Peter Sellers ended up playing the part. Others seem more serious: Kosinski's account of the Polish bureaucrats he invented appears in the 1971 interview and then in a fictional

version in *Cockpit* a few years later. Klinkowitz suggests that the deception might not have taken place. "More pointedly, several critics not at all hostile to his work assured me that Kosinski's tale of forged documents and surreptitious flights sounded like a needless fabrication. 'He left late in 1957,' they said. 'That was during a six-month thaw in relations with the West: you can look up the announce- ments from the Party Congresses here and in Moscow. Visas were very easy to get; going West was encouraged' " (Klinkowitz, "Betrayed," 168). But in order for this assumption to prove that Kosinski did *not* use deception to leave Poland, it is necessary to believe that visas were easy to get for every Pole who wished to go to the West, from those whose dossiers held political liabilities to those completely trusted by the authorities. In short, the issue is unverifiable. We have no way of knowing how Kosinski was perceived by his superiors. My own position is that however Kosinski left, he had no intention of returning in spite of leaving behind his parents, and he has consistently regarded the system as repressive. If the bars of the cage widened briefly in 1957 for Kosinski to step through, he surely narrowed them against any safe return by later publishing books in the West highly critical of the socialist system. His sense of himself as one who has escaped seems to me valid.

6. Kosinski's fascination with "fairy tales, märchen, fables, bestiaries, and allied folk-rooted forms" links him—argues Jack Hicks—with writers such as John Barth, Thomas Pynchon, Donald Barthelme, and Robert Coover (Jack Hicks, *In the Sing- er's Temple: Prose Fictions of Barthelme, Gaines, Brautigan, Pierce, Kesey, and Kosinski* [Chapel Hill: University of North Carolina Press, 1981], 198). Joe David Bellamy's 1974 collection of interviews with "innovative" fiction writers placed Kosinski in the company of Donald Barthelme, William H. Gass, and Ronald Sukenick (Joe David Bellamy, *The New Fiction: Interviews with Innovative American Writers* [Urbana: University of Illinois Press, 1974]). In 1975 Jerome Klinkowitz saw Kosinski as a "fictionist of the new disruptive school," along with writers like Kurt Vonnegut, Jr., and Donald Barthelme (Klinkowitz, *Literary Disruptions: The Making of a Post-Contemporary American Fiction* [Urbana: University of Illinois Press, 1975], ix).

7. Klinkowitz, "Jerzy Kosinski," 150. Kosinski was apparently still dialing telephone operators in 1971. "I would dial the telephone operator . . . I did it hundreds of times—I still do it" (Charles Moritz, ed., *Current Biography Yearbook: 1974*, [New York: H. W. Wilson Company, 1974], 213).

8. Klinkowitz, "Jerzy Kosinski," 153.

9. Gail Sheehy, "The Psychological Novelist as Portable Man," *Psychology Today* 11 (December 1977): 56.

10. Jerzy Kosinski, *Tijd van leven—tijd van kunst*, (Amsterdam: Uitgeverij de Bezige Bij, 1970), translated by Jerome Klinkowitz, 11.

11. Klinkowitz, "Jerzy Kosinski," 154.

12. Klinkowitz, "Jerzy Kosinski," 156. See also Frederick R. Karl's discussion of Kosinski's minimalism in Karl, *American Fictions 1940/1980: A Comprehensive History and Critical Evaluation* (New York: Harper and Row, 1983), 407.

13. Daniel J. Cahill, "Jerzy Kosinski: A Play on Passion," *Chicago Review* 32 (1980): 132.

14. Kosinski, [Joseph Novak, pseud.], *The Future Is Ours, Comrade* (Garden City: Doubleday and Company, 1960). Subsequent page references to this edition appear in the text in parentheses. The state of Kosinski's English at the time of his arrival became a matter of dispute after the publication of Geoffrey Stokes and Eliot Fremont-Smith, "Jerzy Kosinski's Tainted Words," *Village Voice,* June 22, 1982, 1, 41–42. Kosinski's most recent statements stress his preparation for and relatively rapid familiarity with English around this time. See Dave Smith, "Kosinski Whodunit: Who Ghost There If Not Jerzy?" *Los Angeles Times,* August 1, 1982, Calendar section, 3–5. See also appendix, 158–71.

15. Kosinski described this anecdote about truck driving to Daniel Cahill: he was a long-distance driver "transporting hats—an object I have never worn" (Cahill, "Life at a Gallop," *Washington Post,* September 16, 1979, 10). Details about his life in Poland and early years in the United States appear in a number of publications, and there are some discrepancies, such as whether he "docked" or "landed" in New York. Cameron Northouse, "Jerzy Kosinski," in *Dictionary of Literary Biography,* edited by Jeffrey Helterman and Richard Layman (Detroit: Gale Research, 1978), 2: 266–75, seems the most reliable (although with one omission: Kosinski's 1966 divorce). Kosinski has circulated copies of his own typed corrections of—and disagreements with—Northouse, and I will indicate when I refer to this corrected version. For instance, Kosinski corrects Northouse's statement that he was born the "son of Russian parents" to "Polish-born, Russian educated." This 1979 correction presumably supersedes the statement in Cleveland Amory, "Trade Winds," *Saturday Review,* April 17, 1971, 16, in which Kosinski is said to have claimed of his father, "He was born in Russia," and which is repeated in Norman Lavers, *Jerzy Kosinski* (Boston: Twayne Publishers, 1981), 3. See also Sally Johns, "Jerzy Kosinski," in *Dictionary of Literary Biography Yearbook: 1982,* ed. Richard Ziegfeld (Detroit: Gail Research Company, 1983), 169–74. Seven months after his arrival in New York, Kosinski received a Ford Foundation grant for $2,000 per year, renewed during the years 1958 to 1961 for a total of $8,000 (Smith, 4–5). While attending Columbia University, Kosinski began translating his notes into English (Moritz, 213). See also Lavers, 16.

16. One obvious reason why Kosinski chose a pseudonym was to protect his parents, who were still living in Poland. Yet "Novak" also provided Kosinski with an attitude of detachment: he could see himself as a complex character, not merely a passive observer. As he later said about *The Painted Bird,* "The most essential stage of the writing process, it is often argued, is the process whereby the writer comes to stand outside the experience he intends to mirror in his book" (Kosinski, *Notes of the Author on The Painted Bird* [New York: Scientia-Factum, 1965, 1966, 1967], 9).

17. Norman Lavers, commenting on Kosinski's "novelistic methods" in *The Future Is Ours, Comrade,* suggests that a person "sympathetic to the Soviet regime might conceivably have taken the same raw material and selected and arranged it in such a way as to give an impression quite different from Kosinski's" (Lavers, 18). But it is difficult to imagine how this scene—and so many like it—could be "arranged" to produce an impression complimentary to the Soviet Union.

18. Kosinski's observations on bribery, denunciation, and the pressure of collective living appear as current as those made by Alexander Zinoviev, the Soviet exile and dissident, in 1984. "He (the average Soviet student) will take small and cunning steps within the system. He will act in such a way as to convince his superiors that he is the right man to be given promotion. And how will he do that? He will do it by offering 'presents' or straightforward bribes to the right people, and even by writing denunciations. . . . Let me say that denunciations are an accepted practice in Soviet society. They are a way of life and quite natural. In a tough struggle for survival, you help yourself as best you can" (George Urban, "An Interview with Alexander Zinoviev," *Encounter* [May 1984], 30–39).

19. Emanuel Litvinoff confirmed Novak's accuracy with respect to Soviet anti-Semitism. "I am particularly convinced of his accuracy because, in his chapter on the vexed problem of Soviet Jews, I am able to corroborate all he says from direct experience and specialized knowledge" (Litvinoff, *Guardian*, October 21, 1960, 8). W. H. Chamberlin said, "Novak's story is well worth reading and pondering" (Chamberlin, "Life in Russia: What It's Like," *Chicago Sunday Tribune*, May 29, 1960, 2). J. G. Harrison, who was to write the introduction to *No Third Path* two years later, urged that the book be read "thoughtfully and carefully" (Harrison, "Conversations with the Russians," *Christian Science Monitor*, May 25, 1960, 13). R. C. Hottelet touched on Novak's technique of setting a scene and leaving the conclusion to the reader. "It is an interesting personal document, grimly fascinating and important not so much for the author's conclusions as for the testimony which permits the reader to draw his own" (Hottelet, "From Collective to Kremlin, It's One Big State of Nerves," *New York Times Book Review*, May 22, 1960, 3). Only Joseph Ruef expressed skepticism about the authenticity of the conversations: "These conversations are very lively, but at times this reviewer questioned (perhaps unjustly) their authenticity" (Ruef, *Library Journal* 85 [April 15, 1960]: 1585).

20. Kosinski [Joseph Novak, pseud.], *No Third Path* (Garden City: Doubleday and Company, 1962). Subsequent page references are to this edition and appear in the text in parentheses. Kosinski dedicated the book to "Mary Haywood Weir, who has combined warm encouragement with knowledgeable criticism in the preparation of this book."

21. Lavers, 17.

22. Already in *No Third Path* large sections were composed of comments on events described in Russian publications available to readers in the United States in the form of *The Current Digest of the Soviet Press* and others like it. Much of the material for the chapters "The Sleepless Enemies" and "Homo Sovieticus" is drawn from Soviet publications printed after 1960, three years after Kosinski left Poland. Novak's discussion of the severity with which the Soviet Union views foreign journalists who collect information from Russian citizens is illustrated by an article in *Izvestia* entitled "Miss Sally Found a Friend," published December 27, 1960. Novak refers to "the newspapers of 1960" for a series of anecdotes for his chapter, "Sleepless Enemies," among them *Izvestia* and *Pravda* (Kosinski, *No Third Path*, 143, 147, 171).

23. Klinkowitz, "Jerzy Kosinski," 168.

24. Kosinski, *Painted Bird*, xii.

25. R. E. Nowicki, "An Interview with Jerzy Kosinski," *San Francisco Review of Books*, March 1978, 12.

26. Kosinski, *The Art of the Self: Essays a Propos Steps* (New York: Scientia-Factum, 1968), 14.

27. See Hicks, *In The Singer's Temple*, 179, for a discussion of the influence of Hegel on Kosinski.

28. Jerome Klinkowitz is one of a number of individuals who has witnessed the evolution of a Kosinski anecdote from phone call to talk-show chatter to published fictional version. See Klinkowitz, "Betrayed," 167.

one   Meat in Cans

1. Reviews of Kosinski's first novel were enthusiastic, in spite of a few reservations about the violence of certain scenes. Elie Wiesel said of *The Painted Bird*, "Rendered with economy, skill and insight, this metamorphosis of the boy's mind and heart constitutes one of the terrifying elements of the narration." Wiesel thought that the narrator was a Christian: "And their victim was neither Jew nor gypsy, but a forlorn Christian child of good Christian parents" (Wiesel, "Everybody's Victim," *New York Times Book Review*, October 31, 1965, 5). Andrew Field said, "One's primary response to *The Painted Bird* can scarcely be literary, but it would be a great mistake to assume that the events of this book possess an intrinsic power of their own which requires no literary skill" (Field, "The Butcher's Helper," *Book Week*, October 17, 1965, 2). Anne Halley said, "The various episodes, no doubt based on experience, seem to embody and play on recognizable folk-tale motifs, always with that 'realistic' twist, or reversal, which shows that there is neither justice, nor reason, nor black or white magic to help one in extremity" (Halley, "Poor Boy Spreads his Wings," *Nation*, November 29, 1965, 424). Kosinski himself joined the group of commentators on *The Painted Bird* by publishing *Notes of the Author on The Painted Bird* (1965, 1966, 1967). The pamphlet is rich with suggestions, but one comment relates to my point about writing and power: "*The Painted Bird*, then, could be the author's vision of himself as a child, a *vision*, not an examination, or a revisitation of childhood. This vision, this search for something lost, can only be conducted in the metaphor through which the unconscious most naturally navigates. The locale and setting are likewise metaphorical, for the whole journey could actually have taken place in the mind" (Kosinski, *Notes of the Author*, 13). Here, the text in which a child searches for power is also a metaphor for the now-grown writer's search for the right language to articulate that text.

Kosinski discussed further *The Painted Bird* in his introduction to the 1976 edition. His remarks differ from *Notes of the Author* not only by its more autobiographical details (his account of his dying wife and the destruction of all but three of "some 60 members of my family") but by his insistence that the reader of *The Painted Bird* is a victim, analogous to those Jews forced to enter the concentration camps for the purpose of "learning" another language. As an illustration, Kosinski quotes from a letter composed by a Jewish camp victim written shortly before his ~new language~ death: "They tattoo the newcomers. Everyone gets his number. . . . Our brain has grown dull, the thoughts are numbered: it is not possible to grasp this new language." He then states why he began *The Painted Bird*: "My purpose in writing a novel was to examine 'this new language' of brutality and its consequent new counter-language of anguish and despair" (Kosinski, *The Painted Bird*, [1965], 1976, xii).

2. Kosinski emphasizes in another context the link between creativity and hatred. "For hate takes on a mystical aura; to possess hate is to possess great power, and the wielder of that power has control of magnificent gifts. Like Prospero he rules his kingdom, and justice is meted out according to his will. Things are as he sees them to be; if not, they soon submit to his vision of the world. He can shape his world as he wills: Prospero's wand becomes revenge" (Kosinski, *Notes of the Author*, 27).

3. Kosinski, in discussing the viewpoint of a child, refers to Jung's essay, *The Psychology of the Child Archetype* (Kosinski, *Notes of the Author*, 13). See also Professor Jack Hicks's analysis of the influence of both Jung and "fairy tales, märchen, fables, bestiaries, and allied folk-rooted forms" in *The Painted Bird* (Hicks, *In the Singer's Temple*, 198–218).

4. Stanley Kauffmann praised the "large achievement" of "this small book," claiming that "through all its smoke and fire and pain, a curious pride persists" (Kauffmann, "Out of the Fires," *New Republic*, October 26, 1968, 22). F. Y. Blumenfeld said, "These terse, ghoulish episodes will return to the memory at unexpected moments, stirring up uneasy images, disturbing the reader in the very depths of his own fantasies" (Blumenfeld, "Dark Dreams," *Newsweek*, October 21, 1968, 104). Hugh Kenner was taken with the style of *Steps*: "Low-keyed, efficient, controlled, the prose of *Steps* encompasses the banal, the picturesque, the monstrous, with never a flicker of surprise" (Kenner, "Keys on a Ring," *New York Times Book Review*, October 20, 1968, 5). Granville Hicks judged *Steps* "more frightening" than *The Painted Bird* because it suggests "the complete collapse of human values" (Hicks, "Sadism and Light Hearts," *Saturday Review*, October 19, 1968, 29).

5. Kosinski describes the vignettes as "episodes" and suggests that the relationship between them can be inferred by the reader with considerable leeway, as if the reader were cocreator of the fiction. "The reader may perceive the work in a form of his own devising, automatically filling in its intentionally loose construction with his own formulated experiences and fantasies" (Kosinski, *The Art of the Self*, 13).

6. Kosinski's intention in using nonfigurative language, he claims, is not only to avoid specific identification with a time or place but to increase "the moral ambiguity of the work" (Kosinski, *The Art of the Self*, 18).

7. There is some ambiguity about the number and nature of the italicized sections of *Steps*. Professor Jack Hicks counts fourteen, apparently by dividing the episode on pages 42–45 into two parts: 42–43 and 43–45 (Hicks, *In the Singer's Temple*, 231). Paul Bruss sees thirteen, viewing pages 42–45 as one continuous episode, a reading I prefer (Paul Bruss, *Victims: Textual Strategies in Recent American Fiction*

[Lewisburg: Bucknell University Press, 1981], 191). But both Bruss and Hicks include the italicized sentence on page 136 as a "conversation" like the other italicized sections. I would exclude this section ("*If I could become one of them, if I could only part with my language, my manner, my belongings*") because it does not imply the presence of the lover as do the others. Rather, this passage echoes the previous unitalicized section (132–35) in which the narrator wanders alone through the black "districts" of the city, reflecting: "If I could magically speak their language and change the shade of my skin . . . I would transform myself into one of them" (133).

8. For Kosinski's intention on a "sequel" to *The Painted Bird*, see David H. Richter, "The Three Denouements of Jerzy Kosinski's *The Painted Bird*," *Contemporary Literature* 15 (Summer 1974): 370–85. See also Jerome Klinkowitz's response to this essay in "Two Bibliographical Questions on Kosinski's *The Painted Bird*," *Contemporary Literature* 16 (Winter 1975): 126–28.

9. Kosinski is direct on this point. "From the viewpoint of the protagonist of *Steps* the only truly satisfying relationship, then, is one of growing domination, one in which his experience—a certain form of the past—can be projected onto the other person. Until this hold is gained (assuming that the 'prey' has some awareness of the protagonist's purpose), the 'prey' maintains some superiority over the protagonist and remains his rival" (Kosinski, *The Art of the Self*, 20).

10. Kosinski explains the narrator's surrender to mutism as a search for a more efficacious language: "The abandonment of linguistic expression signifies his desire to rely on the power of gesture; his destiny is thus *made* and not *expressed*. This secession from language performs a further function in *Steps*: it increases the moral ambiguity of the work in which the reality is always manipulated and seldom judged" (Kosinski, *The Art of the Self*, 19).

11. "Deliberately to choose as a victim an individual or a group with a definable past to eliminate spontaneity from murder, surpasses in its impersonality even ritual killing, since it is devoid of emotion. Rational murder is the ultimate anti-theatre" (Kosinski, *The Art of the Self*, 26).

12. To this nest of cages Kosinski would add still another—the cage of the woman's mind: "The woman's madness is also a cage, as is her being set aside by the village, her relegation to a secret place" (Kosinski, *The Art of the Self*, 33).

13. Literature as a "threat" has been proposed by Kosinski on a number of occasions. See Klinkowitz, "Jerzy Kosinski," 149. See also Plimpton and Landesman, 205: "Literature does not have this ability to soothe. You have to evoke and by evoking, you yourself have to provide your own inner setting."

two   Blank Pages

1. Barbara Jane Tepa, "Jerzy Kosinski's Polish Contexts: A Study of *Being There*," *The Polish Review* 22, no. 2 (1977): 52–61. Professor Tepa is the translator of the passage from *The Career of Nikodem Dyzma*. She suggests that *Being There* also alludes to other possible writers who supply for Kosinski "his Polish contexts,"

among them Joseph Wittlin's *The Salt of the Earth*. But her essay deals primarily with parallels between *Being There* and *The Career of Nikodem Dyzma*.

2. Kosinski's working title for the manuscript of *Being There* was "Blank Page" (Plimpton and Landesman, 2).

3. Kosinski's comments on the negative effects of television are well known. See Frank Frymer, "Novelist Kosinski Is Afraid Television Is 'Castrating Our Children,' " *Newsday*, July 1, 1971, 14–17. See also Plimpton and Landesman, 204.

4. The reviews of *The Devil Tree* range from puzzlement to outright scorn. Peter Dollard said, "The characterization is bad, the narrative boring and many parts are simply sophomoric: for example, a wealthy lady's wickedness is revealed by her admission that she had never heard of the Bowery. All in all, the book reads more like a bad first novel than the work of a mature writer" (Dollard, *Library Journal*, December 15, 1972), 4003. Robert Alter said in the *New York Times Book Review*, "From beginning to end this is a loose web of stylistic and cultural cliches. Kosinski's prose, with its series of short sentences occasionally embellished by an elaborate simile, runs readily to the characteristic vice of 'simple' styles, which is to fall into the hackneyed formulas of mass journalism and pulp fiction." (Alter, "Pulp-fiction Style, Pop-psychology Jargon, and a Genuinely Sadistic Imagination," *New York Times Book Review*, February 11, 1973, 2). James Finn remarked, "At intervals in this short novel there are brief reminders of the Kosinski of his sometimes striking first two novels—a certain power of evocation—of mystery, of starkness, of cruelty, of void; but these fragments appear fleetingly in the book's vacuum only to disappear without a trace; flicker and go out" (Finn, "In Brief," *New Republic*, March 10, 1973, 34). Compare these remarks with the generally approving tone of the reviews of *Being There*, such as Arthur Curley: "He rivals Borges in economy, precision, and deceptive simplicity. And he writes with the cool assurance of one who possesses some deep secret knowledge about all of us" (Curley, "By One Who Possesses Some Deep Secret Knowledge," *Library Journal*, April 1, 1971, 1239); and John Aldridge: "For *Being There* exists simultaneously on the levels of fiction and fact, fantasy and contemporary history. It is a novel ingeniously conceived and endowed with some of the magical significance of myth" (Aldridge, "The Fabrication of A Culture Hero," *Saturday Review* 54 [April 24, 1971]): 25.

5. Daniel Cahill, "*The Devil Tree*: An Interview with Jerzy Kosinski," *North American Review* 258 (Spring 1973): 57.

three   The Wheelgame of Words

1. In reliving Tarden's life, following the "trace" word by word, the reader becomes the victim of Tarden's book. This relationship between victim and oppressor is like the one described by Kosinski as operating in *Steps*: "In the fissure separating these possibilities the struggle between the book (the predator) and the reader (the victim), *the agon*, takes place" (Kosinski, *Art of the Self*, 14).

2. For a discussion of Kosinski and the picaresque, see Lavers, 33–36.

3. Klinkowitz, "Jerzy Kosinski," 149.

4. Duncan's career in fact parallels Kosinski's at the time of the writing of *Cockpit*. Both Duncan and Kosinski had written four novels; each had experienced a decline in sales after an initial success, and each deliberately invites his readers to entertain connections between his unusual and sometimes danger-ridden life-style and the disquieting revelations narrated in the fictions.

5. This episode seems an expanded version of the narrator's encounter with the woman watching the octopus in *Steps* (22–23). A comparison between the two versions reveals the extent to which Kosinski moved from the stark and understated style of *Steps* to *Cockpit*'s richer vocabulary, more conventional dialogue, and increasing willingness to name actual places such as Combray and Paris rather than, as in *Steps*, the "capital of the neighboring country" (23).

6. Kosinski's quotation from Proust in his *Notes of the Author* summarizes the desperate nature of Tarden's search for reality: "Marcel Proust stated this very clearly: 'The grandeur of real art . . . is to rediscover, grasp again and lay before us that reality from which we live so far removed and from which we become more and more separated as the formal knowledge which we substitute for it grows in sickness and imperviousness—that reality which there is grave danger we might die without ever having known and yet which is simply our life' " (10).

7. Kosinski, *The Painted Bird*, 1976, xi.

8. Cahill, "An Interview with Jerzy Kosinski on *Blind Date*," *Contemporary Literature* 19 (Spring 1978): 133.

9. Kosinski develops this point further in his interview. "Tarden perceives and lives his life as if it were a cumulative process. . . . To Levanter, life is composed of moments, each one commencing with one's awareness of its beginning. . . . In *Cockpit*, it is Tarden's language, his narration that is the sole dramatic agent that recasts what the protagonist claims has been his life's experiences. In *Blind Date*, objectively narrated events of Levanter's life provide the novel's outward expression" (Cahill, "An Interview with Jerzy Kosinski," 134).

10. Hicks, *In the Singer's Temple*, 258.

11. One critic, Norman Lavers, argues that Pauline is really Nameless grown up. Two objections to this interpretation rise up at once: In order for Pauline to become the kind of pianist who gives solo performances in Carnegie Hall, she would have had to be an accomplished pianist at sixteen, when Levanter dates her a year after the rape. The narration describes her only as a student. Second, it is unlikely that Nameless would not recognize Levanter twenty years or so after she had recognized him as her rapist. Lavers, 134.

four   The Sacred Flame Flickers

1.   Jerome Klinkowitz faults the novel for its "unconscionably sexist" tone and "anti-democratic fascination with the very rich" (Klinkowitz, "The Aging Kosinski

Knight, Questing on the Polo Field," *Chicago Sun-Times*, Sunday, September 2, 1979, 9). Stefan Kanfer argues that the "centerfold prose disfigures the novel and makes a few paragraphs indistinguishable from Harald Robbins at the gallop"; still, he offers praise for Kosinski's descriptions of polo playing (Kanfer, "When Going Is the Goal," *Time* 114 [September 17, 1979]: 105). John Leonard calls the book "lugubrious fiction" in which "a kind of rationalism is suggested that metastasizes into fascism" (Leonard, "Books of the Times," *New York Times*, September 13, 1979, C21). Ivan Gold praises Kosinski's "virtuoso writing about sex and horsemanship," but the book is hurt by a "leaden, arbitrary tone" (Gold, "Picaresque Sport," *New York Times Book Review*, September 30, 1979, 9). Grove Koger says that "every writer is entitled to a mistake now and then, but *Passion Play* is more on the order of a disaster; . . . some good sequences on horsemanship merely accentuate the sad poverty of the surrounding material" (Koger, *Library Journal* 104 [September 1, 1979]: 1719). William Kennedy notes Kosinski's new direction ("much plottier than usual") as ultimately promising: "What seems new is Kosinski's interest in unmanipulative life, life in which the protagonist is neither victim nor hero but a spiritual substance subject to forces that can neither be challenged directly nor can be more than barely understood" (Kennedy, "Kosinski's Hero Rides On," *Washington Post, Book World*, September 16, 1979, 1, 11). Daniel J. Cahill cites Kosinski's willingness to rewrite numerous times in order to achieve his "art of imaginative extraction" (Cahill, "Life at a Gallop," 10).

2. Cahill takes a more optimistic view of the close parallel between Kosinski and Fabian. "Fabian is the alter ego of Kosinski and *Passion Play* is—of all his novels—the most personal and most intimate, because submerged in its narrative is an essentially new awareness on the part of the author of his own destiny" (Cahill, "Jerzy Kosinski," 134).

3. Kosinski, "Packaged Passion," *American Scholar* 42 (Spring 1973): 193–204. See also David Sohn's interview with Kosinski, "A Nation of Videots," *Media and Methods* 11 (April 1975): 24.

4. The passages describing Fabian telling tales to hospital patients closely resembles Kosinski's brief essay, "Time to Spare," *New York Times*, May 21, 1979, A19.

5. *Pinball* suffered even more at the hands of the critics. Christopher Lehmann-Haupt suggests that Kosinski's "long affair with the English language is not going well," and that, "lacking a sense of the language, and thus lacking any style of his own, the author gropes for any passable cliche. It is just what happens in bad pornography" (Lehmann-Haupt, "Books of the Times," *New York Times*, February 25, 1982, C20). Benjamin Demott concedes that some of *Pinball*'s "music talk" is "well informed and earnest," but the book is a "descent into self-indulgent laxness" and "sadly unrewarding" (Demott, "Grand Guignal with Music," *New York Times Book Review*, March 7, 1982, 8). Joshua Gilder dismisses *Pinball* as "nothing more than a pornographic thriller" (Gilder, "Pinball" *Saturday Review*, March 1982, 63). Stefan Kanfer is the most sympathetic, arguing that Kosinski in *Pinball* "deftly lampoons contemporary lyrics, his scenes of the South Bronx seem torn from a Bosch triptych, and his discussions of classical music are informed"; still, "What a

waste!" is all he can imagine that admirers of Kosinski could say of *Pinball* (Kanfer, "Trebles," *Time* 119 [March 22, 1982]: 85).

6.   Leo Tolstoy, *The Complete Works of Count Tolstoy*, vol. 18, (London: J. M. Dent and Sons, Ltd., 1908; reprint, 1968), 390.

7.   An earlier version of this sentence appears in an interview by Daniel J. Cahill: "Writing is the essence of my life—whatever else I do revolves around a constant thought: could I—can I—would I—should I—use it in my next novel?" (Cahill, "Life at a Gallop," 10).

8.   Klinkowitz describes *Blind Date* as an "auto-bibliography, a book telling the story of its own imaginative ancestry and birth," a phrase that would work as well for *Pinball* (Klinkowitz, "Jerzy Kosinski: Puppetmaster," *Chicago Daily News*, October 22, 1977, 22).

9.   Chuck Ross, "Rejected," *New West* 4 (February 12, 1979): 39–42. See also "Polish Joke," *Time* 113 (February 19, 1979): 94, 96.

10.   Barbara Gelb, "Being Jerzy Kosinski," *New York Times Magazine*, February 21, 1982, 52.

11.   See Michiko Kakutani, "The Strange Case of the Writer and the Criminal," *New York Times Book Review*, September 20, 1981, 1.

Conclusion

1.   Kosinski, "A Passion for Polo," *Polo: Official Publication of the United States Polo Association*, May 1985, 118.

2.   Kosinski, "Passion for Polo," 115, 116, 118.

3.   Kosinski, "Exegetics," *Paris Review* 97 (Fall 1985): 94, 95.

4.   Kosinski, "Death in Cannes," *Esquire*, March 1986, 82.

5.   Kosinski, "Death in Cannes," 84, 86, 89.

6.   R. Langen, "Jerzy Kosinski," *Canadian Review*, Fall/Winter 1982, 21.

7.   Langen, 23.

8.   Kosinski, *Notes of the Author*, 27.

9.   Hicks, *In the Singer's Temple*, 199.

10.   Langen, 24.

11.   Karl, (see Introduction, Note 14), 506.

12.   Irving Howe, "From the Other Side of the Moon," *Harper's* 238 (March 1969): 105.

Appendix

1.   The origins of the article are as controversial as its contents. Elizabeth Pochada, former literary editor of the *Nation*, claimed that she was interested in Kosinski as symptomatic of the power of celebrityhood. "That's what got me started. Why do we protect our celebrities? Everybody talked about Kosinski's

writing methods. Why were they never written about?" (Jan Herman, "She May Be a Kidder, But She's Not Crazy," Chicago *Sun-Times*, July 11, 1982, 2, 3). She asked Geoffrey Stokes to do an investigative piece on Kosinski for the *Nation*, but he thought his own paper, the *Village Voice*, might want to do it. Meanwhile, Fremont-Smith called Pochada and she told him of Stokes's prior conversation. Eventually, Stokes and Fremont-Smith decided to team up for the essay. In assessing her motives, Pochada stated that "in our cultural life in general we've been unable to tell the real from the fake," using as an example the incident of Chuck Ross's submission of a freshly typed and retitled manuscript of Kosinski's *Steps*: "Do you remember the story of the kid who typed up *Steps* and sent it around to editors after it was published to show that editors didn't know anything? They all rejected the manuscript, but that wasn't the real story." (Pochada overlooks the fact that eleven years had elapsed between the publication of *Steps* and Ross's prank.) That there is no love for Kosinski at either the *Nation* or the *Village Voice* goes without saying. John Corry pointed out the sequence of some of these events: The American Writer's Congress, sponsored by the *Nation*, was criticized by Kosinski for its political nature: the *Village Voice* attacked the Committee for a Free World, of which Kosinski was a member, in an article published June 8, 1982, two weeks before the Stokes-Fremont-Smith essay (Corry, "Case History," 1, 28, 29). Still, because the editors of the *Nation* and the *Village Voice* had previously expressed distaste for Kosinski's political views does not mean that the accusations in the article by Stokes and Fremont-Smith are necessarily without substance, as Corry's response seems to suggest. "Is it not possible," asks the *New Republic*, "that an enemy of totalitarianism does not write all of his books?" ("Notebook," *New Republic*, November 29, 1982, 9).

    2. Among the letters was one by Austin Olney, editor in chief, Houghton Mifflin Company: "I have been sometimes overwhelmed by his flamboyant conceits and his artful social manipulations, but I never had any reason to believe that he has ever needed or used any but the most routine editorial assistance" (Olney, Letter to the *Village Voice*, July 6, 1982, 3).

    3. See John Mutter, "Kosinski Denies *Village Voice* Charges of Extensive Help," *Publishers Weekly*, July 9, 1982, 11, 18. Richard Hayes confirmed the account by Stokes and Fremont-Smith of Hayes's contribution to *Passion Play*, saying that he worked for Kosinski "seven months from 9:30 to 4:30, six or seven days a week. I think that's systematic." See also Michele Slung, "The Wounding of Jerzy Kosinski," *Washington Post*, July 11, 1982, 15. Slung includes the comments of a number of Kosinski's editors all of whom defend his compositional practices. Joyce Hartmann, a former editor at Houghton Mifflin, said, "Whether or not they're good or bad, all of his books have the same exact voice." The two most detailed defenses of Kosinski before the publication of John Corry's essay in the *New York Times* are Smith, 3–5, and Jan Herman, "Did He or Didn't He: Village Voice Sees Ghosts and CIA Spooks—But Kosinski Says They're Imagining Things," *Chicago Sun-Times*, July 25, 1982, Show/Book/Week Section, 25.

    4. David Schneiderman acknowledges the error in Stokes's article about a passage in *The Painted Bird* but insists that the other charges are essentially true: "But

despite the efforts of Corry, Gelb, and Rosenthal to politicize the *Voice* story, it has nothing to do with politics. It was and still is about literary ethics" (Schneiderman, "Kosinski's Friends See Red," *Village Voice*, November 16, 1982, 3). Alexander Cockburn dismisses the Corry article as the result of "the paranoiac world view characteristic of Rosenthal and his henchman Gelb" (Cockburn, "Expect the Unexpected: Kosinski and the Times," *Village Voice*, November 16, 1982, 16). Andrew Kipkind dismissed the Corry essay as an "emotional diatribe against an elaborate ideological conspiracy determined to 'discredit' the life and art of an anti-Communist hero" (Kipkind, "Kosinski Redux," *Nation*, November 20, 1982, 516). See also Charles Kaiser, "Friends at the Top of the *Times*," *Newsweek*, November 22, 1982, 125–26; and Junette A. Pinkney, "*New York Times* Articles on Kosinski Questioned," *Washington Post*, November 15, 1982, C3. The *New Republic* suggested that "maybe the *Voice* owes Mr. Kosinski an apology. Clearly the Times owes the Voice one" ("Notebook," *New Republic*, 9).

5. Johns, "Jerzy Kosinski," 169–74.

6. Stokes and Fremont-Smith, (see Introduction, note 16), 41.

7. Stokes and Fremont-Smith, 41.

8. Stokes and Fremont-Smith, 41.

9. Herman, "Did He or Didn't He?" 24.

10. Stokes and Fremont-Smith, 41.

11. Herman, "Did He or Didn't He?" 24.

12. Stokes and Fremont-Smith, 43.

13. Smith, 4.

14. Schneiderman, 3.

15. Cockburn, 16.

16. Stokes and Fremont-Smith, 42.

17. Smith, 4.

18. Corry, 29.

19. Stokes and Fremont-Smith, 41.

20. Stokes and Fremont-Smith, 42.

21. Mutter, 11.

22. Corry insists that it was Kosinski who was taking drugs for an optic disorder and that he did not accuse his former assistant of using drugs. But Schneiderman retorts that Stokes did quote Kosinski correctly: "We offer the following from the tape of the interview. Kosinski said: 'John Hackett was articulate, nice, pleasant, but just couldn't sit steady. There were drugs, there was going back and forth, he was on the balcony, this and that.' At no time in the discussion did Kosinski 'point' to himself, and in any case gestures could not alter the unambiguous meaning of his words" (Schneiderman, 3).

23. Smith, 5.

24. Stokes and Fremont-Smith, 42.

25. Barbara Mackey, Letter to the Editor, *Village Voice*, August 10, 1982, 3.

26. Stokes and Fremont-Smith, 42.

27. Mutter, 11.

28. Mutter, 11.

29. Kosinski, "Time to Spare," A19.

30. Corry, 29.

31. Smith, 5.

32. Smith, 5.

33. Schapp, 6.

34. Plimpton and Landesman, 193, 196.

35. Klinkowitz, "Jerzy Kosinski: An Interview," 151.

36. Klinkowitz, "Jerzy Kosinski: An Interview," 151.

37. Richard Rosen, "Heirs to Maxwell Perkins," *Horizon* 24 (April 1981): 51.

38. On February 24, 1982, the Authors Guild held a symposium, "Authors, Editors, and Editing," at the New School for Social Research. The *Bulletin* that presented the transcript of the symposium states that because of "the revolving door policy" and quick turnover "of editors and at publishing houses" it has been recognized for years as a valid practice of the publishing industry to "have author's books edited and proofread or copy-edited by an outside copy-editor of the author's choice" (*Authors Guild Bulletin*, April-May 1982, 21).

39. Smith, 5.

Bibliography

I. Novels by Jerzy Kosinski

The Painted Bird. Boston: Houghton Mifflin, 1965. Revised with new introduction, 1976.

Steps. New York: Random House, 1968.

Being There. New York: Harcourt Brace Jovanovich, 1971.

The Devil Tree. New York: Harcourt Brace Jovanovich, 1973. Revised, 1981.

Cockpit. Boston: Houghton Mifflin, 1975.

Blind Date. Boston: Houghton Mifflin, 1977.

Passion Play. New York: St. Martin's Press, 1979.

Pinball. New York: Bantam Books, 1982.

II. Nonfiction by Jerzy Kosinski

[Joseph Novak, pseud.]. *The Future Is Ours, Comrade*. Garden City: Doubleday, 1960.

[Joseph Novak, pseud.]. *No Third Path*. Garden City: Doubleday, 1962.

Notes of the Author on The Painted Bird. New York: Scientia-Factum, 1965, 1966, 1967.

The Art of the Self: Essays a Propos Steps. New York: Scientia-Factum, 1968.

"Against Book Censorship." *Media and Methods* 12 (January 1976): 20–24.

"Dead Souls on Campus." *New York Times*, October 12, 1970, 45.

"The Reality behind Words." *New York Times*, October 3, 1971, 3.

"The Lone Wolf." *American Scholar* 41 (Fall 1972): 513–19.

"Packaged Passion." *American Scholar* 42 (Spring 1973): 193–204.

"To Hold a Pen." *American Scholar* 42 (Fall 1973): 56–66.

" 'The Banned Book,' as Psychological Drug—a Parody." *Media and Methods* 13 (January 1977): 18–19.

"Is Solzhenitsyn Right?" *Time* 111 (June 26, 1978): 22.

"Time to Spare." *New York Times*, May 21, 1979, A19.

"Telling Ourselves Tales to Make It through the Night." Review of *The White Album. Los Angeles Times Book Review*, May 27, 1979, 1, 29.

"Our 'Predigested, Prepackaged Popular Culture.' " *US News and World Report*, January 8, 1979, 52–53.

"Combining Objective Data with Subjective Attitudes." *Bulletin of the American Society of Newspaper Editors* 43 (July/August 1981): 19.

"A Brave Man, This Beatty. Brave as John Reed." *Vogue*, April 1982, 316, 318, 319.

"A Passion for Polo." *Polo: Official Publication of the United States Polo Association*, May 1985, 115–18.

"Exegetics." *Paris Review* 97 (Fall 1985): 92–95.

"Death in Cannes." *Esquire*, March 1986, 82–89.

III. Interviews and Newspaper Articles

Abrams, Garry. "Jerzy Kosinski Leaves 'Em Amused, Bemused, and Confused." *Los Angeles Times*, Wednesday, November 14, 1984, View section, 1, 12.

Amory, Cleveland. "Trade Winds." *Saturday Review*, April 17, 1971, 16–17.

Baker, John. "Kosinski—and Beyond." *Publishers Weekly* 222 (December 3, 1982): 20.

Base, Ron. "Jerzy Kosinski." *Washington Post*, February 21, 1982, Style section, G1, G10, G11.

Cahill, Daniel J. "*The Devil Tree*: An Interview with Jerzy Kosinski." *North American Review* 258 (Spring 1973): 56–66.

―――. "An Interview with Jerzy Kosinski on *Blind Date*." *Contemporary Literature* 19 (Spring 1978): 133–42.

―――. "Life at a Gallop: Interview with Jerzy Kosinski." *Washington Post Book World*, September 16, 1979, 10.

Corry, John. "A Case History: Seventeen Years of Ideological Attack on a Cultural Target." *New York Times*, November 7, 1982, Arts and Leisure section, 1, 28–29.

Elkin, Michael. "Words Don't Fail Jerzy Kosinski's Vivid Memories of the Holocaust." *Jewish Exponent*, April 13, 1984, On the Scene section, M84, M88, M94.

"Flogging It." *Time* 107 (April 5, 1976): 76–77.

Frymer, Frank. "Novelist Kosinski Is Afraid Television Is 'Castrating Our Children.' " *Newsday*, July 1, 1971, 14–17.

Gallo, William. "Jerzy Kosinski: Writing by Chance and Necessity." *Rocky Mountain News* (Denver), November 30, 1977, 63, 65.

Gelb, Barbara. "Being Jerzy Kosinski." *New York Times Magazine*, February 21, 1982, 42–46, 49, 52–54, 58.

Griffin, Patricia. "Conversation with Jerzy Kosinski." *Texas Arts Journal* (1977), 5–11.

Herman, Jan. "Did He or Didn't He: *Village Voice* Sees Ghosts and CIA Spooks—But Kosinski Says They're Imagining Things." *Chicago Sun-Times*, July 25, 1982, Show/Book/Week section, 25.

Holland, Peter. "Holocaust Survivor Says Writing Is His Spiritual Spine." *Concord Journal*, Thursday, June 14, 1984, 8.

"Jerzy Kosinski." In *Current Biography Yearbook: 1974*, edited by Charles Moritz. New York: H. W. Wilson Co., 1975, 212–15.

Kaiser, Charles. "Friends at the Top of the *Times*." *Newsweek*, November 22, 1982, 125–26.

Kakutani, Michiko. "The Strange Case of the Writer and the Criminal." *New York Times Book Review*, September 20, 1981, 1.

Kane, John. "Jerzy Kosinski." *Yale Lit* 141 (August, 1972): 12–16.

Klinkowitz, Jerome. "Jerzy Kosinski: An Interview." *Fiction International* 1 (Fall 1971): 30–48. Reprinted in *The New Fiction: Interviews with Innovative American Writers*, edited by Joe David Bellamy. Urbana: University of Illinois Press, 1974, 142–68.

————. "Jerzy Kosinski: Puppetmaster." *Chicago Daily News*, "Panorama," October 22, 1977, 16, 22.

Kopkind, Andrew. "Kosinski Redux." *Nation*, November 20, 1982, 516.

"Kosinski: Most Obsessive." *New York Post*, February 7, 1979, 6.

Langen, R. "Interview with Jerzy Kosinski." *Canadian Literary Review* 1 (Fall/Winter 1982): 18–28.

Lawson, Carol. "Behind the Best Sellers." *New York Times Book Review*, October 21, 1979, 58.

Leaming, Barbara. "*Penthouse* Interview: Jerzy Kosinski." *Penthouse*, July 1982, 128–30, 167–71.

Mills, Hilary. "Publishing Notes: Jerzy Kosinski Strikes Again." *Washington Star*, August 19, 1979, A6.

Movius, Geoffrey. "A Conversation with Jerzy Kosinski." *New Boston Review* 1 (Winter 1975): 3–6.

Muro, Mark. "They Can't Keep Jerzy Kosinski Down." *Boston Globe*, June 26, 1984, 27, 29.

Mutter, John. "Kosinski Denies *Village Voice* Charges of Extensive Help." *Publishers Weekly*, July 9, 1982, 11, 18.

Nathan, Paul S. "Multiple Kosinskis." *Publishers Weekly*, April 30, 1973, 48.

————. "Rights and Permissions." *Publishers Weekly*, January 8, 1979, 46.

Nicholls, Richard E. "His Life Has Been an Open Book." *Philadelphia Inquirer*, April 14, 1984, 1D, 6D.

Northouse, Cameron, and Donna Northouse. "Jerzy Kosinski: Vanhome of the Mind." *Lone Star Book Review*, November 1979, 6, 7, 24.

Nowicki, R. E. "Interview with Jerzy Kosinski." *San Francisco Review of Books*, March 1978, 10–13.

Pinkney, Junette A. "*New York Times* Articles on Kosinski Questioned." *Washington Post*, November 15, 1982, Style section, C3.

Plimpton, George, and Rocco Landesman. "The Art of Fiction." *Paris Review* 54 (Summer 1972): 183–207.

"Polish Joke." *Time* 113 (February 19, 1979): 94, 96.

Romano, Carlin. "Whose Book Is It Anyway?" *Philadelphia Inquirer*, September 21, 1982, People/Home/Entertainment section 1E, 4E.

Rosen, Richard. "Heirs to Maxwell Perkins." *Horizon* 24 (April 1981): 50–53.

Rosenbaum, L. P. "Jerzy Kosinski: The Writer's Focus: An Interview." *Index on Censorship* 5 (Spring 1976): 47–48.

Ross, Chuck. "Rejected." *New West* 4 (February 12, 1979): 39–42.

Safire, William. "Suppressing Fire." *New York Times*, November 18, 1982, 27.

Schapp, Dick. "Stepmother Tongue." *Book Week* 14 (November 1965): 6.

Schneiderman, David. "Kosinski's Friends See Red." *Village Voice*, November 16, 1982, 16.

Sheehy, Gail. "The Psychological Novelist as Portable Man." *Psychology Today* 11 (December 1977): 52–56, 126, 128, 130.

Silverman, Art, L. Lee, and D. Bordette. "The Renegade Novelist Whose Life Is Stranger Than Fiction." *Berkeley Barb* 641 (November 25–December 1, 1977): 8–9.

Slung, Michele. "The Wounding of Jerzy Kosinski." *Washington Post*, July 11, 1982, Book World section, 15.

Smith, Dave. "Kosinski Whodunit: Who Ghost There If Not Jerzy?" *Los Angeles Times*, August 1, 1982, Calendar section, 3–5.

Sohn, David. "A Nation of Videots." *Media and Methods* 11 (April 1975): 24–26, 28, 30–31, 52, 54, 56–57.

Spring, Michael. "Kosinski on TV." *Literary Cavalcade*, December 1978, 19.

Stokes, Geoffrey, and Eliot Fremont-Smith. "Jerzy Kosinski's Tainted Words." *Village Voice*, June 22, 1982, 1, 41–43.

Szonyi, David M. "Profile: Jerzy Kosinski on the Writer and the Holocaust." *Jewish Times*, April 9, 1982, 69, 79.

Tartikoff, Brandon. "Exclusive Interview with Jerzy Kosinski." *Metropolitan Review* 2 (October 26, 1971): 3, 14–15.

Teicholz, Tom. "A Blind Date with Jerzy Kosinski." *East Side Express*, February 2, 1978, 1, 13–17.

Varro, Barbara. "Jerzy Kosinski." *Chicago Sun-Times*, November 24, 1976, 27, 45.

Walter, John. "The Anguish of Jerzy Kosinski and His Film." *Washington Star*, February 13, 1979, D2.

Warga, Wayne. "Jerzy Kosinski Reaches Down into Life and Writes." *Los Angeles Times*, April 22, 1973, Calendar section, 1, 54.

_____ . "Jerzy Kosinski Collides with Pop Culture." *Miami Herald*, October 26, 1976, 1D.

Wetzteon, Ross. "Jerzy Kosinski: Existential Cowboy." *Village Voice*, August 11, 1975, 37, 39.

IV. Selected Criticism

Aldridge, John W. "The Fabrication of a Cultural Hero." *Saturday Review* 54 (April 24, 1971): 25–27.

Anderson, Don. "The End of Humanism: A Study of Kosinski." *Quadrant* 113 (1976): 73–77.

Bolling, Douglass. "The Precarious Self in Jerzy Kosinski's *Being There*." *Greyfriar* 16 (1975): 41–46.

Boyers, Robert. "Language and Reality in Kosinski's *Steps*," *Centennial Review* 16 (Winter 1972): 41–61.

Brown, Earl B., Jr. "Kosinski's Modern Proposal: The Problem of Satire in the Mid-Twentieth Century." *Critique: Studies in Modern Fiction* 22 (1980): 83–87.

Bruss, Paul. *Victims: Textual Strategies in Recent American Fiction*. Lewisburg, Pa.: Bucknell University Press, 1981.

Cahill, Daniel J. "Jerzy Kosinski: Retreat from Violence." *Twentieth Century Literature* 18 (1972): 121–32.

_____ . "Jerzy Kosinski: A Play on Passion." *Chicago Review* 32 (1980): 18–34.

Carter, Nancy Corson. "1970 Images of the Machine and the Garden: Kosinski, Crews, and Pirsig." *Soundings* 61 (1978): 105–22.

Coale, Samuel. "The Quest for the Elusive Self: The Fiction of Jerzy Kosinski." *Critique: Studies in Modern Fiction* 14 (1973): 25–37.

―――. "The Cinematic Self of Jerzy Kosinski." *Modern Fiction Studies* 20 (Autumn 1974): 359–70.

Corngold, Stanley. "Jerzy Kosinski's *The Painted Bird*: Language Lost and Regained." *Mosaic* 4 (Summer 1973): 153–68.

Cunningham, Lawrence S. "The Moral Universe of Jerzy Kosinski." *America* 139 (November 11, 1978): 327–29.

Daler, John Kent von. "An Introduction to Jerzy Kosinski's *Steps.*" *Language and Literature* 1 (January 1971): 43–49.

Gogal, John M. "Kosinski's Chance: McLuhan Age Narcissus." *Notes on Contemporary Literature* 4 (January 1971): 8–10.

Gordon, Andrew. "Fiction as Revenge: The Novels of Jerzy Kosinski." In *Third Force: Psychology and the Study of Literature*, edited by Bernard J. Paris. Cranbury, N.J.: Associated University Press, 1985, 280–90.

Harpham, Geoffrey Galt. "Survival in and of *The Painted Bird.*" *Georgia Review* 35 (1981): 142–57.

Harpur, Howard. "Recent Trends in American Fiction." *Contemporary Literature* 12 (Spring 1971): 213–14.

Hazlett, Bill. "Writer Nearly Shared Fate." *Los Angeles Times*, August 12, 1969, 3, 18.

Hicks, Jack. *In the Singer's Temple: Prose Fictions of Barthelme, Gaines, Brautigan, Piercy, Kesey, and Kosinski.* Chapel Hill: The University of North Carolina, 1981.

Hirschberg, Stuart. "Becoming an Object: The Function of Mirrors and Photographs in Kosinski's *The Devil Tree.*" *Notes on Contemporary Literature* 4 (1973): 14–15.

Howe, Irving. "From the Other Side of the Moon." *Harper's* 238 (March 1969): 102–5.

Hutchinson, James D. "Authentic Existence and the Puritan Ethic." *Denver Quarterly* 7 (Winter 1973): 106–14.

Johns, Sally. "Jerzy Kosinski." In *Dictionary of Literary Biography*

Yearbook: 1982, edited by Richard Ziegfeld. Detroit: Gail Research Company, 1983, 169–74.

Karl, Frederick R. *American Fictions 1940/1980: A Comprehensive History and Critical Evaluation*. New York: Harper and Row, 1983.

Kennedy, William. "Who Here Doesn't Know How Good Kosinski Is?" *Look* 35 (April 20, 1971): 12.

_____ . "Kosinski's Hero Rides On." *Washington Post*, September 16, 1979, Book World section, 1, 11.

Klinkowitz, Jerome. "Insatiable Art and the Great American Quotidian." *Chicago Review* 25 (Summer 1973): 172–77.

_____ . "Two Bibliographical Questions in Kosinski's *The Painted Bird*." *Contemporary Literature* 16 (1975): 126–28.

_____ . *Literary Disruptions: The Making of a Post-Contemporary American Fiction*. Urbana: University of Illinois Press, 1975. Revised, 1980.

_____ . "Betrayed by Jerzy Kosinski." *The Missouri Review* 6 (Summer 1983): 157–71.

Klinkowitz, Jerome, and Daniel J. Cahill. "The Great Kosinski Press War." *The Missouri Review* 6 (Summer 1983): 171–75.

Lale, Meta, and John Williams. "The Narrator of *The Painted Bird*: A Case Study." *Renascence* 24 (Summer 1972): 198–206.

Lavers, Norman. *Jerzy Kosinski*. Boston: Twayne Publishers, 1982.

_____ . "Jerzy Kosinski." *Critical Survey of Long Fiction*. New York: Salem Press, 1983, 1556–66.

Lilly, Paul R., Jr. "Comic Strategies in the Fiction of Barthelme and Kosinski." *Publications of the Missouri Philological Association*, April 1979, 25–32.

_____ . "Jerzy Kosinski: Words in Search of Victims." *Critique: Studies in Modern Fiction* 22 (1980): 69–82.

_____ . "Vision and Violence in the Fiction of Jerzy Kosinski." *The Literary Review* 25 (Spring 1982): 389–400.

Lustig, Arnost. "Love and Death in New Jerzy." *Washington Post*, November 27, 1977, E1.

Mason, Michael. "A Sense of Achievement." *Times (London) Literary Supplement*, February 10, 1978, 157.

McGinnis, Wayne D. "Transcendence and Primitive Sympathy in

Kosinski's *The Painted Bird.*" *Studies in the Humanities* 1 (August 1980): 22–27.

Mortimer, Gail L. " 'Fear Death by Water': The Boundaries of Self in Jerzy Kosinski's *The Painted Bird.*" *Psychoanalytic Review* 63 (1976–77): 511–28.

Northouse, Cameron. "Jerzy Kosinski." In *Dictionary of Literary Biography*, edited by Jeffrey Helterman and Richard Layman, 1: 266–75. Detroit: Gale Research, 1978.

Packman, David. "The Kosinski Controversy." *Crosscurrents* 3 (1984): 265–67.

Petrakis, Byron. "Jerzy Kosinski's *Steps* and the Cinematic Novel." *Comparatist*, February 1978, 16–22.

Prendowska, Krystyna. "Jerzy Kosinski: A Literature of Contortions." *Journal of Narrative Technique* 8 (1978): 11–25.

Richey, Clarence W. "*Being There* and *Dasein.*" *Notes on Contemporary Literature*, 2 (September 1982): 3–15.

Richter, David H. "The Three Denouements of Jerzy Kosinski's *The Painted Bird.*" *Contemporary Literature* 15 (Summer 1974): 370–85.

Rider, Philip R. "The Three States of the Text of Kosinski's *The Painted Bird.*" *Papers of the Bibliographical Society of America* 72 (1978): 361–84.

Russell, Charles. "The Vault of Language: Self-Reflective Artifice in Contemporary American Fiction." *Modern Fiction Studies* 20 (Autumn 1974): 349–59.

Sanders, Ivan. "The Gifts of Strangeness: Alienation and Creation in Kosinski's Fiction." *Polish Review* 19 (1974): 171–89.

Sloan, James Park. "Literary Debunking, Or How to Roast Your 'Favorite' Author." *Third Press Review* 1 (September/October 1975): 10–11.

Sherwin, Byron L. *Jerzy Kosinski: Literary Alarmclock*. Chicago: Cabala Press, 1981.

Spendal, R. J. "The Structure of *The Painted Bird.*" *Journal of Narrative Technique* 6 (1976): 132–36.

Stade, George. "The Realities of Fiction and the Fiction of Reality." *Harper's* 246 (May 1973): 90–94.

Stone, Elizabeth. "Horatio Algers of the Nightmare." *Psychology Today* 11 (December 1977): 59–60, 63–64.

Tepa, Barbara Jane. "Jerzy Kosinski's Polish Contexts: A Study of *Being There.*" *Polish Review* 23 (1978), 104–8.

Ziegler, Robert E. "The Disconnected Eye: Vision and Retribution in Kosinski's *The Painted Bird.*" *Par Rapport* 5/6 (1982–83): 67–70.

Index

Paul R. Lilly, Jr. is Professor of English at State University of New York College at Oneonta.